# ACCOUNT

OF THE

# POOR FUND

AND

## OTHER CHARITIES

HELD IN TRUST BY

## THE OLD SOUTH SOCIETY,

CITY OF BOSTON;

WITH COPIES OF ORIGINAL PAPERS RELATIVE TO THE CHARITIES AND TO THE LATE TRIAL BEFORE THE SUPREME COURT OF MASSACHUSETTS IN 1867.

BY JOSEPH BALLARD.

---

"BETTER IS A LITTLE WITH RIGHTEOUSNESS, THAN GREAT REVENUES WITHOUT RIGHT." *Prov.* xvi. 8.

---

BOSTON:
PRESS OF GEO. C. RAND & AVERY, 3 CORNHILL.
1868.

Entered, according to Act of Congress, in the year 1868, by
JOSEPH BALLARD,
In the Clerk's Office of the District Court of the District of Massachusetts.

PRESS OF GEO. C. RAND & AVERY, BOSTON.

# PREFACE.

I SHALL, without apologizing, use the words of a preface to the Parliamentary Commissioners' inquiry concerning the "Endowed Charities of the City of London," they being more appropriate to the object in view than any I could offer as a justification for this publication. The compiler of that work says, —

"The present age cannot be more sensitively alive to the calls of humanity than our forefathers were. Every species of misery met its appropriate relief. But, in numberless instances, the all-changing hand of time has counteracted the pious intentions of these honorable benefactors. The variations of trustees, the inattention of the proper officers, the almost criminal heedlessness of some, the absolutely criminal peculation of others, the misappropriation or even the embezzlement of the resources of an immense number of these institutions, public changes or private vicissitudes, — have occasioned their being diverted to purposes never intended or contemplated by the liberal and benevolent persons by whom they were originally planned, established, and endowed. Of these charities the nation itself is trustee: shall it through insensibility become heedless of this trust? shall it through careless indolence neglect this trust? shall it through unfeeling indifference abandon this trust? shall it through avarice violate this trust? Humanity forbids it. Conscience forbids it. Mercy forbids it. Justice forbids it. Christianity forbids it. Received from our ancestors, we must transmit them to our posterity, undiminished, uninjured; and the only permissable alteration is, that they may be increased according to increase of means and of wants. If all such institutions had been perfectly well conducted, faithfully administered, and fully enjoyed by those whose wants justly constitute them the recipients of such munificent bounties, a work like the present would have been of no use, except as an incentive to others to continue adding to the funds of beneficence, as the increasing numbers and wants of the population would still demand an increase of relief; but, under present circumstances, a different, a more urgent necessity appears, — to assist the public, to whom the endowments belong, in obviating the effect of any further defalcation of these revenues, in preventing any ulterior misappropriation of these beneficial resources, to constitute every individual a guardian of those supplies, which, whatever may be his present circumstances or future prospects, he knows not but may hereafter be the source of his future well-being, or of others near and dear to him, who, by the unforeseen occurrences of which every day shows examples, may hereafter rely on those very institutions which are now upheld by his own disinterested endeavors."

How far the above may be strictly applicable to the poor-fund and other property in possession of the Old South Society I will not at present undertake to say, but think the general principles embodied in the quotation are worthy of profound consideration by all who take an interest in the affairs of that institution.

# CONTENTS.

### CHAPTER I.

PAGE.

Authorities referred to in this Compilation. — Finding the Deacon's Account-Book. — Nathaniel Cunningham's Estate, and Lawsuit to recover it . . . . . 9

### CHAPTER II.

Resolution offered for Adoption at Annual Meeting of Old South Proprietors. — Mrs. Norton's and other Charities. — Pious and Charitable Fund. — Ministers' Widows' and Children's Fund. — Josiah Willard. — Dr. Wisner . . . . . . . 10

### CHAPTER III.

Sacramental Collections. — Their Discontinuance. — Money paid to Ministers. — Remark upon the Administration of the Sacrament. — Mode of keeping Accounts. — Relief of Poor. — Church or Poor-fund Stock. — Ministers' Pay. — Church Delegates. — Funds of Society . . . . . . . . . . . . . 26

### CHAPTER IV.

Mrs. Norton's Gift of Land. — Building of Stores proposed. — Committee of Year 1800. — Report of Church Stock. — Treasurer Phillips, Sen.'s, Account of the same. — Treasurer Hubbard's 1761 Account of Church-Stock. — Proceedings for the Erection of Stores. — History of Part of the Stocks belonging to Poor-Fund . . . 33

### CHAPTER V.

Theophilus Parsons's and Jeremiah Mason's Opinions. — Mrs. Norton's Deed and Will. — Dr. Blagden's Relinquishment of Parsonage House. — Mr. Manning's Non-relinquishment . . . . . . . . . . . . . . . 44

### CHAPTER VI.

Poor-Fund. — Account of $5,245.00, Amount of Loan to the Society. — Parish-Houses Proposed. — Vote of Society to borrow Poor-Fund. — Ministers' and Treasurer Phillips's (Trustees) Obligation to Loan $14,000 to pay for Houses. — Extraordinary Report respecting the $5,245.00 due from the Society. — Cost of Parsonage-Houses. — Account of Stocks furnished from the Poor. — Amount of Society's Indebtedness to Fund . . . . . . . . . . . . 51

## CHAPTER VII.

Milk-Street Stores. — Amount of Profit made by their Erection. — Non-performance of Trustee-Duties by Ministers. — Relief to Poor only granted to Church-members. — Conditions of the Poor-Fund Bequests. — Mrs. Norton's Conditions as to Ministers' Houses. — Society's Rights in the Parsonage-Houses. — Trustees' Powers and Duties. — Mistakes in the Use of Property. — Present Value of it. — Dangers arising from its Wrong Use . . . . . . . . . . . . . . 58

## CHAPTER VIII.

Supreme-Court Decision in the Church-Green Case. — Its Applicability to the Case of the Old South. — Close-Corporation Practices. — Chambers-Street Chapel. — Mode of Managing the Business of the Old South . . . . . . . . . 64

## CHAPTER IX.

Prince Library. — Information. — Master's Report. — Complaints. — Brief. — Defendants' Points and Authorities before the Supreme Court of Chancery. — Estimation of Amount paid by Society, as per their Answer . . . . . . . . 68

## CHAPTER X.

Rescript and Final Decree . . . . . . . . . . . . . . 125

## CHAPTER XI.

Poor Fund as a Public Charity. — Regret at Small Amount Awarded. — Deacons' Book Account. — Accounts from 1708 to 1755. — General Accounts. — Extracts from Old Accounts of the Church. — Ministers' Pay. — Collections and Assessments on Pews. — £192 Loan to Ministers. — Pious and Charitable Fund. — Thomas Hubbard and William Phillips, Sen. — Discontinuance of Sacramental Collections. — Mingling of Funds. — Old South Stores. — Eckley and Huntington Parsonage-Houses. — Mrs. Norton's Real Estate Gift. — Accounts of Pious and Charitable Fund. — Church Stock of 1761, 1766. — Particular Account of the £186.19s.8½d., "Sacramental Balance;" and also of the "Interest, £119.14s.8½d, Account." — General History of the Poor-Fund. — Parsonage-House Rent. — Responsibility of the Old South for the Whole Fund. — Utter Uselessness of the Decision as to the True Amount due the Poor . . . . . . . . . . . . . . . . . 128

## CHAPTER XII.

Result of Examination. — Trustees' Obligation. — Regret of Lawsuit. — Conduct of Members of the Old South. — Extraordinary Preaching by one of the Ministers. — More Extraordinary Records of the Standing Committee. — Remarks on the Trial. — Removal of the Poor-Fund. — Gratitude to the Memory of its Founders. — Duties devolving upon each Member of the Society. — Spiritual Interest of the Church. — Advantages and Dangers in Example. — Public Charities of McLean and Peabody. — Committees for Examination of Public Charities in England. — Their Success. — Necessity of similar Examination here . . . . . . . . . . 139

APPENDIX, No. 1, 151. Deacons Book . . . . . . . . 157

# OLD SOUTH POOR FUND.

# THE POOR FUND.

## CHAPTER I.

Authorities referred to in this Compilation. — Finding the Deacon's Account-Book. — Nathaniel Cunningham's Estate, and Lawsuit to recover it.

THE authorities relied upon to substantiate the facts in this relation are the Church Records from 1705, and the Standing Committee's Records, together with those of the Probate both of Suffolk and Middlesex. To the last, reference can be readily had, as the folio, leaf, and date are noted for that purpose. These alone would furnish sufficient proof of the existence of a poor-fund, even if the Deacon's Cash-Book, which was supposed to be irrecoverably lost, had never been found. In that book, all the accounts relative to the charities were accurately kept for nearly a century. This book, after being missing for a long time, was found in the law-office of the late Abraham Moore, Esq., by his son, who presented it as an antiquarian curiosity to his friend and classmate, the Rev. Caleb Davis Bradlee, and was by him deposited in the New-England Historic-Genealogical Society, from whence it reverted to the Old South Society. As Mr. Moore was connected by marriage with a descendant of Nathaniel Cunningham, Esq., he thereby became interested in a suit at law brought to recover some lands formerly owned by that person. It is quite probable that the book was obtained from the Old South Society to furnish some proof in the case, as Mr. Cunningham was an influential member of the Old South, and bequeathed a considerable legacy to the poor-fund. This suit was brought some fifty years ago, and the lands in question are thus described in the inventory of Mr. N. Cunningham's estate: "A house, and eight and two-thirds acres of land, at the bottom of the Common." In 1812, after previous protracted law proceedings, the case was closed by a quit-claim deed to Messrs. Otis, Mason, and Joy, from Susannah Cunningham, of the land in question. This land must have embraced within its bounds a portion of the Common, and Beacon Street extending to Cambridge Street, including the site of the "Old Powder House."

## CHAPTER II.

Resolution offered for Adoption at Annual Meeting of Old South Proprietors. — Mrs. Norton's and other Charities. — Pious and Charitable Fund. — Ministers' Widows' and Children's Fund. — Josiah Willard. — Dr. Wisner.

IN the year 1858, at a special business-meeting of the Old South Society, the following motion was made: —

"*Whereas* doubts have been expressed as to the regularity of certain proceedings of this Corporation, and whereas it is important that all legal forms should carefully be observed in the management of the valuable property held in trust for religious and charitable purposes, it is therefore *voted*, That a Committee of five be appointed to investigate the past proceedings of this Corporation, and all matters which may affect the legality of the present or past doings of its officers, or seem to be in any degree a departure from a strictly lawful and economical administration of said trust, to report the result of their examination at a special meeting of the Pew Proprietors, to be called by said Committee for that purpose, and to propose such measures as they may deem to be expedient in the premises. And the said Committee is hereby empowered to take the advice of legal counsel with relation to such questions and matters as they may think proper."

This motion, at that and a subsequent meeting, was defeated in such a manner as to raise some doubts of the motives of so determined and persistent an opposition to an inquiry only offered in view of correcting any past errors which might thereby be discovered, and adopting measures for future action conformable to the obligations of law, and more consistent with the present financial condition of the Old South Church and Society. In January, 1859, a publication was issued, and distributed to those concerned in the affairs of this institution, inviting their attention to many departures from correct business-principles practised by the government of the Society, in which a remark was made "that the Ministers' and Deacons' Fund may prove a most important subject for consideration, both to the Society and the Trustees." Subsequently the identical old Account-Book, kept by the Deacons of the Old South Society, was found; by the aid of which a clear, full, and complete investigation of the whole of this important matter could be made. This invaluable book, kept by the respective Deacons and Treasurers of the Old South Society from 1708 to 1798, contains a very particular and accurate account of the numerous charities bequeathed in trust to the Old South Church Ministers and Deacons officially, to whom the income was to be given; the manner in which the fund was kept, invested, and augmented; the rise and progress of the "Church Stock;" amount of sacramental and other contributions and collections; and the periodical settlement of correct audited accounts. There is but little doubt that the absence of this book might, in some degree, be the cause why the Poor Fund of the Old South had well-nigh passed among the things "lost upon earth." Still it was not by any means the whole cause; for an inspection of the church-records from the earliest period wherein the entries were made, by those eminent men, Drs. Sewall and Prince, and others, furnishes full and abundant evidence as to the particulars of that trust. It is therefore believed, that, had the motion for a committee of investigation been carried, the Society would have been spared the consequences, be they what they may, resulting from the institution of legal proceedings, which a sense of duty towards a portion of much-wronged persons called for.

The affairs of the Old South Society, so far as they may be connected directly or indirectly with all the Trust Property, will be now considered.

The first in magnitude, being the foundation of all the property now under consideration, is

### Mrs. Mary Norton's Charity.

This comprises all the land upon which the five stores in Washington Street, — erected A.D. 1800, — and the Old South Church, now stand, also that upon which the three stores in Milk Street stand. As this part of the property is so intimately connected with the financial transactions of A.D. 1800, its further history will be much better understood by a reference to events of that period.

It may not be improper here to state, that the Old South Chapel, in Spring Lane, now joined to the Norton property, was not obtained by the original gift, but from purchase, in A.D. 1816 and 1819, by the Society; who must have derived the means of so doing from the income of the Norton estate and improvements, as there is no other visible way that they could have paid for it. Consequently, that is as much a part of the Trust Property as any other part of the property now in the possession of the Old South Society. The next procedure will be to give an account of the charities bestowed by sundry persons, with extracts from their wills, all of which, with the exception of one (Mrs. Mills's), are registered in the records of Suffolk Probate Court, the lib. and fol. of which are noted for reference.

### John Bolt's Charity.

Will proved April 20, 1711; lib. 17, fol. 34. "Item, I give and bequeath unto the Poor, being communicants of the South Church in Boston aforesaid, the sum of Twelve Pounds, current money of New England, to be paid unto the Deacons of said Church for the use of said Poor." Cash received and credited in the Deacons' book, Feb. 12, 1712. £12. 0s. 0d.

### Samuel Moore's Charity.

Will proved Aug. 22, 1716; lib. 19, fol. 201. "Item, all the rest and residue of my money and plate I give, devise, and bequeath unto the use and benefit of the First Meeting House, and to the use and benefit of the South Meeting House, being equally divided between them." Credit in Deacons' book, "Received 30 oz. plate, and bills of credit £36. 0s. 0d."

### Simon Daniels's Charity.

Will proved May 21, 1722; lib. 22, fol. 266. "Item, I give and bequeath to the Poor of the Old South Church in Boston Fifty Pounds, to be disposed of according to the discretion of the Ministers and Deacons of said Church." Dec. 12, 1722, credit in Deacons' book, "£50. 0s. 0d."

### John Walley's Charity.

Will not found. Jan. 4, 1725, credit in Deacons' book, "Received of Mr. John Walley Twenty Pounds, it being a legacy left by his Father to the Poor of said Church."

### Andrew Belcher's Charity.

Will, lib. 20, fol. 26, dated Oct. 17, 1717. "Imprimis, I give to the Old South Church in Boston, whereof I am a member, the sum of Fifty Pounds." In the church-records there is a vote of grateful thankfulness to the memory of the late Andrew Belcher for his legacy to the Old South Church; but its receipt is not credited upon the Deacons' book.

## Mary Saltonstall's Charity.

Will proved Jan. 16, 1729; lib. 27, fol. 227. "Item, I give to the poor of the Town of Boston One Hundred Pounds, to be disposed of to them at the discretion of the Overseers of the Poor of the said Town; also to the poor of the now Old South Church in Boston Twenty Pounds, to be disposed of at the discretion of the said Church."

Credit in the Deacons' book, March 9, 1730, "Received £20."

## William Manley's Charity.

Will proved June 26, 1732; lib. 31, fol. 16. "Item, I give and bequeath to the poor of the New South Brick Church, whereof I am a member, the sum of Twenty Pounds, to be raised and levied out of my estate, to the poor of the Church."

March 5, 1723. Credit in Deacons' book, "Received £20."

## Joseph Maylem's Charity.

Will proved Feb. 13, 1732; lib. 31, fol. 140. "Item, I give unto the Rev. Mr. Joseph Sewall and Mr. Thomas Prince, the present Pastors of the Old South Church, Five Pounds to each, to be paid them in public bills of credit, in convenient time after my decease, by my executors herein named. I also give unto the poor of the said Church the sum of Twenty Pounds, in Province bills of credit, to be also paid out of my estate in convenient time after my decease by my said executors unto the deacons of the said Church, to be by them distributed, according to the best of their discretion, for the ends intended."

Credit in Deacons' book, "Received £20."

## Abigail Duckaline's Charity.

Will proved Nov. 1, 1737; lib. 33, fol. 159. "Item, I give and bequeath unto the poor of the Old South Church, in Boston, the sum of Five Pounds in money."

Nov. 3, 1737. Credit in the Deacons' book, "Received £5."

These legacies (with the exception of Mr. Belcher's £50) were received and credited in the Deacons' book to the amount of £183. 3s. 0d., Old Tenor, with the contribution money; and out of these combined sums were paid the ordinary sacramental expenses and donations to the poor, whose names are registered, and the balance on hand Oct. 8, 1735, £441. 11s. 0d., carried to a new account.

## NATHANIEL CUNNINGHAM'S CHARITY.

Will proved Dec. 13, 1748. "I give and bequeath unto the poor of the aforesaid meeting-house (Old South), that is, the church and congregation, Five Hundred Pounds, in passable bills of credit, such as may be passing at the time of my decease, of the Old Tenor."

In the church-records (which have always been open for inspection to the church members, and have never been mislaid or lost) is the following entry: "May, 1749, *Voted*, That the Deacons be empowered to received £500, Old Tenor, left to the poor of the church and congregation by Mr. Nathaniel Cunningham, deceased, and give a full discharge, with the full acknowledgments of the church and congregation for so generous a benefaction." "1751, March 25. *Voted* the Deacons be desired to put to interest the donation of Mr. Cunningham, deceased, being £500, Old Tenor, to keep good the principal, and distribute the interest among the poor of the church and the congregation."

In account of church-stock 1761, the amount realized from this bequest was £66. 13s. 4d., lawful money, which was invested in a Treasury Note, together with Eliza Loring's legacy of £13. 6s. 8d.; and from 1757 to 1761, Deacon Hubbard, as Treasurer, had received £22. 15s. 7d. interest on the Cunningham legacy, which was paid to the poor. In the Deacons' book there is no account of how much they received from Mr. Cunningham's executors, or how it was invested; although subsequently, it appears, the business was correctly transacted so far as amount is concerned. It was the custom, from 1708 to 1761, to thus invest, without making specific entries thereof; general mention being made of bonds and province notes of various amounts. This continued until Deacon Hubbard resigned his office as Treasurer; who, when he paid over the assets of church-stock in 1766, gave a particular account, whereby the amount of this and other legacies are known to have been received.

## FARR TOLMAN'S CHARITY.

Will proved Oct. 22, 1751; lib. 45, fol. 235. "I do hereby give and bequeath unto the poor of the church whereof the Rev. Dr. Joseph Sewall and Mr. Thomas Prince are ministers the sum of Three Hundred Pounds, Old Tenor, or Forty Pounds lawful money, the same to be put out at interest, and said interest to be paid yearly to the poor forever." In 1761 account of church-stock, this legacy was invested in a note of £40. July 5, 1763, it was again invested, together with the legacy of Deacon Henchman, in a treasury note of £106, the interest on which was credited; and in January, 1766, in the account of church-stock, this legacy is estimated as an item of the amount £874. 14s. 3d., lawful money.

## ANN MILLS'S CHARITY.

Will of Ann Mills, of Watertown, Middlesex County. Probate Records, lib. 17, fol. 17: date Nov. 27, 1725. "My Will is that all the rest and residue of my estate, of what kind or denomination soever, be equally divided as followeth; viz., one-quarter part to the Old or First Church in Boston, and one-quarter part to the Old South Church in Boston, and one-quarter part to the Church in the east part of Watertown, and one-quarter part to the Church in the west part of Watertown. To be improved for the relief of the poor of said churches, and such poor as usually congregate with said churches, at the discretion of the minister or ministers and deacons. To be paid by my executors within five years after my decease." Upon the Old South Church records, heretofore referred to, is the following: "At a church-meeting of the Old South, in Boston, Jan. 21, 1728. *Whereas*, through the good Providence of God, there is a considerable legacy bequeathed to this church by Mrs. Ann Mills, of Watertown, to be improved for the relief of the poor of this church and congregation, *Voted*, Antony Stoddard, Esq., Deacon Henchman, and Mr. James Pemberton, be a committee to receive this legacy according to the tenor of the will, and give proper discharges to the executors."

In the Deacons' book this legacy was credited, "Received as follows:—

| | | | |
|---|---|---|---|
| Joseph Garfield's Bond | £22 | 16s. | 8d. |
| Daniel Whitney's Bond | 29 | 4 | 0 |
| William Smith, and James and John Simpson's bond | 22 | 5 | 10 |
| Cash invested in Treasurer's notes, Church Stock, 1761 | 26 | 13 | 4 |
| | £100 | 19s. | 10d." |

It appears that Mrs. Mills must have left quite a large estate, as the following memorandum in the Deacons' book will show:—

| | | | |
|---|---|---|---|
| 1728, South Church, By Six Bonds, from sundry persons, am't | £280 | 0s. | 0d. |
| A Note under hand, and Cash | 2 | 3 | 1¼ |
| | £282 | 3s. | 1¼d. |

The sum of £282. 3s. 1¼d. as above is the one-quarter part of the residue of the estate of Ann Mills, deceased, which she gave by her last will and testament " to be improved for the relief of the Poor of the Old South Church and Congregation, at the discretion of the Ministers and Deacons of said Church." The Committee of 1800, in their report, say, " We also find an old bundle of papers that is wrote on, 'Six Bonds, from sundry persons, for £280. 0s. 0d., due the Old South Church, the interest whereof to be disposed of to the Poor of the Church and Congregation, Dec. 31, 1729.' Note, — It appears that these moneys were never paid by the debtors." In the Deacons' book, 1762, the interest on amount received from this legacy of £100. 19s. 10d., up to date, was paid to the poor.

### CAPTAIN JOHN ARMITAGE'S CHARITY.

Will proved May 7, 1751; lib. 45, fol. 46. " Item, I give and bequeath unto the Old South Church, that I now belong to, One Hundred Pounds, Old Tenor, or Thirteen Pounds, six shillings, and eight pence, lawful money of the Province aforesaid, to be put out at interest by the Ministers and Deacons of the aforesaid Church, and the interest of it to be given to the poor members of the aforesaid Church as the Ministers and Deacons shall see fit."

June 1, 1758, in Deacons' book is credited Capt. Armitage's donation and four years' interest: the latter was debited as paid to the poor, while the principal, £13. 6s. 8d., was invested in a Treasurer's note of £40, with that part of Mrs. Mills's legacy received in cash, as noted in Church Stock of 1761.

### DEACON DANIEL HENCHMAN'S CHARITY.

Will proved March 6, 1761; lib. 58, fol. 104. " I give unto the Old South Church, whereof the Rev. Dr. Sewall is minister, the sum of Sixty-five Pounds, thirteen shillings, and four pence, lawful money, and order the same to be put out on interest, and the interest thereof to be paid to such of the Poor of said Church as the Ministers and Deacons shall in their prudence judge proper, forever."

In the accounts of Church Stock, 1761 and 1766, it is called £66, and was invested July 5, 1763, in a Treasurer's note. In an interest account of bonds and notes, it also is credited in the Deacons' book for interest on Treasurer's note.

### MRS. ELIZA LORING'S CHARITY.

In the account of Church Stock, 1761 and 1766, it is called the same amount, £13. 6s., 8d. in each. In 1761 it was invested in a

Treasurer's note, together with the legacy of Nathaniel Cunningham. 1757 to 1761, Treasurer Hubbard collected as interest £6. 13s. 6d., and paid it to the poor.

### Rev. Ebenezer Pemberton's Charity.

Rev. Ebenezer Pemberton's will, proved Feb. 28, 1716, lib. 19, fol. 281. "I give Fifty Pounds, to be put out at interest by my executors and overseers, the interest annually to be distributed to the Poor of the town of Boston."

In the account of Church Stock, 1761 and 1766, is James Mirrick's note for £17. 7s. 9d., received for part of the Rev. E. Pemberton's legacy, 1761, to the "Poor of Boston." 1757 to 1773, the Treasurers regularly received the interest until May 8, when the note was paid.

### Mary Ireland's Charity.

Will proved Oct. 17, 1763; lib. 62, fol. 225. "I give unto the Old South Church, whereof the Rev. Drs. Joseph Sewall and Alexander Cummings are pastors, the sum of One Hundred and Thirty-three Pounds, six, and eight pence, lawful money, and order that the same be put out on interest, taking Province security, or, instead thereof, good land security for the same, the interest thereof to be annually paid to such of the Poor of said Church as the Ministers and Deacons thereof shall in their prudence judge proper, forever, an account of such disposition to be laid before the Church yearly." Extract from the church records, which, be it remembered, were never lost: "1776, the Pastor and Deacons laid before the Church the distribution of Mrs. Ireland's legacy for one year, being Eight Pounds, L.M., agreeably to the tenor of her will."

1764, credit in the Deacons' book: "Cash received, Mrs. Ireland's legacy, by Deacon Jeffries, £133. 6s. 8d. 1764, Nov. 6, Treasurer Phillips invested the same in Treasurer's notes, together with other assets."

In Deacon Phillips's accounts (Treasurer twenty-nine years) the interest from 1766 amounting to £206. 13s. 4d., was paid to the poor as per account, 1791.

| | | |
|---|---|---|
| 1795. Interest accrued | £17 14s. 0d. | |
| Legacy | 133 6 8 | |
| Principal and Interest | | £151 0s. 8d. |

### Dr. Joseph Sewall's Charity.

Oct. 29, 1764, in Deacons' book, "Gift of the Rev. Dr. Joseph Sewall, £20, the income of said sum to be distributed to the Poor of the Old South Church in Boston, yearly, by the Deacons of said Church."

Nov. 6, 1764, credited as received by Deacon Jeffries, £20. 0s. 0d. Dr. Sewall was for many years pastor of the Old South.

### John Simpson's Charity.

Will proved Aug. 2, 1764, lib. 63, fol. 133. "Item, I give unto the Poor of the Church whereof Dr. Sewall is minister the sum of Thirty Pounds, lawful money, to be paid to the Deacon or Deacons of said Church, to be by them distributed among the said Poor." 1764, Nov. 6, credited in Deacons' book, "Received by Deacon Jeffries, and paid over to Treasurer Phillips, £30. 0s. 0d."

### John Osborn's Charity.

1769, June 16, credited in Deacons' books, "Received from Deacon Hubbard, John Osgood, Esq.'s legacy of £13." Jan. 9, 1777, in accounts Church Stock, this is mentioned among the assets as Mr. Osborn's legacy.

### Benjamin Pemberton's Charity.

Will proved 1782, June 25, lib. 81, fol. 144. "I give and bequeath unto the University of Cambridge, and to the South Church in Boston, unto each Twenty Pounds. Also to Nathaniel Taylor, Esq., Ten Pounds, all deficiencies to be made up to lawful money." 1783, May 5, credit in Deacons' book, "Received of Samuel Whitwell and Jonathan Mason, Esqs., Executors of the will of Benjamin Pemberton, Esq., deceased, for his legacy to the Old South Church, £20."

### Thomas Bromfield's Charity.

Will proved 1778, April 21, lib. 77, fol. 58. "Item, I give to the Old South Church in Boston, New England, whereof the Rev. Dr. Joseph Sewall is now Pastor, the sum of Twenty-five Pounds, lawful money aforesaid of Great Britain, to be paid into the hands of the Deacons of said Church, and to be by them let out at interest, and the interest applied to the supporting of the Poor of said Church."

1789, May 1, credit in Deacons' book, "Received Thomas Bromfield's Legacy (see extract from his will), £33. 6s. 8d."

## Thomas Hubbard's Charity.

Will proved 1773, July 23, lib. 73, fol. 36. "I give to the Charitable and Pious Fund of the Old South Church, so called, in Boston, Fifty Pounds."

1773, Aug. 17, credit in Deacons' books, "Received of the Executors of the late Thomas Hubbard, Esq., for his legacy to the Charitable and Pious Fund, £50."

This sum was specially invested and re-invested as belonging to this fund for many years, when it became commingled with the Deacons' and Ministers' Fund. Mr. Hubbard was deacon and treasurer of the Old South, which offices he "filled with fidelity, uprightness, and integrity."

The forementioned twenty-two legacies are all given to the church, and ministers and deacons, for the use of the poor, and, with a few exceptions, they are specifically directed to be put out at interest, the income to be distributed to the poor, at the discretion of the Ministers and Deacons. There seemed at this time to be but one object in view, — the spiritual and physical relief of the poor; and it is curiously worthy of notice that no small part of these testamentary devises show more than slight evidence of the influence of the same hand in their concoction. There were, however, other objects prominently in view in the minds of those who then conducted the affairs of the church, as the following vote will show:—

Church Records, March 25, 1725. *Voted,* That there be a public collection on our anniversary Fasts and Thanksgivings, to be bestowed on pious uses, for the advancement of Christ's kingdom among the poor, and other proper objects of such charity, first among ourselves, and then in other places, as we shall find " we are able, " by putting into their hands Bibles, catechisms, and other books of piety, or by promoting religion among them, or any other way as you shall deem and determine upon. Upon which the church very generally came into the vote, that there be a public collection on our anniversary Fasts and Thanksgivings, to be bestowed on pious uses, and for the advancement of Christ's kingdom. The church voted that the Hon. Edward Bromfield, and Daniel Oliver, Esq., be joined with the deacons, as trustees of this evangelical treasury. The church also voted that the concurrence of the congregation be asked in this affair.

Joseph Sewall.<br>Thomas Prince.

The above vote was the first step towards the adoption of the Pious and Charitable Fund, instituted in 1739, the history of which, having indirect relation to the subject under consideration, will particularly be noted.

At a meeting of the brethren of the South Church and congregation, May 1, 1738. *Whereas* there has been a proposal made that some part of the money which is or may be collected for charitable and pious uses should, as we shall find ourselves able from time to time, be made a stated fund, the income of it to be improved for such uses as the brethren of the church and congregation shall from time to time determine, *Voted*, that a Committee be chosen to consider of said proposal, and make report to this meeting on Monday, the 15th of the instant. *Voted*, that the Hon. Ezekiel Lewis, Josiah Willard, Anthony Stoddard, Samuel Welles, Esq., Col. Edward Winslow, Esq., Mr. Thomas Hubbard, William Foye, Joshua Winslow, Esq., and Mr. Nathaniel Cunningham, with the deacons, be of this Committee. There were several adjournments to the first Monday in October. At a meeting, Oct. 2, 1738, of the brethren of the church and congregation, it being also proposed that a certain fund be established for the support of the widows and fatherless children of the pastors of said South Church from time to time, *Voted*, that the Committee to consider the proposal for a Fund for Charitable and Pious Uses take this also into their consideration, and make the report at the next meeting; and that Messrs. Andrew Oliver and Benjamin Hollowell be added to the said Committee. December, 1738, at a meeting of the Brethren, *Voted*, that the report of the Committee appointed by the brethren of the church and congregation to consider of the proposals to establish a Fund for Charitable and Pious Uses be accepted, and recommended to the South Church, in order, if they see cause, to its being voted and established.

At a Church-meeting, April 9, 1739, —

.... "And *Whereas*, Dec. 18, 1738, at a meeting of the brethren of the South Church and Congregation, there was a report relating to a Fund for Charitable and Pious Uses agreed upon, and recommended to the said church, in order, 'if they see cause, to its being voted and established,' said report was read and established accordingly, and is as follows: —

'At a meeting of the committee of the brethren of the Old South Church and Congregation in Boston, of which Messrs. Sewall and Prince are pastors, to consider of the proposals to establish a certain Fund for Charitable and Pious Uses, as well as for the support of the widows and fatherless children of the pastors of the Old South from time to time, as other uses of charitable and pious nature, the said committee, after divers consultations, propose that the said fund be begun, continued, and established under the following regulations: —

I. As divers brethren of the said church and congregation have declared that they contributed, at the last general collection for such uses, with a view to put the moneys into the said fund, which had been a little before moved, that committee propose that twenty pounds of silver be purchased with part of the moneys then collected, and be appropriated and settled as the beginning of said fund for said uses; but yet no addition shall be made to said fund out of the public collection, for time to come, but by the particular appropriations of persons inclined to encourage the same, expressed by writing annexed to their moneys appropriated.

II. That the Pastors and Deacons of the said church, for the time being, be the trustees of said fund, to manage the same in behalf of the said church; the major part of said trustees to have power of acting, and all and each of them to be accountable to the said church, or their committees, from time to time.

III. That the principal stock of said fund, together with all additions that shall be made to the said principal by persons disposed thereto, either by contributions, presents, deeds, wills, or otherwise, shall be kept perpetually entire, without being broken in upon any occasion; but the principal moneys shall be either constantly let out to interest, or laid out in some real estate bringing in some income, or building on or improving the real estate which shall belong to said church, as the said church shall at their half-yearly meeting from time to time determine.

IV. That in the bonds for moneys belonging to said fund let out to interest by the said trustees, the principal and interest shall be expressed by ounces of silver, and to be made payable to the major part of the trustees; the borrower and two sufficient sureties to be bound both jointly and severally for the same, and neither the borrower, nor either of the sureties, to be of the church and congregation.

V. That, while there shall be no widow or fatherless child of the pastors of said church, the interest and incomes of that part of the fund raised for them shall be added to the principal stock, not to be divided again. But when there shall be a widow, or fatherless child or more, of said pastors, it shall be left to the said church to judge and order how much of the interest and income shall be disposed of for their support from time to time, and when to cease supporting them. But of all other parts of said fund it shall be left to the said church at their half-yearly meetings to dispose both of the interest and income to any kind of charitable and pious use whatever.

VI. That there shall be a stated half-yearly meeting of the brethren of the said church; viz., one in the Spring and another in the Fall, annually; that at the said meeting in the Spring they shall choose a committee, which shall consist of members of said congregation as well as of said church, to stand for the year ensuing, and continue till others shall be chosen in their room, to examine into the state of said fund, both into principal stock and income, and consider how to order the same according to the preceding articles, and make their report to the said brethren at their stated half-yearly meeting, both in the Spring and Fall ensuing, for the said brethren to consider and vote upon as they shall judge proper.'"

VII. Lastly, *Whereas* there are stated half-yearly meetings of the brethren, both of the South Church and the congregation with them, for the preservation of mutual harmony and good agreement, it is further proposed that the said committee shall, at the said half-yearly meetings from time to time, lay their aforesaid reports before the said brethren, that the said brethren may express their minds thereupon, and give their advice, when they see cause, to the said church accordingly.

"Oct. 18, 1738. Unanimously agreed to by the said committee present, to be offered as their report by the brethren of the South Church and congregation at their next meeting, in order to its being agreed upon and recommended, if they see cause, to the said South Church, to be voted and established."

"Dec. 18, 1738. At a meeting of the brethren of the South Church and Congregation, this report was agreed upon, and recommended to the said South Church, in order, if they see cause, to its being voted and established."

"Voted and established at a church-meeting, April 9, 1739."

JOSEPH SEWALL,
THOMAS PRINCE.

It appears extraordinary that there should have been so large a committee as thirteen, not only of the most prominent men belonging to the Old South Church, but of those also who were at that time distinguished in the public affairs of both the Province and Town of Boston, appointed to frame rules for the government of a fund with so small a beginning as this institution possessed; viz., "twenty ounces of silver," or about twenty-three dollars. That so elaborate a document should for this purpose alone have been the result of their protracted labors is not probable; but when it is considered that at that time many charitable gifts had already been placed in trust of the Old South Church, for the use of the poor, and to the pastors especially, with most of the committee, it must have generally been known that in time similar ones would be received, the fair inference therefore must be, that this production was not alone intended for the Charitable and Pious Fund, but a special Constitution for the perpetual preservation of all Trust Funds, both real and personal, which were and might be confided to the Old South Church. Its provisions were, —

That the Pastors and Deacons shall, from time to time, be the trustees to manage said fund, the major part to rule.

That the principal stock shall be kept perpetually entire, without being broken in upon on any occasion.

That it shall be kept at interest, laid out in real estate, or may be lent to the church for the improvement of the real estate of the church.

That the money shall always be specified in gold or silver, and, when loaned to individuals, that neither borrower and the two securities required should either be of the church or congregation.

The whole appropriating power is lodged in the church, to whom the trustees, at specified periods, are to make a report of their doings as to the state of the fund, half-yearly.

Finally, the congregation are to have a voice in the conducting the whole fund, from which nothing but the interest and income is ever to be appropriated.

The amount of this fund (forming no inconsiderable part of the trust-property) is now in the possession of the society in common with their general assets. With what propriety, therefore, can any person who is *ex officio* a trustee, or any member of the church and congregation, accept an office of emolument, the pay of which is in any way derived from a fund so carefully guarded upon this very point as this was by its founders? This report was in all probability the work of Josiah Willard, the son of the Rev. Dr. Willard, pastor of the Old South. Mr. Willard was a man of great distinction in the time in which he lived; was a graduate of Harvard College, afterwards tutor of the same; held for a period of fifteen years the office of colonial secretary under the provincial government; was judge of probate, and member of the Old South Church. It was said in (Judge Oliver's) poem, published at the time of his death, —

> "He stands distinguished in the important cause
> Of widow and of orphan."

For one moment let us imagine a man capable of a production which would do honor to the most accomplished conveyancer of the age; so well adapted to its purposes; so carefully and clearly expressed; so guarded in its restrictions against fraud, peculation, and mismanagement; in a word, so exquisitely fitted, not only for the time for which it was particularly intended, but for all future times and conditions in which the society might be placed as trustees of other charitable funds. Great would be his astonishment to learn that the only recorded result of the careful labors of those pious men and women with whom he in this instance was associated, was the payment, from that part of the fund belonging to the "minister's widow and children," unto Deborah Prince, of one pound; and that the capital stock, which was to be "kept perpetually entire without being broken upon on any occasion," is now merged in common with the real-estate trust-property of Mary Norton, possession being obtained on the very principles laid down in Mr. Willard's report, and now augmenting an enormous income, profusely distributed in large salaries, heavy expenses, indirect gifts to forbidden incumbents, and official emoluments, — one partaker of which is, *ex officio*, a trustee of the very property from which they are derived. It is greatly to be regretted that Dr. Wisner, in his history of the Old South, when he praised the church and congregation "from the beginning for having always been kind and liberal to the widows and orphan children of the ministers,— quoting largely from this very report, and that of the committee of 1800 also, — did not with his acknowledged ability and zeal pursue the subject to the end. It would, without any doubt, have modified the high encomium then expressed; and, possibly, would have led to a thorough investigation of the whole financial concerns of the society.

An account of the fund belonging to this part of the Trust will now be given from the Deacons' book: —

| | |
|---|---:|
| In 1761, there was invested in Province notes | £58 0s. 0d. |
| " 1766, the part in church-stock amounted to | 66 19 2½ |
| " 1733, amount of Deacon Hubbard's legacy received | 50 0 0 |
| Interest and profits credited to 1795, as received | 54 3 2¼ |
| | $570.35 or £171 2s. 4¾d. |

In the church-stock accounts of 1761 to 1766, this fund is identified; afterwards it was not separately invested, and no particular notice was taken of it, except when the interest was received and duly credited, until 1773, when the legacy of Deacon Hubbard (one of the most prominent founders of this very charity) was received, credited, and invested as belonging to the "Charitable and Pious Trust."

The respective amounts of all the legacies (with the exception of that from Mr. Belcher of Fifty Pounds, Old Tenor) were credited as "received," together with the balance of the sacramental account, as belonging to the Poor Fund or church-stock. This was kept carefully, and profitably invested, while the income was faithfully applied, liberally, as far as it was found necessary, to the relief of the poor, the names of whom were recorded for inspection in the church-books. In some instances, in conformity with the will of the donor (that of Mrs. Ireland), a report was made of the doings of the trustees in special cases. A particular account was at first kept of all the charities; but, in time, the benefactions became so numerous, and a large majority of them being decidedly for the same purpose, — "the relief of the poor," — the method of keeping the accounts separately was changed for one less complicated, though equally correct; the entire accounts from 1708, after a critical examination, proving that the only object which actuated those good men who had this charity in their charge, believing as they did "that we should always have the poor with us," was to hand its blessings down unimpaired, and increased "to the latest posterity." When the church was first organized, the funds necessarily required for its expenses, including the salaries of the ministers, were obtained by subscription, and collections from the church and congregation. There were collections also occasionally taken for aid to sufferers by fire, also to soldiers and sailors engaged in the country's defence; and a permanently-established contribution upon Fast and Thanksgiving Days for missionary and charitable purposes, at which the contributors were requested to mark their gifts, designating for whom, or for what purpose, they were bestowed; and they were credited in the Deacons' book in accordance, and faithfully applied. This rule was most applicable to the "Charitable and Pious Fund." The building and repairs of both the meeting and minister's houses were defrayed by subscription; and the account-book affords undisputed evidence that in its own corporate capacity *the society did not possess any other pecuniary means*, excepting a very inconsiderable rent received irregularly for the use of the meeting-house cellar, which was bestowed upon the ministers. They were so cramped for money in July, 1747, that they were obliged to borrow of the "church-fund for the poor" £192. 0s. 7d. to pay off "the deficiency of our ministers."

## CHAPTER III.

Sacramental Collections. — Their Discontinuance. — Money paid to Ministers. — Remark upon the Administration of the Sacrament. — Mode of keeping Accounts. — Relief of Poor. — Church or Poor-fund Stock. — Ministers' Pay. — Church Delegates. — Funds of Society.

UNDER all these pecuniary trials, their zeal for aiding the poor was undiminished, inasmuch as they held and maintained, in common practice with sister churches, that important part of the sacramental service denominated the "offertory," the proceeds from which, after deducting the expenses incidental to the observance of that ordinance, were paid to the poor-fund as a thank-offering, and used and invested with, and as part of, that fund. This custom continued to be observed for more than a hundred years, when it was abolished by a vote of the church, as the following extract from the records will show: —

Dec. 28, 1849. At the regular church-meeting, after remarks from Deacons Cutler, Stoddard, and Dimon, showing that the omission of the church to take a collection at the close of each communion for the benefit of the poor of the church would not in the present circumstances of the Old South in any degree hurt the interests of the poor, and would contribute greatly to the more solemn and appropriate observance of the ordinance, it was unanimously voted, on motion of Deacon Cutler, seconded by Deacon Stoddard, that the contribution hitherto taken on that occasion be hereafter omitted, and that the pastor give notice of this vote at the close of the next communion service. Attest,

GEORGE W. BLAGDEN,
*Pastor of the Church.*

Tuesday evening, Jan. 8, at the close of communion on Sabbath, 6th ultimo, the pastor gave notice of the omission of the usual contribution, in accordance with the above vote. Attest,

GEORGE W. BLAGDEN,
*Pastor of said Church.*

The particulars of this abrogation of what had hitherto been considered by most churches a vital part of this sacred ordinance is not directly pertinent to the prominent object of this history, but, in connection with the answer to the "information," in the Supreme Judicial Court, of the nine members of the standing committee, the two pastors, two deacons, and treasurer of the Old South Church and Society, with the testimony of the witnesses before the auditor relative to the question of the sacramental collection, it is interesting, to show how matters of the gravest importance to present and future interests are passed upon without that calm, deliberate, and careful consideration which should never be disregarded, or set aside by the technicalities of form, or the unwillingness to acknowledge and correct errors. The extract from the answer is as follows : —

> And these defendants further answering admit, that it was formerly the custom in said Old South Church to take up a contribution on Communion Sundays; but they deny, on their information and belief, that such contributions were specially and specifically designed for any specified and certain objects and purposes, as alleged in the bill of complaint : on the contrary, they say, on their information and belief, that the said contributions were given generally to the Old South Church, to be appropriated to any object or purposes desired by said church.

Two witnesses appeared before the "master," for the purpose of sustaining the belief of the defendants, both of whom had taken a prominent part in the abrogation act of Dec. 28, 1849. One testified that he "knew" that the sacramental contribution balance was not specially designed for the poor, but that the contribution was always considered to be applied for any purposes the church might choose; and that, among other ways of its expenditure, "they had made presents to ministers." The other witness, when asked "whether he knew for what purposes this collection was taken in the Old South and other churches," answered, "that he was not so well acquainted as to the practice of other churches; but, in the Old South, it was for the use of the poor." The confession made by the first witness in the abrogatory document, which passed under his own supervision, "that the omission to take a collection at the close of each communion would not, in the present circumstances of the Old South, in any degree hurt the interests of the poor," with the following extract from the records of the standing committee in whose charge the financial matters are, will show the egregious mistake this witness was led into by his zeal to have this very important point — viz., the ownership of the " sacramental balance " — settled against the " poor-fund : " —

Extract, " April 15, 1822.

| | | |
|---|---|---:|
| Received on account of church, for interest | | $91.92 |
| " | rent of house Milk Street | 650.00 |
| " | balance of communion table | 85.37 |
| " | lighting and warming church, for charity lecture | 10.00 |
| | | $837.29 " |

Is not the foregoing sufficient proof that this sacramental balance is justly a part of the poor-fund, this extract also dispelling the obscurity thrown over "the lighting and warming of the church," which was neither more nor less than that each of the nine churches belonging to the Charity-Lecture Association paid to the Old South Church their proportionate part of the expense incurred on the evening when that lecture was given, and the twelve preparatory lectures also bore their part of the cost? With respect to gifts being made to ministers out of this money, as stated by this witness, the books of the church are silent. In those of the society, there are accounts of many liberal grants of money to our own ministers and their families, and one other also, which is noted for its entire absence of those common forms generally used by officials as indispensably requisite to substantiate the payments of such large sums of money.

March 15, 1857, " Paid Professor Park one thousand dollars."

No one of these sums of money, it is believed, were connected directly with the sacramental collections, as they were all passed in the treasurer's annual accounts. It may be that money donated to ministers is recorded in some account-book not furnished for the inspection of the auditor, as the books of the Old South had to be legally demanded before they could be obtained for use in the lawsuit.

The vote of the church in the "omitting" the customary sacramental collection appears to be based entirely upon the convenience of supplying the wants of the poor from its own abundant treasury, absolutely eschewing every consideration arising from the important fact that the offertory was in itself no inconsiderable part in the celebration of that ordinance.

The connection essentially subsisting for more than a hundred and forty years between this ordinance and the poor-fund, the interest of the latter being both directly and indirectly affected by the abrogation, [indirectly, more especially, by its severing the last tie which connected the parties together, will lead to some appropriate selections, which are respectfully offered for the serious consideration of the members of the Old South Church, as being particularly applicable in this case : —

At the celebration of the Lord's Supper, or Holy Communion, almsgiving is a necessary duty, without which our faith would be dead, being alone; the first way of expressing which is by dedicating some part of what God has given us to his use and service, which is strictly commanded in the Gospels, hath the best example for it, and the largest rewards promised to it, being instead of all the vast oblations and costly sacrifices which the Jews did always join with their prayer, and the only chargeable duty to which Christians are obliged. It is, in a word, so necessary to recommend our prayers, that St. Paul prescribes to the ancient church, that every one lay by him in store, as God has prospered him, as a collection for the saints, when the sacrament is received, at which time it is by no means to be omitted. When the Jews came before the Lord at the solemn feasts, they were not allowed to appear empty; but every one was required "to give as he was able," according to the blessing of the Lord which had given him. And our Saviour supposes we should never come to the altar without a gift. And it is very possible that at the time of receiving the sacrament were those large donations of houses, lands, and money made. For, when the first converts were united to Christ and one another in the feast of love, their very souls were mingled, they cheerfully renounced their property, and freely distributed their goods to those to whom they had given their hearts before. None were allowed to receive without giving something, and to reject any man's offering was to deny him a share in the benefit of those comfortable ministrations. At first, this offertory embraced the moneys paid for the maintenance of the ministers. Now, indeed, while they have a stated income, the money collected at these times is generally appropriated to the poor.

In early times, bishops and clergy were the only dispensers of alms to the poor: the whole of the income of the church was directed to support of the clergy, and the poor, and the ransom of captives. "Those who appropriated to their own use the property of the church, if they persisted in their evil courses, drew upon them the malediction of Judas, that they might die excommunicated and accursed."

A reference is also recommended to that apposite and beautiful selection from the Scriptures, appointed by the Episcopal Church to be read during the taking the sacramental offertory; believing that its perusal may induce an opinion, that, if the worldly "interests of the poor are not hurt" by the act of omission, the spiritual interests of both rich and poor were entirely lost sight of and forgotten in that transaction.

From 1708 to 1761, the sacramental accounts were kept, in common with the general legacy accounts, in old tenor, which at the latter time was changed to lawful currency, as will be seen by a reference to Deacon Hubbard's general account of the church and society, wherein the whole accounts to the above date are settled, and which is the only account in the books in which these affairs are stated together. From that time also, the balance, being the unexpended portion of the sacramental collection, was received from the respective deacons, and credited to the church-stock or poor-fund account, in common with the legacies to the poor and the emoluments therefrom, thus becoming a part and parcel of that fund. The manner in which this church-stock or poor-fund was kept was to credit the cash as it was received for the whole or a part of a legacy; while bonds or notes comprising also another part of the same were separately accounted for in periodical statements of church-stock, the amount of which was charged to each successive treasurer, so that an accurate account of all the trust assets was shown in the settlement of these accounts, which were always audited by three persons, and authenticated by their signatures. A memorandum or special legacy account was kept of the income and disposition of the largest legacies; and when any of the bonds, notes, mortgages, or bank-stock belonging to them, were realized, the money was placed in the church-stock, and invested with the money of that fund. These legacies, being designed for one purpose, in course of time became merged in one common stock. The ordinary accounts of the parish expenditures, relating to meeting-house, ministers' houses, salaries to ministers, and all other expenditures which generally belong to public worship, were always kept separately and distinct by themselves.

At this time there were no institutions in this country, similar to the incorporated companies of the city of London, in which property designed for charitable uses could be placed in safety. Consequently these benevolent donors of the poor-fund confided their gifts to the Old South Church, believing that sanctuary, whose own poor was especially interested in its preservation, would insure to future generations the benefits they intended to perpetuate after they had passed away. For many years the money of this fund was invested in province notes, which were purchased at going rates when the province required money. When the currency became debased, this was redeemed in Spanish dollars at a great discount, and the proceeds invested in old tenor province notes, which again was changed into lawful money, and again invested in province notes. But, when the political troubles between the mother country and this country commenced, these were sold, and the money was placed on bond and mortgage of good real estate, where it remained during the Revolutionary War, — in one instance, the interest on a very large sum remaining unpaid for over ten years. All the property — with the exception of a slight amount lost — being available, was, after the adoption of the Federal Constitution, invested in United-States and Massachusetts State stocks, purchased at the most favorable prices for ready money at that day. When the Massachusetts Bank was established, these stocks were sold at an advance, and, with the accumulated income, were invested in that bank, from which it received an income of over nine per cent per annum, a small part of this stock being among the assets of this fund at the present time. The church was at this period intimately connected in its social relations with the bank, and seemed to be well posted up in its knowledge of money affairs. Several of its members were directors of the bank, and the solicitorship of the bank and of the church were united in the same person.

While the "cruse of oil" failed not abundantly to supply this "treasury of the Lord," a distribution to the poor corresponding to its receipts was made ; for, in 1797, the amount appropriated for their relief was five hundred and ninety-two dollars, being within eight dollars of the sum set apart by the society in their by-law donation at the present time, when their yearly income is over forty thousand dollars from the rents of their real estate, which real estate was enhanced in value by the application of the money of the poor-fund to its improvement.

The rise and improvement of the church-stock, or poor-fund, is as follows, as shown in the Deacons' book from 1708 to 1798, and in the society's report of 1800 : —

| | | | | | | |
|---|---|---|---|---|---|---|
| In Oct. 31, 1761, amt. bonds, notes, &c., per D. Hubbard's acc., | | | | | | £513 14s. 3d. |
| " Jan. | 1766, | " | " | " | " W. Phillips, | 874 14 3 |
| " Jan. | 1767, | " | " | " | " " | 911 13 3¼ |
| " Jan. | 1771, | " | " | " | " " | 1,071 8 4 |
| " Sept. | 1773, | " | " | " | " " | 1,314 10 8 |
| " Nov. | 1793, | " | " | " | " " | 3,052 13 9 |
| " April, | 1800, as per committee's report to the society, | | | | | $16,062 71 |

This church-stock, from so small a sum as £98. 8s. 5d., old tenor, in 1708, was greatly increased by the gifts and bequests of charitable persons. It was these gifts and bequests, combined with the zealous and disinterested labors of truly good men, who exercised a wise discretion and Christian liberality in relieving the wants of the poor, which enabled the Trustees to present the large amount of assets in 1800. So very scrupulous were they in regard to its proper use and preservation, that no instance can be adduced where any part of the trust-property was ever used for the general purposes of the society, excepting that of the before-mentioned sum of £192, old tenor, "lent out of this stock" to the society "to pay deficiency to the ministers," and a trifling expenditure from the sacramental collection for expenses of delegates to sister churches on ecclesiastical business. So particular were they against the infringement of this rule, that the society had to pay for wine taken from the sacramental supply for the entertainment of their ministerial guests. And in 1798, while the church had in their hands funds of the net amount of over fourteen thousand dollars, the meeting-house and steeple were out of repair, and the only way devised by a committee of ways and means to consider the subject was to obtain a subscription, which was done, and thus the object effected.

If these funds had been considered by the society, at that time, justly available for their own purposes, would they not, in the absence of other means, in this case, have been resorted to? It has been before stated how the ordinary parish expenses were paid before the erection of the present meeting-house. Subsequently to that time, a tax upon the pews was laid for that purpose, the rate of which has been but slightly altered until the present day.

## CHAPTER IV.

Mrs. Norton's Gift of Land. — Building of Stores proposed. — Committee of Year 1800. — Report of Church-Stock. — Treasurer Phillips, Sen.'s, Account of the same. — Treasurer Hubbard's 1761 Account of Church-Stock. — Proceedings for the Erection of Stores. — History of Part of the Stocks belonging to Poor-Fund.

It will here be necessary, for a clear understanding of this financial history, to give an elaborate account of Mrs. Norton's gift of land to the Old South, and the relation which it bears, not only to the entire property now in possession, but to the poor-fund in particular. Mrs. Norton had given the land in question to the society, in trust for certain purposes, as expressed in her conveyances of the same. The society had, from A.D. 1677 to 1800, used the same for the special purposes of that trust; and, to use her own words, "for noe other intent or purpose whatever." At this time, 1800, a project was entertained by some of the society, to occupy the vacant part of the land fronting on what now is Washington Street, by erecting five brick stores thereon, with a view of obtaining an income from their rental, whereby they might be enabled "amply to pay, with the present tax on the pews, not only the present minister (Dr. Eckley), but an additional one." To effect this object, funds adequate became necessary; and as the society, as such, possessed no means whatever, either real or personal, either to borrow upon, or otherwise convert into money, the only alternative was to resort to the assets belonging to the Ministers' and Deacons' Fund, thus profiting by the permissive intimation shadowed forth in the Charitable and Pious Fund foundation, whereby the funds of what Drs. Sewall and Prince denominated that "evangelical treasury" "should be laid out in some real estate bringing some income, or building on or improving the real estate which shall belong to said church."

In 1800, an entire revolution was effected in the manner of managing the real and personal trust-property, by changing the former from a strict trust, and nearly annihilating the latter, by mixing them together, until it was with great difficulty that each could be discerned through the obscure medium of a fragile annual " six-hundred-dollar law," which, fortunately, afforded a clew to unravel the mystery of the well-nigh-forgotten poor-fund.

### MARY NORTON'S CHARITY.

Deed entered and recorded, lib. 6, fol. 26, Suffolk Records, 1st April, 1669. Attest, Edward Rawson, Reg. The second deed was acknowledged 30th June, 1677; and recorded Jan. 13, 1804, lib. 207, fol. 241, — one hundred and twenty-seven years afterwards. William Alline, Register.

As this second deed conveys a very important part of the Norton property as to quantity and conditions, and as Mr. Theophilus Parsons's opinion of the year 1800 is considered a standard rule as to the manner of its use by the society, it may be curious to inquire how such a rule could have been made infallible, taking into consideration the date of the above registrary.

### DEED.

To all Christian People to whom these presents shall come: I Mary Norton, the Relict, Widow, and sole Executrix to the last Will and Testament of the late Reverend my Deare and Honoured Husband Mr. John Norton, teacher of the First Church of Boston in the County of Suffolk in the Colony of Massachusetts, in New England, Send Greeting. Know yee that I the said Mary Norton for divers good causes and considerations mee thereunto moving, and more especially for and in consideration of that indeared affection, that my late deare husband, in his life time did beare, and myself doe beare, unto his and my assured friends — Captaine Thomas Savage, Capt. William Davis, Mr. Hesekiah Usher, Mr. Edward Rawson, Mr. John Hull, Mr. Peter Oliver, Mr. Josiah Scottow, Mr. Edward Raynsford, Mr. Richard Trewsdall and Mr. Jacob Elliot, all of the said Boston, and in confidence of their faithfullness to performe that Trust which I shall repose in them, Have absolutely Given, granted, allened, enfeofed, and confirmed, and by these presents doe fully, clearly, and absolutely, Give, Grant, alliene, enfeof, and confirme unto them the above named Thomas Savage, William Davis, Hesekiah Usher, Edward Rawson, John Hull, Peter Oliver, Josiah Scottow, Richard Trewsdall, Edward Raynsford, and Jacob Elliot, for the use and purpose and purposes hereafter mentioned, conditioned, and expressed; one parcell of land situate lying and being within the Limmetts of Boston Towne, above named, and is part of the land that is adjoining, to my now mansion-house, the said given and Granted premises, containing by estimation, fifty five poles or pearches, more or less, and is bounded from the corner post next Nathaniel Reynolds, along the high street leading from Roxbury to Boston; seaven length of rails being seventy nine foote and a halfe, from thence to the middle fence now standing and parting of orchard, and the pasture six length of rails, from the lane or street leading to Mr. Peter Olivers, and soe back into the pasture, ninety five foote, the said length of rails conteyning seaunty one foote or thereabouts, from thence to the dividing fence betweene the said pasture and Mr. Richard Price, his Garden, one hundred foote and alongst the said fence, this lane aforesaid sixty foote and from thence to the said corner aforesaid, next the said Nathaniel Reynolds his dwelling house Two hundred thirty eight foote and one halfe foote, bee it more or less. To Have and to Hold the above granted Premises bee the same more or less with all the priviledges and appurtenances to the same apperteyning or in anywise belonging unto them the said Thomas Savage, William Davis, Hesekiah Usher, Edward Rawson, John Hull, Peter Oliver, Josiah Scottow, Richard Trewsdall, Edward Raynsford, and Jacob Elliott, and to such as they shall associate to themselves, their heirs, and successors forever, for the erecting of a house for their assembling themselves together publiquely to worship GOD. As also the erecting of a dwelling-house for such minister or ministers as shall bee by them and their successors from time to time orderly and regularly admitted for the Pastor, or teacher to the said Church or Assembly, and for the accommodation of the meeting house, with convenient passages of ingress, egress, and regress, for the people, that shall, there from time to time assemble as aforesaid, and for noe other intent, use, or purpose whatever. " And I the above Mary Norton, sole Executrix as above is expressed for mee, my heires Executors and Administrators doe Covenant, promise and grant to and with the said Thomas Savage, William Davis, Hesekiah Usher, Edward Rawson, John Hull, Peter Oliver, Josiah Scottow, Richard Truesdall, Edward Raynsford, and Jacob Elliott, their, and every of their heires Executors, Administrators, and Assigns, by these presents that I the said Mary Norton ; now am and at the Ensealing hereof stand and bee the true and proper owner of the above Granted premises, and that I have good right, full power and lawful Authority, to Give, Grant bargaine, and confirme, the same, unto them the said Thomas Savage, William Davis, Hesekiah Usher, Edward Rawson, John Hull, Peter Oliver, Josiah Scottow, Richard Trewsdall, Edward Raynsford and Jacob Elliott, their heires and successors forever." And that the said Thomas Savage, William Davis, Hesekiah Usher, Edward Rawson, John Hull, Peter Oliver, Josiah Scottow, Richard Trewsdall, Edward Raynsford, and Jacob Elliott, and company, which they shall associate to themselves and their successors shall and may at all times, and from time to time forever hereafter, have, hold, possess, and enjoy all the above given and granted premises, to the use, and uses, intents, and purposes, as above is Expressed, without the least denyall or Contradiction of mee the said Mary Norton, my heires, Executors, Administrators and assigns, or by any other person, or persons, whatsoever, having, clayming or pretending to have or clayme, any Lawful right and use or interest therein, by from or under mee, or by from or under my late Reverend and deare husband Mr. John Norton deceased, or any of his estate, or either of our heires, Executors, Administrators, or assigns. In Witness hereof I the above mentioned Mary Norton have hereunto putt my hand and seale the first day of Aprill, One thousand, Six hundred and sixty nine, being the one and twentieth yeare of the Reigne of Sovereigne Lord Charles the second of England, Scotland, France & Ireland, King: Defender of the Faith yr 1669.

Signed Sealed and with seal appending delivered after possession was given and taken of the within granted premises in presence of us.

MARY NORTON.

J. HINKSMAN
JOHN GREENLEAF
SALOMON RAYNSFORD & acknowledged before
THOS. DANFORTH Assistant.

In the second deed, an additional "piece of land is given" "for the ends and purposes in the first above-mentioned deed of April 1, 1669, as fully and amply declared, reference thereto being had, may appear;" and the following is a copy of the clause in her will which gave the remainder of the property: —

Suffolk Records, lib. 297, fol. 241. " Item, I give and bequeath unto the Third Church of Christ, in Boston, my now dwelling-house, with all the land belonging to the same, as it is situated near the Third Meeting House, in Boston aforesaid, with all profits, privileges, rights, and appurtenances whatsoever to the same belonging or appertaining, for the use of the ministry in the said church forever."

When the plan for erecting the stores was first proposed to the society, many members, especially the more aged ones, were doubtful of its expediency, fearful of jeopardizing the title to the land on account of Mrs. Norton's conditions as to its use, and the difficulty of raising means, being aware that the society were cramped to pay their bills, and had recently to resort to a voluntary subscription to pay for repairs upon the meeting-house and steeple. A committee had been chosen in the preceding year, 1799, to take into consideration the right and propriety of building a number of stores on the land held by the society, adjoining the meeting-house. Their report was twice read by the moderator. It is as follows: —

Boston, March 20, 1800. Your committee, having met together at different times to consider the subject referred to them by the South Society, are of opinion it would be for the interest of the said society to erect, on the land belonging to them fronting the main street, five handsome brick stores, agreeably to a plan exhibited some time since by Mr. Dawes.

Your committee, wishing to be possessed of the opinion of able lawyers respecting the society's right of building on land given by Mrs. Norton, have called on Theophilus Parsons, Esq., attorney at law, whose opinion they have in writing; which is, that the society have a clear right to make use of said land *in any way they please*, as said land, in the opinion of your committee, cannot be improved to the benefit of the said society in any better way than by erecting said stores; it appearing, by estimate, that the whole expense will not exceed ten thousand dollars to complete them, and they may be rented, without any difficulty, to good tenants, for the sum of two thousand or two thousand five hundred dollars per annum, which will give an interest from twenty to twenty-five per cent for their money.

If this statement is a true one, and the society's money can be borrowed for erecting said buildings, even if the society pay the interest for the same at the rate it is now said to produce, which is nine per cent, there must remain an overplus of from eleven to sixteen per cent, which would enable the society amply to pay, with the present tax on the pews, not only the present minister, but an additional one, provided the society should choose to expend it in that way; in doing which, it is the opinion of your committee, the views of the donors, not only of the land, but those who have left legacies from time to time, will be fully answered, as the poor of the society will have as much as they now receive, and the other will be laid out in pious uses for the support of public worship. All of which is submitted. By order.

Wm. Holmes,<br>*Chairman of Committee.*

Fast Day, April 3, 1800. After the foregoing report had been duly conversed upon at a numerous meeting of the society, the question was moved and put whether the same should be accepted. *Voted* to accept the same, *nemine contra dicente.*

A reference to a report of the standing committee of the Old South Society, March 22, 1809, hereafter noticed, will show that denominating the poor-fund in the present report "The Society's Money" was partly the occasion by which a very large part, $5,245, belonging to that fund, was wrongfully diverted into the uses of the society, and is now due, principal and interest.

*Voted,* That there be a committee of five appointed to examine into the state of the society's funds, and report the sums of moneys and their different appropriations.

The committee was appointed April 22, 1800; and the following is their report: —

Your committee, appointed to examine into the state of the funds of the South Church and congregation, to endeavor to find from what source they have arisen, and the intentions of the donors, have attended to that business, and beg leave to report, that, on examining, they find them to have arisen as follows; viz. : —

| | | | |
|---|---|---|---|
| Given by sundry persons of the church to the care of the deacons of the church | | | £102 18s. 4d. |
| Given by sundry persons, for the poor of said church, to the care of the ministers and deacons of the church | | | 153 6 8 |
| Given, for the poor of the church and congregation, to the care of the ministers and deacons | £5 12s. 0d. | | |
| Given by Mrs. Mills | 100 19 10 | | |
| Given by Mr. Cunningham | 66 13 4 | | |
| | | | 173 5 2 |
| Collected at sundry times the interest, to the use of ministers' widows and children | | | 66 19 2 |
| Given to the poor of the church, not mentioned to whose care, | | | 6 0 0 |
| Given, and not mentioned whether to the use of the church, or the church and congregation | | | 8 0 4 |
| Collected from May, 1757, to 1773, for use of palls | | | 46 7 6 |
| Balances arising from the sacramental collections at different times, to the year 1766, over and above what paid the expenses | | | 186 19 5 |
| We find by the church-book, given by sundry persons, which we find no minutes in the papers for what use, but, as they are entered in the church-account, suppose for their use | | | 136 14 5 |
| Amount of the whole, lawful money | | | £880 11s. 0d. |

Annexed to this is the notice of the old bonds alluded to in the account of Ann Mills's charity.

This was in possession in 1766, and at interest, and has been used ever since, the war coming on in about nine years after this time; and the moneys remaining during that period must have accumulated considerably. After peace came on, the money was generally called in, and invested in public funds, where it now remains, and is as follows; viz.: —

| | | |
|---|---|---|
| Massachusetts Bank shares, sixteen, at $500 each | | $8,000 00 |
| Forty-two and one-half Union Bank shares, at $8 | | 340 00 |
| Samuel Hinkley & Co.'s bond | | 416 66 |
| Three per cent stock | $2,391 40 | |
| Ditto | 194 35 | |
| Ditto | 2,350 00 | |
| | | 4,935 75 |
| Eight per cent stock | | 600 00 |
| Five and one-half per cent stock | | 1,000 00 |
| Massachusetts State notes, 5 per cent | | 709 37 |
| Deferred stock of United States | | 60 93 |
| | | $16,062 71 |

All of which is submitted per order.

The committee acknowledge that they took as a basis of their report the account of 1766. This fact is also completely substantiated by the mention of the item £186. 19s. 5d., which is *only* found in that document, and in no other, in the whole accounts. The original report of church-stock was made by William Phillips, sen., both deacon and treasurer of the Old South Church; which account was audited separately for church and congregation by Deacon Hubbard, Andrew Oliver, and Joshua Winslow, while Mr. Phillips charged the amount, £874. 14s. 3d., to himself in his account of treasurership, as follows : —

| | | | |
|---|---|---|---|
| Rev. Mr. Pemberton's legacy . . . . | £17 7s. 9d. | | |
| Mr. Cunningham's " . . . . | 66 13 4 | | |
| Mrs. Mills's " . . . . | 100 19 10 | | |
| Mrs. Eliza Loring's " . . . . | 13 6 8 | | |
| Capt. John Armitage's " . . . . | 13 6 8 | | |
| Mr. Farr Tolman's " . . . . | 40 0 0 | | |
| Daniel Henchman's " . . . . | 66 0 0 | | |
| Mr. John Simpson's " . . . . | 30 0 0 | | |
| Mrs. Mary Ireland's " . . . . | 133 6 8 | | |
| Rev. Dr. Sewall's " . . . . | 20 0 0 | | |
| | | £501 0s. 11d. | |
| Pious and Charitable Fund . . . . | 63 12 6 | | |
| Ministers and Widows . . . . . | 3 6 8 | | |
| | | 66 19 2½ | |
| Sacramental Stock . . . . . | 186 19 5¼ | | |
| Interest received on above . . . . | 119 14 8¼ | | |
| | | 306 14 1½ | |
| | | £874 14s. 3d. | |

In the discovering committee's report, the amount is £880. 11s. 0d., being £5. 6s. 9d. more than Mr. Phillips's account, and designating but two names of persons who bestowed legacies to the poor (Cunningham and Mills), and stands in relation to each as follows : viz.,

| | |
|---|---|
| Amount same both accounts . . . . . . . | £421 11s. 9d. |
| Amount not explained in committee's account . . . | 458 19 3 |
| | £880 11 0 |

Besides leaving unmentioned the names of eight persons or more who were early benefactors of the poor-fund, whose gifts must form a larger portion of the above unexplained amount in this committee's report.

Mr. Phillips's account being kept in accordance with ancient usages practised by his predecessors, and being transferred to and credited by him, with every particular legacy identified, as well as the unexpended and uninvested balance of both income and interest, as exhibited in the two last items, — balance £186. 19s. 5¼d., balance and interest £119. 14s. 8½d. = £306. 14s. 1¾d., — go far to prove its correctness.* To this church-stock account, in course of time, were added, as "received," the respective legacies of John Osborn, Benjamin Pemberton, and Thomas Bromfield, with fifty pounds bequeathed by Thomas Hubbard to the Pious and Charitable Fund some years before 1771, when it was credited to that account.

In 1766, when all the accounts, including those of the early old-tenor legacies, eight in number, were settled by Mr. Hubbard, the money invested prior to that date was re-invested in a note of £134. 0s. 0d., which comprises a larger part of the sum £186. 19s. 5¼d. attributed in this spurious report to the sacramental collections, but which had but little to do with it. Was not this committee, instructed, as they were, "to examine into the society's funds, and report the sums of money and their different appropriations," truly unfortunate in their labors, as exhibited in this production? and was not also the society more unfortunate still, in view of all its deplorable consequences, in giving heed to representations so incompatible with the actual condition of its financial situation? . . . A fair examination of the whole subject inevitably leads to the conclusion, that this report was purposely intended to divert the attention of the society from the true condition of the property held by them in trust, both real and personal.

This subject, being intimately connected with another important action of the society's financial operations, will be considered in its due course, in a further and more comprehensive relation of it, which will then be presented.

At the same meeting it was —

*Voted*, That so much moneys in the hands of the treasurer, belonging to them as church and congregation, be borrowed and improved, by erecting the five brick buildings on the land belonging to them, agreeably to a vote passed the third day of April last.

*Voted*, That a committee of five, three of the church and two of the congregation, be desired to apply to the trustees, the ministers and deacons, for the loan of the sum necessary to defray the expenses of building the stores.

The committee was then chosen.

May 11, 1800. At a meeting of the brethren of the church and congregation, —

* This interest was balance of interest account received by Mr. Phillips in the settlement, when he assumed the treasurership, the assets being estimated at par value by payer and receiver.

*Voted*, That the committee appointed on 22d April last, to borrow moneys of the minister and deacons to defray the expense of erecting stores on the society's land, be hereby discharged from that duty. And it is —

*Voted*, That the ministers and deacons be requested, and they are hereby authorized, to pay and deliver from the money of the church and congregation, to the committee, contractors appointed on 22d April, and to any other committee that may be employed to erect said stores, all such sums of money as may from time to time be found necessary by such committees for building said stores; said committees rendering regular accounts thereof to said minister and deacons, so that it may appear how much of said money shall be transferred and changed from their present situation to the property in said stores. And whatever moneys shall be so paid and delivered shall be considered as having been duly accounted for by said minister and deacons, the present trustees thereof. And the said minister and deacons shall at all times be entitled to receive so much of the rents and income of said stores as shall amount to six per cent per annum upon the moneys they shall pay and deliver as aforesaid, to the end that they may be enabled to appropriate the same in like manner as the interest of said moneys has heretofore been appropriated, according to the pious intentions of the donors thereof.

And as it is highly probable that the rents and income of said stores will exceed the rate of six per cent per annum upon said moneys, by reason that the value of the land will be added to the value of the stores, it is therefore

*Voted*, That whatever rents and income said stores shall produce, over and above the legal interest on said moneys, shall go into the hands of the treasurer, *distinct from any funds of the society*, and shall be used and applied for the purposes set forth in the committee's report of 20th March last, and which was accepted the 3d April last, in such manner as the church and congregation shall from time to time vote and determine, or for such other ecclesiastical purposes as they shall order.

This document, if any proof was requisite further than that previously offered, affords unquestionable evidence that these funds, or any part of them, never belonged to the church and congregation; for, if that had been the fact, why any need of borrowing upon the part of the society? Why not use them as such?

It shows that they were trust-funds, in charge of the society, the income of which was under the direction of the minister and deacons.

That these funds were invested, and produced more than legal interest.

That, in this agreement, provision was made against the diminution of that income.

That a provision also was made (so far as was possible) for the security of the principal borrowed, making the store-property accountable for the same. And, as the income from the moneys had already been legally disposed of under the provisions in the wills of the donors thereof, the church and congregation had no right to alter or divert the same, the distributive power having been vested with the ministers and deacons of the Old South Church, *ex officio*.

The trust-funds were in amount, nominally, $16,062.71, consisting of sixteen shares of the Massachusetts Bank, par-value $8,000.00; and other assets estimated at the value of $5,221.40, which were by a special vote ordered to be sold, and produced the sum of $5,245.00, leaving the bank-shares for future operation. The cost of the five stores, as per the treasurer's account, amounted to the sum of $14,065.90.

To show that the securities, valued at $5,245.00, were justly inseparable from the shares of the bank, valued at $8,000.00, and were equally the assets of the poor-fund, an abstract from the Deacons' book will show the date when the purchases were made, —

| | | | | £ | s. | d. | |
|---|---|---|---|---|---|---|---|
| 1784, Aug. 7, | purchased | 2 bank shares | . | £300 | 0s. | 0d. | |
| "   " 20, | " | 2    " | . | 300 | 0 | 0 | |
| "   Sept. 2, | " | 1 treasurer's note | . | 109 | 13 | 9 | |
| 1789, | " | 1    " | . | 300 | 0 | 0 | |
| " | " | 1    " | . | 100 | 0 | 0 | |
| 1790, May 1, | " | 1    " | . | 200 | 0 | 0 | |
| 1791, Jan. | " | 4 shares in bank | . | 660 | 0 | 0 | |
| 1792, June 2, | " | 6    " | . | 900 | 0 | 0 | |
| "   July 2, | " | 2    " | . | 300 | 0 | 0 | |
| 1793, Nov. | " | $2,300 U. S. stock | . | 379 | 0 | 0 | |
| 1794, April, | " | treasury note, | . | 158 | 7 | 9 | |
| | | | | £3,707 | 11s. | 6d. | $12,358 58 |
| 1796, Jan. | " 5 per cent U. S. stock at 20 per cent discount | | | $1,000 | | | |
| Oct. | " 42 shares Union Bank | | | 417 92 | | | |
| | | | | | | | $1,417 92 |
| | | | | | | | $13,776 50 |

Assets on hand belonging to the trust, $13,380.00

A.D. 1800 was the beginning of a new era in the management of the money concerns of the society: "old things were to be done away, and all things become new;" these long-cherished funds, so wisely and carefully kept and augmented, so prudently yet liberally administered to relieve the necessities of the poor and needy, were hereafter to be indiscriminately mixed with the general financial concerns of the society. Hitherto, they had always been scrupulously kept apart; and although the society at times suffered much in their temporal concerns during the vicissitudes of the Revolutionary

War, yet but a slight loss was incurred by the poor-fund, every precaution that carefulness could indicate for its safety being taken by those who held it in their charge. At this period also, a great change in the religious opinions of many, as to the duties incumbent upon Christians in relation to doing good, agitated the public mind. Churches, ministers, and societies became greatly enthusiastic in disseminating their views and doctrines for Christianizing the world, and establishing universal benevolence, while the still unruffled stream of personal, practical charity, smoothly and unostentatiously making its way, refreshing all around, "blessing those who gave as well as they who received," was almost unheeded amid the general clamor which prevailed. It was therefore not unlikely that a prominent institution, like the Old South, should have partaken of the excitement.

## CHAPTER V.

Theophilus Parsons's and Jeremiah Mason's Opinions. — Mrs. Norton's Deed and Will. — Dr. Blagden's Relinquishment of Parsonage-House. — Mr. Manning's Non-relinquishment.

In the committee's report of 3d April, they say, " Wishing to be possessed of the opinion of able lawyers respecting the society's right of building on land given by Mrs. Norton, having called on Theophilus Parsons, Esq., attorney at law, whose opinion they have in writing," of which the following is a copy: —

### CASE.

Mary Norton by her deed executed April 1, 1669, conveyed a lot of land, in Boston, to Thomas Savage and others and their associates, who are now the Old South Society, in Boston, to them and their heirs and successors, forever, for the erecting an house of public worship, and also of parsonage-houses for their ministers; and for the accommodation of the parsonage, and also of the meeting-house, with convenient passages; and for no other use, intent, or purpose whatsoever. The grantees entered under the said conveyance, and they and their successors have ever since been seized of the premises. On the same they erected a meeting-house and two parsonage-houses. One of the parsonage-houses has been down for some years, and the site of it is vacant ground. Question, Can the society erect buildings or stores on that vacant site, to let out, for the purpose of applying the rents for the support of public worship, and for the benefit of the said society? Answer, As the conveyance is to the grantees, their heirs, and successors, forever, without any words of condition or limitation annexed to the fee, it is my clear opinion that the society may erect the building or stores aforesaid for the said purposes; that the words " and for no other use, intent, or purpose whatsoever " contain only a direction, a deviation from which will not defeat the title of the society.

Signed, THEOPHILUS PARSONS.
March 14, 1800.

There being also upon the records of the society an opinion of an equally eminent professional man, the Hon. Jeremiah Mason, upon a part of the same estate, given on a similar occasion, it is thought proper to place them in proximity, although in anticipation of its history, which will be otherwise continued in regular course.

## JEREMIAH MASON'S OPINION ON DEEDS RELATING TO OLD SOUTH PROPERTY.

The said parish, in 1810, erected two dwelling-houses on the vacant land in Milk Street. One of said dwelling-houses has been occupied by the minister of the parish as his parsonage; the other has been leased, and the rents applied to the support of public worship of the parish.

An opinion is requested, whether the parish can rightfully build warehouses on the land adjoining Milk Street, on which the two dwelling-houses stand, and let them to tenants, applying the rents to the support of public worship, and other necessary expenses of said society.

### OPINION.

This case raises two questions: first, whether the first-mentioned deed of Mary Norton, under which the parish hold the premises in question, created a condition as to the perpetual use of said premises, for the non-performance of which a forfeiture may be incurred, and which her heirs may enter, and defeat the grant. Second, whether the said deed created a trust, limiting and confirming the said premises for the sole use of a parsonage-house for the ministers of the said parish forever, which a court of chancery, on due application therefor, will enforce. A copy of an opinion of the late Chief Justice Parsons has been shown me, given in 1800, in which he says, that the terms used in the aforesaid deed do not constitute a condition, a deviation on which a forfeiture may be incurred, but only a direction, a deviation from which will not defeat the title of the society. I fully concur with that opinion: none can carry with it a greater authority. Indeed, were it doubtful whether the provisions of that deed might not be construed to amount to a condition, little danger to the title of the parish need be apprehended from such construction; none but the heirs of the grantor can take advantage of the breach of condition. In her will she mentions no descendants, which she would have been likely to have done, had she have left any; and it is in the highest degree improbable that any person now living can be able to establish his heirship to Mary Norton by any line of collateral kindred, after the lapse of so long a period. I am of opinion, therefore, that there is no ground for any reasonable apprehension of danger from forfeiture by breach of condition. As to the question whether the deed creates a trust, I think it apparent from the language of the deed, that the grantor intended that the granted premises should be forever applied to the use of a meeting-house thereon, to be erected by the parish, then about to be established, and for a parsonage-house for the use of the ministers of such parish. This in my opinion created a valid trust; and I think the parish now holds the land subject to that trust. At the time when Chief Justice Parsons gave his opinion on the "case," no court in this State had power to enforce the execution of trusts. The Supreme Court of Judicature now has jurisdiction competent for that purpose. A court of chancery, in dealing with trusts for charitable uses, will never vacate or set aside a trust, if it has been abused or misused, and restore the property to the heirs of the donors, but will, in a proper case, compel the specific execution of this trust for the benefit of the *cestuie que trust*. The only person interested in the specific execution of this trust (that is, in having always a parsonage-house on the land granted in trust) is the minister of the parish for the time being. The great change of circumstances since the time of conveyance has rendered this land an inconvenient and ineligible site for a dwelling-house. The present minister is desirous of a residence in a more retired situation. Under these circumstances, I am of opinion that the parish may, without the abuse of the trust, apply this land to the use of warehouses, and provide for the minister a suitable dwelling-house in a more convenient situation. So long as the income derived from the warehouses shall be faithfully applied to the support of the minister, and other necessary expenses of the parish, no court of chancery will, I think, ever hold this to be an abuse or mismanagement of the trust. More especially will this be deemed not an abuse or breach of trust when it is done with the consent of the *cestuie qui trust*, — the minister of the parish, the only party in interest. Such consent the present incumbent, it is said, is ready to give in authentic form. A similar consent, by way of release of all claims to a parsonage-house on that land, may be required by the parish of all their future ministers, at the time of their respective settlements. This may be readily done by the parish inserting in their votes for the call and settlement of their future minister, immediately after the vote of the salary, that the same is to be in full satisfaction and discharge of any supposed right or claim to have a parsonage-house on the land adjoining the meeting-house, and requiring him, in his acceptance of the call, especially to assent to such a discharge. I do not think this necessary; but the parish can, if they please, require it out of abundant caution.

Signed,     J. MASON.

It must be admitted that there cannot be a doubt as to the legal ability of those eminent professional men who were consulted in this case; but as the questions are involved in doubt and difficulty, upon which different minds might well be led to different conclusions, who is to say how far any court (a court of chancery, for instance), having the whole subject before them, may concur with their opinions and the consequences flowing from them, particularly when the questions involved would be determined upon a clear and legal view of the whole ground, instead of a partial representation, presented for consideration to private counsel, for an answer conformable to pre-conceived opinions, with a sole view to an ultimate object? That Mrs. Norton's intention of making this a strict trust for the placing a meeting and parsonage houses upon the land bequeathed and given by her, and for "no other intent, use, and purpose whatsoever," seems as plain as language can make it; and that it was always so understood and practised upon for over one hundred years by her cotemporary friends, trustees, and their immediate successors, who would be most likely to know her wishes, is unquestionable. During that period, the expenses attendant upon building and repairing both meeting and parsonage houses, the ministers' salaries, the expenses of public worship, support of missionary aid to the poor, relief to sufferers by fire and shipwreck, were all sustained by collections, contributions, and pew-taxes, from church and congregation. Would this have been done, had it not been well understood at that time that the Norton property was especially dedicated to another purpose? This property was then, as it is now, centrally situated. North and south of it had been appropriated to dwellings, and places for business, — Old Cornhill, directly contiguous, being the choice stand for the fashionable retail trade of Boston, — nor was there any other vacant lot available, all others having been built upon. It is hardly possible to conceive of any other reason than the one here given why, under these circumstances, the church, who were often straitened for ways and means, should never have entertained, for so long time, the project of using this land as a source of income. Whether Mr. Parsons was made aware of this sentiment as to the use of the land from the time it was received to the time when he gave his opinion, there is no means now of learning; but, as it regards the amalgamating the personal trust-property with it, there appears to be no proper way pointed out by the committee whereby the society could have arrived to a just conclusion upon the subject. If the committee had, it would have been impossible that a conveyance could have been made of it; for, had the Society fully comprehended the nature of the trust-fund, which could not have been derived from that committee's report, they would, in all probability, have taken such measures to secure the repayment of the money loaned, as would have prevented the grievous wrong sustained by that portion of the trust-property.

In the same partial manner must the case have been presented to Mr. Mason as it was to Mr. Parsons; otherwise, it cannot be accounted for why he labored under several misapprehensions in his view of it. Whether or not they might have affected the opinion, it is not here the place to determine. They are only noticed to show that both of the opinions were not based upon such a careful examination as a court of chancery would have made, had the case been presented to them for a decision. Mr. Mason supposed the premises to have been "vacant land," for the future use of which the society designed one more profitable. In fact, the land had, from 1705, always been used according to the express direction of the donor, having a pastor's house erected upon it. This house was removed in 1809, for the purpose of building two other parsonages to accommodate the two pastors of the Old South Church. After the demise of one of them, Dr. Eckley, the rent received from this vacant house was, in the society's annual estimate of "ways and means," reckoned merely as a source of income for paying interest on their debt. When these parsonage-houses were removed, to the great pecuniary advantage of the society, the annual six-hundred-dollar grant to the poor was passed (in which no mention was made as to its perpetuity); and which was, in 1867, by vote discontinued.

It is correct, as Mr. Mason says, that Mrs. Norton left no descendants; but the following clauses in her will show that she was not unmindful that she had collateral ones, whom she particularly named and mentioned in relation to this very matter. All that is known of her previous to her marriage is that, in 1634, " Mr. Norton having married a gentlewoman, both of good estate and good esteem, he took shipping for New England," &c.

Suffolk Records, lib. 6, fol. 223. Item, I give and bequeath unto my cousin John Norton the sum of Twenty Pounds, to be paid unto him within one year after my decease. Also all my husband's books, provided security shall be given that they shall not be taken out of the country.

Item, I give and bequeath unto my sister Mrs. Lucy Norton my silk gown and petticoat.

Item, I give and bequeath unto my cousin Edmund Hornby of Westerly Hall, in the County of Suffolk, in England, to his brother Thomas, and his two sisters Elizabeth and Mary, the sum of ten pounds, in New England money, apiece, to be paid unto them or their order, in New England, within one year next after my decease.

Item, my will is, that, if either my brother William Norton, or either or any of his sons, should trouble or molest my Executors or legatees, by suits of law or otherwise, whereby they shall be damnified, then the damages shall be made good to such party or parties out of the books that I have ordered unto my cousin John Norton.

Then follows the acknowledgment of John Norton: —

Received of, &c., in full of legacy given me by my honored aunt, Mary Norton, &c.     JOHN NORTON.

These conditions, by deed and will, by which the Norton property was held, being well-known to those contemporaneous, created a sensitiveness in their minds towards a strict adherence of the terms, and was a great cause why the unproductive property was not before 1800 improved. By giving undue weight to these "opinions," wrong impressions may have been created by those having this trust in charge, as to its use; for, after all, they are not finally decisive, possessing no more weight than that of emanating from a high legal source, unsanctioned by judicial decision; for Mr. Chief-Justice Parsons, whose official name is often used in connection with this opinion, did not fill the office of chief justice until many years after he gave this "opinion" in the Old South case. Mr. Parsons says, "It is my clear opinion that the society may erect the buildings or stores aforesaid, to be let out for applying the rents for the support of public worship, and for the benefit of the said society." Whereupon the committee of 1800 say in their report, "they have a clear right to make use of said land in any way they please." On the other hand, Mr. Mason, after stating the purposes for which Mrs. Norton gave the land, says, —

This, in my opinion, created a "valid trust; and I think the parish now holds the land subject to that trust," and that the minister of the parish, for the time being, is the *cestui que trust*, without whose consent the land cannot be occupied for any other purpose than the one specified by Mrs. Norton, the donor. From whence, therefore, do the parish derive the power to completely change its use? It certainly cannot be obtained from either trustees or ministers, who in the course of time are ever changing in persons as well as opinions. In an official opinion in the Dedham case, Judge Parker, of the Supreme Judicial Court, says (and the quotation here is made especially both for its applicability, and its significance to the property in question) that "to divert the charity from the poor of the Old South Church to the poor of the church in Park Street would be to violate the will and design of the donor as effectually as to apply it to the support of the town's poor." — Mass. Rep. vol. 16, lib. 507, Baker *v.* Fales.

It thus being the opinion of Mr. Mason, that the property constituted a "valid trust," he, in a very significant and peculiar manner, directed certain proceedings on behalf of the society, in the event of the settlement of another minister. In Dr. Blagden's case, this was done by a relinquishment of his official rights, much to his pecuniary loss; for, instead of providing him a suitable residence, to which he was justly entitled under Mrs. Norton's will, by virtue of his official position, the sum received in lieu thereof became, owing to a great change in money values, disproportionately inadequate for his support, and rendered it necessary for the society to make him a grant of money, which by right was his own. "Abundant caution" was thus used as to the right of a parsonage in Dr. Blagden's case, while in that of Mr. Manning's it was directly opposite. The committee, on his settlement, either not considering it necessary, or neglecting to look into the records for information, omitted to take any discharge of this right; and, when on a suitable occasion a motion was offered by which both pastors were to be placed, as regards this matter, upon an equality, the vote was negatived at the instigation of the treasurer, who strenuously opposed its passage. It is, however, but justice to say, that afterwards, at a meeting for the purpose of adjusting the salaries, the relinquishment of both the pastors was obtained.

## CHAPTER VI.

Poor-Fund. — Account of $5,245.00, Amount of Loan to the Society. — Parish-Houses Proposed. — Vote of Society to borrow Poor-Fund. — Ministers' and Treasurer Phillips's (Trustees) Obligation to Loan $14,000 to pay for Houses. — Extraordinary Report respecting the $5,245.00 due from the Society. — Cost of Parsonage-Houses. — Account of Stocks furnished from the Poor. — Amount of Society's Indebtedness to Fund.

THE history of the poor-fund will now be continued in regular course. The society borrowed of the fund, for the purpose of building the Old South block of stores, five in number (now on Washington Street), sixteen shares of the Massachusetts Bank, par value $8,000.00; sundry specified stock, par value $5,221.40, sold for $5,245.00. By the vote of the society directing the sale, the committee were not empowered to dispose in like manner of the bank-stock, but only of the securities, valued at the $5,221.40, — without doubt, deeming the bank-stock too good an investment to be parted with altogether, — and with the aid of Treasurer Phillips, who was connected with the bank, borrowed of that institution the additional amount required for the payment of building the stores, taking out the interest when the money was received, and, what is a singular fact, charging the discount, $479.46, to the trust-fund account, where it remains unadjusted until this day. Had the bank-stock been sold, there would have been no source of income for the poor; but, that not being the case, the dividends as received were paid over to the poor by the ministers and deacons.

When the stores were finished, they were rented for $2,600.00 per annum; and, as the rents were received, they were applied to pay off the loan due the bank, utterly regardless of any obligation they were liable to by the terms upon which it was borrowed. The loan from the bank being thus paid off, the deficiency in crediting the society's part of the rents, together with the appropriation of the whole of the proceeds arising from the sale of the securities, $5,245.00, soon showed itself in making the society daily richer; while the society in their fiduciary capacity were, in fact, poorer, having only the $8,000.00 bank stock remaining. And it is extremely doubtful if that would not have disappeared also, in the comminglement, had it not been absolutely necessary to retain it, the stated dividends received from it being absolutely requisite to satisfy the accustomed wants of the poor. Six years after, Nov. 17, 1806, it was voted by the society, that the deacons be a committee to procure a plan for a new parsonage-house, and exhibit the same at the adjourned meeting. And at the meeting, April 13, 1807, is the following remarkable report: —

There is due to the church and congregation fund for the poor thereof the interest on $5,245.00, which was vested in the five stores called "South Row," as by vote passed by vote of church and congregation, at a meeting held May 11, 1800; viz., from the first day of April, 1801, to first day of April, 1807, — six years, at 6 per cent per annum, and reckoning compound interest, which amounts to $2,195.12; which interest, by a vote passed as aforesaid, was to be paid from the income of the stores to the ministers and deacons (trustees) for the same. Your committee beg leave, therefore, to suggest whether it would not be well for the society to pass a vote for the treasurer to pay, and place under the direction of the trustees, one thousand dollars out of the balance of income from the stores, in part of the above interest. All of which is submitted.

BOSTON, April 20, 1807. Signed,

SAMUEL SALISBURY.<br>JOSEPH PIERCE.<br>JOHN WINSLOW.

*Voted*, The report of the committee be accepted.

*Voted*, That the treasurer be authorized to pay the balance of the interest due the church and congregation to the 1st October next, out of the income of said stores, when received; and, at the end of every quarter-year afterwards he pay to the ministers and deacons (trustees), for the distribution of said interest money, the quarter's interest, being $78.67½, as the same may become due and payable out of the income arising from said stores.

This sum of $78.67½ per quarter amounts to $314.70 per year, which sum is the interest on $5,245.00, and is more than one-half the sum paid to the poor under the six-hundred-dollar by-law system! Here is indubitable proof of the bargain made when the trust-money was borrowed to build the stores, showing that not a doubt existed in the mind of the committee that $5,245.00 of the poor-fund was "vested in the five stores," on terms specified in the vote of May 11, 1800. How it was possible that obligations then entered into by the parties in interest should for so many years remain unfulfilled is extraordinary; and even more so is it, that, when a particular examination was made for the purpose of rectifying the mistake, the most important feature in the bargain whereby the present and future income was equitably arranged, should have also escaped their observation, — an omission which caused a loss in the interest to the poor-fund of $647.18, as per following statement: —

$5,245, poor-fund, if it had been invested at the income of 9 per cent per year 6 years, would have amounted to . . . . . . . $2,832 30
$5,245, the society allowed 6 years compound interest, 2,195 12

Leaving a loss of . . . . . $647.18

The interest on the $5,245.00 continued to be paid in conformity with the aforementioned vote, no other notice having been taken of it until it is again brought to view in a report attached to an obligation of the ministers and deacons, agreeing to loan $14,000.00 to build two parsonage-houses, to which reference is made. The next subject for consideration is the project for building these two brick parsonage-houses upon the land whereon the society's roughcast parsonage, erected in 1705, still stood.

Boston, May 22, 1809. At a meeting of the church and congregation, met by notice from the desk, yesterday, after divine service in the afternoon; viz., the committee of ways and means for the purpose of building two parish-houses, having considered the subject committed to them, report, That there is in the hands of the treasurer of the society certain capital stock, the interest of which is appropriated to the use of the poor of the church; that, instead of borrowing money of a bank or of an individual, and depositing this stock as security for payment, it should be disposed of, or so much thereof as may be found necessary, and the proceeds permanently invested in those buildings. The interest appropriated to the use of the poor may always be drawn from the surplus of permanent income, as stated in the schedule annexed. By this operation, the business will be simplified, and the society freed from the necessity of borrowing money. Your committee, after mature consideration, could not fall upon any other measure to accomplish the wishes of the society, without being burthened with a debt that would hang upon them many years before it could be extinguished; and it was the desire, if possible, to avoid an increase of the tax on pews, especially at this particular time, when it is expected there will be a secession of some from the society.

ESTIMATE, ETC.

Money of church and congregation . . . . $11,250 00
" pews to be sold . . . . . . . 1,290 00
" pews in gallery . . . . . . . 2,000 00
" in treasurer's hands . . . . . . 2,824 49

$17,364 49

This sum, it is supposed, may be sufficient for the purpose of building the two houses. The interest of $11,250.00 is $675.00, for the use of the poor. This sum, deducted from the surplus income of $1,360.00, (pew-tax), will leave about $685.00 per annum. Out of this income must be paid the rent of two houses for the two ministers, the chief part of one year, while the two houses are building. Afterwards the pew-taxes may be reduced to what they were before the Rev. Mr. Huntington was settled.

In the above report, the right of the society to deposit as collateral security the "certain capital-stock" belonging to the poor-fund for moneys borrowed for their own uses is unequivocally declared, for the purpose of inducing the trustees of this property to loan them a large part of it for realization into cash; and then, at one "fell swoop," by a counter-report unsupported by a particle of evidence, deprive this same poor-fund of another large part. It is not therefore surprising, that, when such opinions were entertained, the final destination of the fund became only a question of time.

Boston, June 6, 1809. The church met according to notice given. *Voted*, That the trustees of certain funds placed in their hands be requested to furnish the society with so much from the same as may be required to complete the building of the parsonage-houses, upon condition that the interest be paid, and the buildings be insured to insure payment thereof.

The houses, after they were finished, were insured at the Massachusetts Insurance Office.

In pursuance of a vote of the church and congregation, on the 7th June following, the standing committee, by a sub-committee, made application to the ministers and deacons, trustees of certain funds, with the request that they would furnish from said funds the means of erecting two parsonage-houses, as expressed in said vote, to which they signified their ready compliance, under their hands, on the paper which accompanies this report.

### MINISTERS' AND DEACONS' AGREEMENT.

*Whereas* in times past there have been legacies, bequests, and donations made to the South Church, to be placed at interest for the benefit of the poor of said church and congregation, and the interest arising therefrom to be distributed among them according to the direction of ministers and deacons of said church, trustees for the purpose; and *whereas* the society have voted to build two parsonage-houses, whereon the old one now stands, and it appears that the church and congregation, at their meeting on 22d May, 1809, voted and accepted the report of a committee by them appointed to devise ways and means to build two parsonage-houses, — which was to appropriate so much of the capital stock as might be found necessary for that purpose, — and the church at their meeting 6th June, 1809, *Voted*, That the trustees of the fund be requested to furnish the society with as much from the same as may be required to complete said houses, upon condition that the interest be punctually paid, and the buildings be insured to secure the said payment; and *whereas* the church and congregation, at their meeting 7th June, 1809, *Voted*, That the standing committee for the year be the committee to contract for building said houses and carry the same into effect, — we, therefore, the undersigned, ministers and deacons, trustees as aforesaid, in compliance with the above request, do hereby agree to pay to said committee, or to any person or persons by them appointed to receive the same, a sum out of said funds not, exceeding fourteen thousand dollars.

BOSTON, Dec. 29, 1809.

        Signed,    JOSEPH ECKLEY.
                 JOSHUA HUNTINGTON.
                 WILLIAM PHILLIPS.

Attest,   E. M. HUNTINGTON.
       JOHN MOREY.

Appended to the report and agreement is the following paper, the singular character of which is most extraordinary, considering that it was offered and accepted by those who were well acquainted with all the circumstances of the case, many of whom had borne testimony in direct contradiction to its purport. Had they but consulted with care the past records of the church, it would have dispelled any doubts they might have entertained respecting the validity of the transaction relative to the "investment of the $5,245.00 in the five stores," and proved that that money was a portion of the benefaction of Mills, Ireland, Cunningham, Bromfield, Henchman, Hubbard, and a host of other worthies, kept sacredly invested from the earliest gift of John Bolt, in 1712, to 1800, when, in an evil hour for the spiritual interest of the church, the property in trust became amalgamated with the land-trust of Mary Norton, and thus became the prolific source of many evils, of which this connection and its consequences are far from being the least; for it initiated a series of measures subversive of that purity of Christian character which ever strives to keep itself " unspotted from the world." This, it is obvious, a religious society, when imbued with an irrepressible desire of progressive accumulation, "growing by what it feeds on," found it difficult to do; for the " cares of this world and the deceitfulness of riches, entering in, choke the word, and it becometh unfruitful;" and it is to be feared that higher interests, at times, were in danger of being sacrificed by the counsels pursued in favor of these temporalities. To such a height did this passion arise that at one time a project was entertained to alter the present Old South meeting-house, by turning the lower floor and cellar into stores for rent, removing the part for worship up-stairs, thus making the "Father's house a house of merchandise." Happily for the interest of the church, and the associations blended with its history, the exterior of this venerable edifice escaped desecration from the hands of those architectural Vandals whose blind zeal for "modern improvements" spare neither age, art, nor historical associations. The singular production appended to the agreement is as follows: —

The standing committee also embrace this opportunity to communicate to the society, that, by the records, it appears that there was a committee appointed April, 1800, to examine into the state of the funds, who reported that the foundation upon which the funds "had arisen" consisted in certain items, as they stood in 1766, — the whole of which amounted to £886. 11s. lawful money. That the funds on 3d April, 1800, consisted of bank-shares, — value, $8,000.00, — and other securities, nominally $8,062.72. At a meeting of church and congregation, 11th May, 1800, it was voted that the ministers and deacons deliver, from the money of the church and congregation, to the committee empowered to erect the stores, such sums as might be necessary for the purpose. This last sum was reduced to specie value, amounting to $5,221.40, — sold afterwards for $5,245.00, — *and was then considered to be the property of the church and congregation, leaving the bank-shares to belong to the church.* By another part of the report of that committee of 3d April, made May 11, 1800, it might seem that the whole, $5,221.40 (or $5,245.00), grew out of certain donations from particular persons. That, however, does not appear to have been the fact, but, on the contrary, arose from the four last items, as stated in that report, amounting to £378. 8s. 3d. lawful money. This statement is founded upon that of the committee of 3d April, 1800, on the state of the funds. The society will therefore consider, whether the ministers and deacons have the disposal of the interest of that part, as was then supposed in said vote. The standing committee are unanimously of opinion, they had not that right. If the society concur in the same opinion, it should seem that the $5,221.40 ($5,245.00) vested in the stores, as well as the income that has since arisen on the same, was the property of the church and congregation, and entirely at their disposal. If so, the vote or votes passed May 11, 1800, as respects the control of the interest by trustees, should be reconsidered. *Voted*, To accept the report of the standing committee. It was then moved, this meeting be dissolved; and it was dissolved accordingly.

Signed,    JOHN WINSLOW,<br>Clerk.

This "simplified" counter-report, by which a large part of the poor-fund is transferred to the society (as will be seen above), is grounded upon the fraudulent report presented to the society, April, 1800, for the purpose of influencing their vote upon the store-building question, and was the original cause of that —

"Legal wrong that bears Astræa's name."

A careful examination of documents relating to that transaction furnishes no proof whatever as to the authenticity of that report, while it affords abundance of evidence to the contrary.

The two parsonage-houses were erected at the cost of $16,310.00. The money was furnished from the property of the poor-fund, as per ministers' and deacons' agreement with the society, as follows: —

| | | | |
|---|---|---|---:|
| 1810. | May 3, | 7 shares Massachusetts Bank, sold for . . . | $4,524 00 |
| | July 1, | 7 " " " " . . . | 4,364 00 |
| 1811. | July 1, | 15 " " " " . . . | 3,245 00 |
| | | 6 per cent United States stock . . . . . . | 650 00 |
| | | Amount furnished in stocks . . . . . | $12,783 00 |

The whole indebtedness of the society to the trust at this time was, —

| | | |
|---|---:|---:|
| For the foregoing amount of stocks delivered . . . . . . | | $12,783 00 |
| "   " amount of the following stocks, nominal, $5,221.40: — | | |
| 3 per cent stock, $4,721.40, sold for . . | $2,406 00 | |
| Hinkley's bond . . . . . . . . . | 135 56 | |
| Deferred United States stock . . . . | 53 41 | |
| Massachusetts State notes . . . . . | 617 40 | |
| 5½ per cent United States notes . . . | 850 00 | |
| 8 per cent United States stock . . . . | 645 00 | |
| 42½ shares Union Bank . . . . . . | 412 00 | |
| 3 per cent U. S. N. stock . . . . . . | 102 03 | |
| | $5,221 40 | |
| Which was sold afterwards for . . . . . . . . . . . | | 5,245 00 |
| For interest paid Massachusetts Bank on note discounted . . . | | 479 46 |
| " compound interest awarded Nov. 17, 1806, on $5,245.00, by vote of society . . . . . . . . . . . . . . . | | 2,195 00 |
| " additional interest on $5,245.00 to date of building houses . | | 944 05 |
| Whole indebtedness of the society to the trust, . | | $21,646 51 |

## CHAPTER VII.

Milk-Street Stores. — Amount of Profit made by their Erection. — Non-performance of Trustee-Duties by Ministers. — Relief to Poor only granted to Church-members. — Conditions of the Poor-Fund Bequests. — Mrs. Norton's Conditions as to Ministers' Houses. — Society's Rights in the Parsonage-Houses. — Trustees' Powers and Duties. — Mistakes in the Use of Property. — Present Value of it. — Dangers arising from its Wrong Use.

APRIL 17, 1843. Another of those speculative projects, the legitimate offspring of the successful financial operations carried into effect in 1800, was at this time entertained, for the purpose of removing the two parsonage-houses built in 1810, and erecting three stores for income, upon part of the trust-land of Mrs. Norton, in Milk Street. This being a portion of the same piece of land upon which Mr. Mason's opinion was given, as will be seen by reference to the proceedings in that case, page 45, the plan was to be effected by borrowing a very large sum of money for the purpose. But, as many members of the Old South objected to this measure, on the ground of its illegality, a protracted discussion on the question ensued, during which it was discovered that the whole proceedings of the society, for the eleven years prior to that period, were extremely doubtful as to their lawfulness, they not being in accordance with the requisitions of the general law of the State regulating all parishes; to which they, as well as all others, were amenable. It therefore became indispensable that an act of incorporation should be obtained; and, as the legislature was then in session, one was hurriedly passed, March 26, 1845. This event caused a change in the measures at first contemplated, and a lease of the land granted for twelve years, at a ground-rent of twelve hundred dollars per year, to parties agreeing to build at their own cost the stores in conformity to the original plan proposed by the society themselves; and, at the expiration of that time, the whole estate with its improvements reverted free and clear to the society. They are now in possession of these stores, and rent them for a large sum. By this operation, it will be seen that the society was benefited financially over one hundred thousand dollars.

| | |
|---|---:|
| Received twelve years' ground-rent | $14,400 00 |
| " rent for stores after they came into possession, to 1860, | 40,000 00 |
| " cost of stores to those who built them | 75,000 00 |
| | $129,000 00 |

Even if there should be deducted from this the amount paid yearly from the easterly parsonage-house rent to the poor, $7,200.00, — a small sum comparatively, — it is largely over the above estimate.

The poor-fund, so far as it was connected with the removed parsonages, being entirely forgotten in this transaction, it seemed as if one of the last ties which held it in recollection was severed. The ministers of the church — being trustees, and supposed on account of their professional position to be more accurately acquainted with the wants and sufferings of the needy — having long ceased to administer the benefits of the charity, the poor-fund had well-nigh fallen into utter oblivion.

It is painful to conceive that such an institution, engaging the hopes, the religious aspirations, and earnest solicitude of the many Christian men and women who founded and endowed this charity, should, in so short a time comparatively, become neglected, nearly forgotten, and its treasures meted out in almost criminal narrow-mindedness, or, being commingled with the general funds of the society, expended for purposes not designed by the donors.

In some, if not in many instances, relief was denied to applicants because they were not members of the church as well as of the congregation; while, in fact, a larger part of the money bequeathed was given expressly to both. And, whenever an examination into the condition of the poor-fund was suggested, it was not unfrequently excused as needless, by members adverse to the measure, saying there were no poor to relieve!

A careful investigation of the accounts of church and society, with the Records of Suffolk and Middlesex, furnishes evidence that all the property, with the exception of the meeting-house, communion-plate, &c., now in possession of the Old South, is held in trust, — the chapel in Spring Lane included, — being purchased by the society with the profits of the united property of the Norton bequest and the assets of the poor-fund. It is fair, therefore, to consider that the whole, other than the part excepted, is altogether held in trust. Should this be essentially so, from whence do the society obtain the right to assume free and uncontrollable ownership over it, and direct its use to purposes never designed by those who placed it in the society's charge? It certainly does not derive it from the opinions of Messrs. Parsons and Mason; for those, at best, can carry no further weight than that of any other persons of like eminence in their profession; and the society themselves stand precisely in the same position as any individual does in assuming a trust, — equally obliged to perform its lawful requisitions, and transmit it unimpaired, as far as is possible, to their successors. The ministers and deacons, being but *ex-officio* almoners, cannot justly alter the duties enjoined upon them, or deprive their successors of rights over which they only possess power for a brief time. Neither can they compromise the future claims (whatever they may be) which the society and its ministers hold under Mrs. Norton's will, as expressed in the following conditions: "For the erecting a dwelling-house for such minister or ministers as shall be by them and their successors orderly and regularly admitted for the pastor or teacher of the Old South Church or assembly." The society having on their part accepted and fulfilled these conditions by erecting three parsonage-houses, it would seem that a proper construction of this part of the bequest would be, that, as the society, without any legal right being first obtained, disregarded this condition by placing the Norton property in such a position as to render an exact compliance with the terms by which it was held almost impossible, they should appropriate from the income received from it a sufficient sum to furnish a suitable and proper "dwelling-house" for each and every "minister or teacher regularly settled by the Old South Society," the said sum to be annually expended for the purpose, in strict conformity with the conditions of Mrs. Norton's will, and for "no other purpose whatever." Whether in its final result it makes any pecuniary difference or not to the pew-owners is a matter in nowise to be considered here. If Mary Norton made provision in her will that the Old South "ministers and teachers" should be provided with land for their parsonage-houses, and the society take both land and houses for money-making purposes, is not the society, to say the least, bound to furnish both house and land for each minister's use and accommodation? The apathetic feelings towards this charity in later years had well-nigh consigned it to utter forgetfulness. Those who formerly took an interest in it had passed away, and its recollection was only faintly remembered by a few of their successors. This, with the erroneous idea that there were but few, if any, poor persons in the Old South requiring aid, and the belief that none but church-members in full communion were entitled to it, had its due influence in fostering the impression that the entire property was one of those lucky waifs which floated into their possession for want of an ownership. Unfortunately, the society would not permit an investigation into this state of affairs, which were conducted altogether by a few, who, by that indifference not unfrequently exhibited in similar cases in other institutions, had become sole managers of these financial concerns.

Such an examination would have shown, that this charity was not intended for the relief of public pauperism alone, but was designed for aid also to persons whose means were limited, and required a small addition to eke out the sum necessary for their maintenance in a manner not entirely different from that to which they had been accustomed, and that no account was made of their religious belief. "They rejected not the supplications of the afflicted: neither did they turn away their face from a poor man." In other words, to require aid was to receive it.

For the aged and infirm, in particular, was this boon bestowed. How often has some weary pilgrim in the last stage of the journey of life had occasion to bless with grateful remembrance the founders of this charity, —

> "Whose hearts contrived for their relief
> More good than their own hands could do"!

The great privilege of dispensing this "good" was for many years enjoyed by their successors in the Old South Church. They also have passed away, and gone, we trust, to receive their reward.

It is scarcely within the bounds of probability (as "the poor will always be with us") that the purposes for which this trust was created cannot now be executed as reasonably as at that time.

If no authority is given to make a change, and the trust is just as capable of being executed now as at the time it was made, they — the trustees — cannot legally change it. But if it is apparent that not only the very purposes for which the trust was created are obsolete, or that a further and more extended application of the trust could advantageously be made, in a similar direction in which the original trust was intended, on application a court of chancery would direct a reference to inquire what object is next *(cy pres.)* such objects; and, after mature consideration, will direct the application of the trust in such a way as they may deem proper. The trustees, being only transitory *ex-officio* agents, have not the legal right either to add to or alter the objects specified by the donor.

Under these plain and comprehensive rules of law, how is it to be accounted for that this trust-property was so lamentably misused? The initial mistake was in borrowing the money of the trustees to build the five stores called the Old South Block, in Washington Street, without adopting the legal obligations commonly used on like occasions between individual parties, trusting to what may be termed family affiance, — a sure way in cases of this nature to produce difficulty. Another and greater one was made in the second transaction, of borrowing more trust-funds to build the two parsonage-houses, previously to which the society, in 1806, had discovered an error in favor of the poor-fund, amounting to the very considerable sum (for that time) of $5,245.00, — which occurred in not carrying out the bargain made by them in 1800, — and honorably rectified it, by a vote which is upon the records of the society. But from some inexplicable reason, or mistake, which cannot now be accounted for, while they made an appropriation for payment of the interest on the $5,245.00 as it became due, that amount of poor-fund stock *was never credited at all on the books of the society*, and was the foundation of that counter-report, founded upon the fraudulent one of 1800, which is before related in the course of this history.

In making these researches into the history of this fund, sufficient evidence was found in the records of both church and society to warrant the opinion that all the property now in possession (with but an inconsiderable exception) is held by them in strict trust, for special purposes; and that the profits and enhanced values, over and above what was expended in the performance of those trusts, are also a part and parcel of the original trusts, and, as such, the Old South Society are accountable for the same.

The question therefore may be asked, From whence do those who are only trustees for specified and distinct purposes derive the power, without legal direction first obtained, to appropriate any part of this property for other purposes than those for which it was designed by the donors, expressed in their wills in the most unequivocal manner?

Should this be the present position of the property, how can any portion of it be justly appropriated for the support of any establishment whatever (however good it may be) in which the members of the Old South are only benefited in common with other members of the community; and with what propriety can an official of this church intrusted with the care and distribution of the poor-fund, holding also an office of compensation in the society, occupy another office in this same establishment whose emoluments are taken from this very trust-property?

The land received in trust from Mrs. Norton is now much the greater part in value of the property, and was given on the only condition, that they (the society) "should assemble themselves together to worship Almighty God,"— a provision broad and expansive enough to prevent any theological objection against the society's changing their religious opinions, by which the whole property could be transferred to any denomination of Christians whatever. If, therefore, a "departure from a strictly lawful administration of its affairs," or a latitudinarian course, be pursued in its management and ownership, may not its very safety be imperilled by any unholy combination formed for the express purpose of obtaining control of so large an amount of property?

This may appear at first sight too problematical to heed; but what do the tendencies of the public mind at the present time show, by which a contrary opinion could be sustained? Is it not almost entirely absorbed in pursuit of material interests? Are even our religious institutions free from this unholy contamination? If not, how is it to be accounted for that so many changes, both in opinions and position, are prevalent with them? Why is so little veneration exhibited towards the preservation of those ancient places of worship which our fathers in the church dedicated as "houses of God, the very gate of heaven,"— with all their historical and religious associations, as well as architectural excellences, so readily sacrificed to that Juggernaut which, under the specious appellation of the "demands of commerce," "spares not the temple's holy ground," but bids fair to deprive also the community of a large and important part of their very habitations? Had such opinions prevailed in older nations, what would have been the fate of those immortal works which are now the wonder and admiration of the world? Would it not be wise, therefore, in view of the past history of the subject now under consideration, and of transactions at the present taking place in other churches, not to be too sanguine that — "as gold can knit and break religions"— the golden prize in the possession of the Old South, at some time or other, superinduced by the "demands of commerce," may be strong enough to break through even this old bulwark of Orthodoxy, and scatter all its treasures, not even sparing the miserable remnant of the poor-fund which remains.

## CHAPTER VIII.

Supreme-Court Decision in the Church-Green Case. — Its Applicability to the Case of the Old South. — Close-Corporation Practices. — Chambers-Street Chapel.—Mode of Managing the Business of the Old South.

SINCE this was written, the Supreme Court of Chancery has decided the "New South Case." The sound principles of law on which this decision is grounded, if applied to this case of the Old South, would show the most astonishing disregard of all legal obligations in the management of the trust-property, since 1800, held by that institution. Rights of pew-holders, in that decision, are said to be as follows: —

As pew-holders, they had no right or title in the real estate beyond a limited usufructuary interest, by virtue of which each had an exclusive right to occupy a particular portion of the church edifice, at certain times, for the special purpose of attending on public worship, and for the customary use to which said edifices may be properly appropriated. And this was the extent of the beneficial use or enjoyment which belonged to the pew-holders as such. They could in no just sense be held to be equitable owners of aliquot parts, or shares, in the property, according to the number of pews held by each; because a right to a pew conferred a limited usufruct only, and not the entire beneficial interest in the property, such as belongs to stockholders in corporations established for pecuniary profits. But the stockholders also became members of the society or parish, and, by virtue of such membership, had a right, according to the duly expressed will of the majority, to control the management of the property. This, however, was not an absolute and unrestricted right. The entire *jus disponendi* was not vested in them. Their power was necessarily limited by the trusts for which the legal title was held. These they could not pervert or destroy by misappropriation of the property. Their right was restricted, from the very nature of the trust, to such direction and control of the affairs of the parish or society, both religious and temporal, as were calculated to subserve and duly administer the trust for which the property was held. But beyond this they could not legitimately act. The trust was not limited by time; it had for its object no temporary purpose; the property was devoted to a use in its nature perpetual. No power to revoke or annul the trust was reserved by implication. It would be plainly inconsistent with its manifest scope and purpose, that the majority of the trustees, or of the *cestuis que trust*, or of both united, should have the power to abrogate such a trust by diverting the entire property from the use to which it was dedicated, and converting it to purposes of private pecuniary gain. This view of the nature of the trust which attached to property belonging to parishes and religious societies, as anciently organized in the town of Boston, is especially applicable to the corporation which is the subject of these proceedings. It did not owe its existence solely to the contributions of those who intended to become beneficial owners in the property, as pew-holders or members. It was founded in part by donations from those who had no expectation of personal benefit or advantage, but who gave money for the special purpose of aiding in the erection of a house of worship for the use of a religious society; and by a voluntary grant of land from the town, conveyed on the express trust that it was to be appropriated to such purpose. It is difficult to see on what principle property so given and held can be justifiably taken and appropriated, either by a majority of the trustees, or of the *cestuis que trust*, to a purpose wholly foreign from that for which it was originally intended to be used. Certainly no case was cited by the learned counsel for the petitioners which lends any sanction to such a doctrine.

It must be admitted that the same principles of law must be applicable to both the Old South and New South cases, whose relative position bears so much resemblance.

Mrs. Norton gave her land to the Old South, the fee of which was invested "in trust, for the erecting of a house for their assembling themselves together publicly to worship God; and also the erecting of a dwelling-house for such minister or ministers as shall be by them and their successors, from time to time, orderly and regularly admitted for the pastor or teacher of the same church or assembly; and for the accommodation of the meeting-house with convenient passages of ingress, egress, and regress for the people that shall from time to time assemble as aforesaid, and for no other purpose whatever."

In a gift by will, she gave her "dwelling-house, and land belonging thereto, for the use of the ministry in the said church forever," the inducement being, as she sets forth, that the society had erected a meeting-house upon the land first given them. The society, having accepted the land, built a meeting-house upon it, which remained until it was removed for the purpose of erecting the present one; the whole expense for both of which, and for necessary repairs thereon, was defrayed by subscription of the society. The society also erected, by the same means, a parsonage-house, which remained until removed to make way for the two brick parsonage-houses occupied by Dr. Eckley and Mr. Huntington; and these were removed for the purpose of making it the site for the present stores which are standing thereon. Until the present meeting-house was erected, the ministers' salaries, and all parish expenses whatever, were paid by private subscription. After that period, a pew-tax was laid, to enable the society to be more systematical in meeting their engagements. In 1738, the society inaugurated the Pious and Charitable Fund, for the purpose of diverting a portion of the gifts which were flowing into the treasury, for one purpose only, to other uses which had not been considered in their bequests. The moneys received for this particular trust, being duly credited in proper order, afterwards became merged in the church-stock.

After the trust-property became mixed together, real and personal, the chapel land in Spring Lane was purchased in the society's own name, for a chapel, and accommodation of the Prince Library, to which purpose it was devoted, until quite recently, when it was rented for business purposes.

From 1711 to 1789, many legacies from benevolent persons, the interest whereof was to be paid annually to the poor, were received, and the accounts of them accurately kept, exclusively, separately, and entire from those of the parish, until 1800; since which they have been mixed together, and have been managed as one, and the society has assumed exclusive ownership over the entire property. In the mean while, in addition to this, the very heavy expenses of salaries to ministers, their house-rents, — since the parsonages were demolished to make room for stores to rent, — repairs of meeting-house and other buildings, support of Chambers-street Chapel, with all other parish expenses, including the six-hundred-dollars grant to the poor, have been defrayed by the income since 1800, — the society meanwhile, as their books will show, not having ever received one cent of income from any source whatever other than from the united trust-property confided to their keeping for special purposes, "their power being limited by the trusts for which the legal title was held," except the annual tax on pews, amounting to about twelve hundred dollars.

For many years past an approximation to close-corporation principles in the business concerns of the society has been gaining ground, which has resulted in utterly disregarding the usual safeguards practised in other well-regulated business communities, and which, in this particular case, where such heavy responsibilities were involved, should have been rigidly observed. It was an ancient usage to have the standing committee composed of nine members, five of the church, and four of the congregation, all being pew proprietors, so as to afford a proper representation of both church and society, — the clerk of the society performing the duties of that office gratuitously. Within a few years the clerk has been paid a yearly salary, the standing committee selecting some young member for that office. It is well known to all, that this place was occupied under this understanding for many years. It is now filled by one who also holds the respective offices of deacon of the Old South, trustee of the poor-fund, and superintendent of the Chambers-street Chapel, — from which is derived a pretty fair income altogether.

It was also customary, when matters involving the expenditure of large sums were to be acted upon by the society, to refer them to a special committee to report thereon at an adjourned meeting. Affairs of the greatest moment, involving vast expenditures as well as future liabilities, are now merely presented for form's sake, and adopted at one and the same meeting. Even the treasurer's account — of the magnitude it must necessarily be — has, unintentionally and carelessly, been sometimes audited by those whose interest therein should have excluded them; and, for the same reasons, the treasurer himself transacted the business of his office, for many years, without giving the legal bonds required to make his acts valid.

The yearly account, thus audited, is merely read over at the annual meeting for the choice of officers and for the transaction of other business, — the brief time allotted to which absolutely forbids its thorough examination; and, as there is never any printed report of it, the knowledge of the business transactions of the society must necessarily be limited. Under this mode of conducting the business of the society, its administration fell into the hands of a few, who inconsiderately thought that the rejection twice of the resolutions of inquiry, offered for the purpose of looking into the entire concern, would (so large was the majority in their favor) forever put the question at rest, not considering so persistent and unreasonable an opposition to such a just and fair proposition would furnish in itself good and sufficient reasons for the inquiry demanded.

## CHAPTER IX.

Prince Library. — Information. — Master's Report. — Complaints. — Brief. — Defendants' Points and Authorities before the Supreme Court of Chancery. — Estimation of Amount paid by Society, as per their Answer.

THE following account of the society's proceedings in relation to the preservation of the library intrusted to their care by their eminent pastor, Dr. Thomas Prince, not having been immediately connected with the main subject of this history, has been deferred until this time.

The library bequeathed by Dr. Prince, under particular conditions designed by him for its preservation, is the only trust-property which has been administered near the terms designed by the donors; but, in the words of the late Dr. Clark, "it proved as totally insignificant for all beneficial purposes as it would do if the books had been deposited in a deep well." The action of the society at large, in relation to this valuable collection, will best be shown by their proceedings in connection with a report of a committee on the subject, Oct. 10, 1848, twenty years ago: —

Your committee have also considered the actual condition of the library.

The foundation laid in the wise and liberal bequest of the late Rev. Mr. Prince, for an historical and ecclesiastical library, seems to demand from us, that the design should be carried forward, and be made more useful than it has hitherto been, either to others or to ourselves. Your committee recommend that an annual appropriation be made for the increase of the library, and that purchases be made, as opportunity shall offer, of the writings of the Puritan Fathers of Old and New England: it should also include polemical and periodical literature, biography, civil and ecclesiastical history, tracts, reports of societies, sermons, manuscripts, and documents relating to ecclesiastical councils, etc.

Your committee recommend that an appropriation be now made to procure a portrait of Rev. Mr. Prince, to be suspended in the library, to testify that we recognize him as our benefactor, and that we honor his generous spirit; the portraits also of Cotton, Baxter, Owen, and Mather, of Henry, Watts, Milton, Knox, Calvin, and Luther, with others "*of whom the world was not worthy,*" should be there; nor should the features of the men of more recent date be wanting, — such as Edwards and Whitefield and Dwight and Stillman and Emmons. The establishment of such a library would be hailed with joy, it is believed, by all the lovers of New-England institutions. It would be something permanent, and increasingly useful to the world. It would be honorable to this church and our city. The advantages of such an institution to ministers and students will appear at a glance. A beginning once made, in a liberal spirit, many donations doubtless would be offered, and such an institution at length arise as would be worthy to be called a Congregational Puritan Library. These views may be new to some of the proprietors; and the committee do not design to have them adopted in full without mature reflection, and at a subsequent opportunity.

This report was written by the late Gov. Samuel T. Armstrong, who evinced the strongest interest in this subject until his death.

The response to this noble and praiseworthy appeal was the following vote of the society: —

*Voted*, That the Committee on the Library cause a portrait of the Rev. Mr. Prince, the beneficent founder of the library, to be placed therein, at an expense not exceeding one hundred dollars.

A few years since, one who was of this committee sent a catalogue of this library to London, by a person professionally well acquainted with books, to ascertain its value. The inquiry was duly made in the proper quarter, and its value was estimated to be far greater than any one in this country could imagine. One who was interested in the foundation of the present Congregational Library, encouraged by the prospective plan in this report for the establishment of almost the same thing which they proposed, made an informal but ineffectual attempt to call the attention of those prominent in Old South affairs to the subject. Under the circumstances at that time, it would have seemed a fortunate period to have carried out the plan shadowed forth in the accepted report of the committee of the Old South. The foundation could then have been laid of one of the noblest evangelical institutions in our country, not only having the means, unattainable at any price otherwise, as to books to begin with, with the pecuniary power of erecting an edifice to contain them, — which would have redounded to the everlasting honor of the Old South, and shown their gratitude for this " wise and liberal bequest of Dr. Prince." It is pleasant to think that an arrangement has recently been made to deposit this collection in the City Library, where it will at least be protected from depredation and harm, and may become more useful than it ever has been heretofore. Yet still it is to be regretted that after the labors of fifty years, which it took to complete this collection, there has never been found some kindred spirit who could have carried out the intentions of its founder. Instead, therefore, of its becoming the corner-stone of a noble structure lasting for ages, it now is only a specimen of the past, isolated, and independent of improvement; kept "free of dust," for the inspection of curiosity-mongers; and the building in which it was kept, with the chapel,— purchased with the property of the trust-funds,— by the transmutation of the "demands of commerce" (more rent), adding thousands of dollars to that huge property now in possession, bringing in a rent of over forty thousand dollars per year.

The above disposition of the library, on this poor-house principle of ridding oneself of an encumbrance which stands in the way, was transacted under close-corporation proceedings, the present opinion of the society at large in the matter never having been legally obtained.

The suit in equity in the Supreme Court was commenced in July, 1859, by the filing of an information in the name of the attorney-general, of which the following is a copy : —

*To the Honorable the Justices of the Supreme Judicial Court of the Commonwealth of Massachusetts.*

Informing sheweth unto your Honors Stephen H. Phillips, Attorney-General of the said commonwealth, at the relation of Joseph Ballard, of Boston, in the County of Suffolk and commonwealth aforesaid, that "The Old South Society, in Boston," is a corporation duly established by the laws of this commonwealth, having been incorporated by an act of the legislature passed on the twenty-sixth day of March, in the year eighteen hundred and forty-five, by which act Samuel T. Armstrong, Pliny Cutler, Charles Stoddard, and others, proprietors of pews in the Old South meeting-house, in Boston, and their successors, were made a corporation by the name of "The Old South *Church*, in Boston," which name was changed to that of "The Old South *Society*, in Boston," by an act of the legislature passed on the seventh day of March, in the year eighteen hundred and fifty-nine.

And the said attorney-general, at the relation aforesaid, further informs your Honors that the ministers and deacons of the Old South Church, in Boston, are, by virtue of sections thirty-nine and forty of chapter twenty of the Revised Statutes of this commonwealth, constituted a body corporate for the purpose of taking and holding in succession all grants and donations, whether of real or personal estate, made either to them and their successors, or to their church, or to the poor of their church.

And the said attorney-general, at the relation aforesaid, further informs your Honors that one Ann Mills, of Watertown, in this commonwealth, by her will, proved 27th of December, 1725, and recorded in Middlesex Registry, liber 17, folio 17, bequeathed a sum of money amounting to £282. $3s. 1\frac{1}{4}d.$

"to the Old South Church, in Boston, to be improved for the relief of the poor of said church, and such poor as usually congregate with said church, at the discretion of the minister or ministers and deacons." That one Mary Ireland, in the year 1761, bequeathed to the said Old South Church " the sum of £133. 6s. 8d., lawful money," and ordered " that the same be put out at interest, taking province securities, or, instead thereof, good land securities for the same, the interest thereof to be annually paid to such of the poor of said church as the ministers and deacons thereof shall in their prudence judge proper, forever, — an account of such disposition to be laid before the church yearly." That one Thomas Bromfield, by his will, dated 14th December, 1764, bequeathed to the said Old South Church " the sum of £25, lawful money of Great Britain, to be paid into the hands of the deacons of said church, and to be by them let out at interest, and the interest applied to the poor of the church." That one Captain Armitage, by will dated May, 1754, bequeathed to " the Old South Church, that I now belong to, one hundred pounds, old tenor, or £13. 6s. 8d., lawful money of the province aforesaid, forever, to be put out to interest by the ministers and deacons of the aforesaid church, and the interest of it to be given to the poor members of the aforesaid church as the ministers and deacons shall think fit." That divers others persons, including John P. Bolt, Nathaniel Cunningham, Simon Daniels, Abigail Duckalien, Daniel Henchman, Elizabeth Loring, Samuel Mores, William Mauley, John Maylem, Benjamin Pemberton, Rev. Dr. Sewall, John Simpson, John Osborn, and others whose names are not known to your informant, at different times between the year 1700 and the year 1800, bequeathed sums of money " to the poor of the Old South Church," " to the poor being communicants of the South Church, in Boston," " to the poor of the Old South Church, in Boston, to be paid to the deacons, to be by them distributed among said poor," etc., etc. That it was formerly the custom in the said Old South Church to take a contribution on each communion Sunday, the proceeds of which, after being applied to meet the expenses of the communion-table, and of sending ministers and delegates to sister churches, were to be distributed among the poor of the church. That from the aforesaid bequests and contributions, extending through many years, a fund was gradually accumulated in the hands of the ministers and deacons of the Old South Church, in Boston, which was known as " The Ministers' and Deacons' Fund," and of which a separate account appears to have been kept until the year 1800; at which time, according to the report of a committee of the Old South Society, made 11th May, 1800 (the correctness of which report, however, your informant does not admit), the said fund amounted to the sum of $16,-062.71, which was invested in United States, State, and bank stock, and in sundry bonds and notes. [A copy of said report is hereto annexed, marked *Exhibit A*.]

And the said attorney-general, at the relation aforesaid, further informs your Honors that, in the year 1801, the Old South Society, being in want of money to enable them to build stores on their land on Washington Street, borrowed of this fund the sum of fourteen thousand dollars, in accordance with a vote passed at a meeting held on 11th May, 1800, — a copy of the record of the proceedings of which meeting is hereto annexed, marked *Exhibit B.* That, as appears from the records of the society [a copy of which is hereto annexed, marked *Exhibit C*] it had been at first proposed that "the society pay the interest for the same at the rate it is now said to produce, which is *nine* per cent;" but it was afterwards voted that "the ministers and deacons shall at all times be entitled to receive so much of the rents and income of said stores as shall amount to *six* per cent per annum upon the moneys they shall pay and deliver as aforesaid, to the end that they may be enabled to appropriate the same in like manner as the interest of said moneys has heretofore been appropriated, according to the pious intentions of the donors thereof." That no interest or profits was paid on the above amount prior to the year 1807, when a vote was passed by the society, stating the sum of $2,195.12 to be due as interest thereon; but whether said sum, or any part thereof, was ever paid over, does not readily appear. That in the years 1809, 1810, and 1811 (a portion of the before mentioned loan of $14,000.00 having previously been refunded), a further sum of over sixteen thousand dollars was borrowed by the society from the Ministers' and Deacons' Fund, partly in accordance with a written instrument, a copy of which is hereto annexed, marked *Exhibit D.* That after this second loan, a small balance of one or two thousand dollars appears to have been left in the hands of the ministers and deacons, of which an account was kept for several years; but this balance is believed to have been finally merged and lost sight of in the general funds of the society. That, instead of the payment of interest for the second loan above-mentioned, the rent of the "easterly parsonage-house," so called, amounting usually to about $600.00 per annum, was paid, as appears by the report of the standing committee, dated 28th April, 1823, "to the ministers and deacons for interest of money borrowed by the society, for the purpose of building the two parsonage-houses; which money was left by a number of persons at different periods to the ministers and deacons of the Old South Church in trust, for the benefit of the poor of said church." That since the removal of the said parsonage-houses, in the year 1845, to give place to the new block of stores on Milk Street, it has been customary for the treasurer of the aforesaid "Old South Society, in Boston," to pay over $600.00 annually, in accordance with a by-law of the said corporation, which provides, among other duties of the treasurer, that "he shall pay annually to the deacons, for the use of the poor, the sum of six hundred dollars." That the whole capital of the large fund which originated and accumulated as above set forth is now in the possession of the said "Old South Society, in Boston," the successors of the society of the *Old South Church*, or *South Church*, as it was originally called, and is mingled with its general funds without any separate account, and even without any recognition of its existence other than may be implied from the above-quoted provision of the by-laws of the said corporation. And that there are now, and always have been since the establishment of said fund, persons answering to the description of "poor of the Old South Church," and, as such, entitled to the benefit of said fund.

But now so it is, may it please your Honors, the funds which in law and justice should be in the hands of the said "ministers and deacons of the Old South Church, in Boston," and which should be applied by them to the use of the poor of said church, are now in the possession of the said "Old South Society, in Boston," and are used by the said corporation to defray its general and current expenses, — for salaries of ministers, organist, and choir; for repairing and ornamenting the meeting-house; for grants to missionary and other societies, and to professors of the Theological Institution at Andover, etc., etc., — and not only the said "Old South Society, in Boston," but also the said "ministers and deacons of the Old South Church, in Boston," neglect and refuse, contrary to equity and good conscience, to take any steps to place the said funds in the proper hands, or to use them for the purposes for which they were intended.

And the said attorney-general, at the relation aforesaid, charges that the funds appropriated to public charity as aforesaid are in danger of being wholly misapplied and perverted.

In consideration whereof, and forasmuch as these matters are remediless according to the strict rules of common law, and can only have relief in a court of equity, where they are properly cognizable and relievable, —

And to the end that the aforesaid corporations may true answer make under their corporate seals to the matters herein charged, and may upon the several and respective corporal oaths of their proper officers, to the best and utmost of their several and respective knowledge and belief, full and perfect answer make to all and singular the several matters aforesaid, as fully as if particularly interrogated thereto; and that the said charity may be established; and that an account may be taken under the direction of this Honorble Court of all moneys so bequeathed, contributed, and accumulated as aforesaid; and that the said "Old South Society, in Boston," may be decreed to pay over such sum as may be found due, upon the taking of said account to the said "ministers and deacons of the Old South Church, in Boston," to be by them held and applied to the purposes for which the said moneys were originally intended, so far as such purposes are now capable of being performed; and that such further and other directions may be given for the establishment and maintenance of the said charity as to your Honors may seem meet, and this case may require, —

May it please your Honors to grant unto your informant a writ of subpœna of this Honorable Court, to be directed to the said "Old South Society, in Boston," and to the said "ministers and deacons of the Old South Church, in Boston," commanding them at a certain day, and under a certain pain therein to be limited, to appear before this Honorable Court, and then and there full, true, perfect, and direct answer to make to all and singular the premises, and further to stand to perform and abide such further order, direction, and decree as to your Honors shall seem meet.

And your informant shall ever pray.

STEPHEN H. PHILLIPS, *Attorney-General.*

URIEL H. CROCKER, *of Counsel.*

## EXHIBIT A.

#### REPORT OF COMMITTEE OF OLD SOUTH SOCIETY.

BOSTON, 18th April, 1800. Your committee, appointed to examine into the state of the funds of the South Church and congregation, to endeavor to find from what source they have arisen, and the intentions of the donors, have attended to that business, and beg leave to report, that, on examining, they find them to have arisen as follows; viz., —

| | | | |
|---|---:|---:|---:|
| Given by sundry persons for the poor of the church to the care of the deacons of the church | | | £102 18s. 4d. |
| Given by sundry persons for the poor of the church to the care of the ministers and deacons of the church | | | 153 6 8 |
| Given for the poor of the church and congregation to the care of the ministers and deacons | £5 12s. 0d. | | |
| Given by Mr. Mills | 100 19 10 | | |
| Given by Mr. Cunningham | 66 13 4 | — 173 5 2 | |
| Collected at sundry times the interest to the use of ministers' widows and children | | | 66 19 2 |
| Given to the poor of the church, not mentioned to whose care | | | 6 0 0 |
| Given, and not mentioned whether to the use of the church or the church and congregation | | | 8 0 4 |
| Collected from May, 1757, to 1773, for the use of the palls | | | 46 7 6 |
| Balances arising from the sacramental collections at different times, to the year 1766, over and above what paid the expenses | | | 186 19 5 |
| We find by the church book, given by sundry persons, which we find no minutes in the papers for what use, but, as they are entered in the church account, suppose for their use | | | 136 14 5 |
| Amount of the whole lawful money | | | £880 11s. 0d. |

This was in possession 1766, and at interest, and has been used ever since. The war coming on in about nine years after this time, and the moneys remaining during that period, must have accumulated considerably. After peace came on, the money was generally called in, and invested in public funds, where it now remains, and is as follows; viz., —

| | | |
|---|---:|---:|
| Massachusetts Bank shares, sixteen, at $500.00 each. | | $8,000 00 |
| Forty-two and a half Union Bank shares, at $8.00 | | 340 00 |
| Samuel Hinkley & Co.'s bond | | 416 66 |
| Three per cent stock | $2,391 40 | |
| Ditto | 194 35 | |
| Ditto | 2,350 00 — | 4,935 75 |
| Eight per cent stock | | 600 00 |
| Five and a half per cent ditto | | 1,000 00 |
| Massachusetts State notes, five per cent | | 709 37 |
| Deferred stock of United States | | 60 93 |
| | | $16,062 71 |

All which is submitted per order.

JOHN WINSLOW, *Chairman.*

## EXHIBIT B.

COPY OF RECORD OF MEETING OF SOCIETY, 11TH MAY, 1800.

May 11, 1800. At a meeting of the brethren of the church and congregation, —

*Voted*, That the committee appointed on the 22d of April last to borrow moneys of the minister and deacons to defray the expenses of erecting stores on the society's land be hereby discharged from that duty. And it is *Voted*, —

That the minister and deacons be requested, and they are hereby authorized, to pay and deliver from the money of the church and congregation to the committee, contractors appointed on the said 22d April, and to any other committee that may be employed to erect said stores, all such sums of money as may from time to time be found necessary by such committees for building said stores; said committees rendering regular accounts thereof to said minister and deacons, so that it may appear how much of said money shall be transferred and changed from their present situation to the property in said stores. And whatever moneys shall be so paid and delivered shall be considered as having been duly accounted for by said minister and deacons, the present trustees thereof.

And the said minister and deacons shall at all times be entitled to receive so much of the rents and income of said stores as shall amount to six per cent per annum upon the moneys they shall pay and deliver as aforesaid, to the end that they may be enabled to appropriate the same in like manner as the interest of said moneys has heretofore been appropriated, according to the pious intentions of the donors thereof.

And as it is highly probable that the rents and income of said stores will exceed the rate of six per cent per annum upon said moneys, by reason that the value of the land will be added to the value of the stores, it is therefore *Voted*, That whatever rents and income said stores shall produce over and above the legal interest on said moneys shall go into the hands of the treasurer, distinct from any funds of the society, and shall be used and applied for the purposes set forth in the committee's report [*see Exhibit C*] of the 20th of March last, and which was accepted the 3d April last, in such manner as the church and congregation shall from time to time vote and determine, or for such other ecclesiastical purposes as they shall order.

Whereas, on the 3d day of April last, the society came into the resolution of building five stores according to a plan exhibited by Mr. Dawes, *Voted*, That, in the article of the depth of said stores, proposed on said plan to be forty feet, the committee for erecting the buildings be authorized to make an alteration, if on further consideration they shall judge it proper.

JOSEPH ECKLEY.

## EXHIBIT C.

COPY OF PORTION OF THE RECORD OF A MEETING OF THE SOCIETY, HELD 3D APRIL, 1800.

The report of the committee chosen in the preceding year, and appointed to take into consideration the right and propriety of building a number of stores on the land belonging to the society, adjoining the meeting-house, was twice read by the moderator. It is as follows: —

Boston, March 20, 1800. Your committee, having met together at different times to consider the business referred to them by the South Society, are of opinion that it would be for the interest of the said society to erect on the land belonging to them fronting on Main Street five handsome brick stores, agreeably to a plan exhibited some time since by Mr. Dawes.

Your committee, wishing to be possessed of the opinions of able lawyers respecting the society's right of building on land given by Mrs. Norton, have called on Theophilus Parsons, Esq., attorney at law, whose opinion they have in writing, which is, that said society have a clear right to make use of said land in any way they please. As said land, in the opinion of your committee, cannot be improved to the benefit of said society in any better way than by erecting said stores, it appearing by estimate that the whole expense will not exceed ten thousand dollars to complete them, and they may be rented without any difficulty to good tenants for the sum of two thousand, or two thousand five hundred dollars per annum, which will give an interest of from twenty to twenty-five per cent for their money. If this statement is a true one, and the society's money can be borrowed for erecting said buildings, even if the society pay the interest for the same at the rate it is now said to produce, which is nine per cent, there must then remain an overplus of from eleven to sixteen per cent, which would enable the society amply to pay, with the present tax on the pews, not only the present minister, but an additional one, — provided the society should choose to expend it in that way, — in doing which, it is the opinion of your committee, the views of the donor, not only of the land, but those also who have left legacies from time to time, will be fully answered, as the poor of said society will have as much as they now receive, and the other will be laid out in pious uses for the support of public worship.

All which is submitted by order.

WILLIAM HOMES,
*Chairman of the Committee.*

After the foregoing report had been duly conversed on, at a numerous meeting of the society, the question was moved for and put, whether the same should be accepted.

*Voted* To accept the same, *nemine contradicente.*

## EXHIBIT D.

COPY OF AGREEMENT BETWEEN THE MINISTERS AND DEACONS OF THE OLD SOUTH CHURCH AND THE OLD SOUTH SOCIETY.

*Whereas* in times past there have been legacies, bequests, and donations made to the South Church to be placed at interest for the benefit of the poor of said church and congregation, and the interest arising therefrom to be distributed among them according to the direction of the ministers and deacons of said church, trustees for the purpose; and *whereas* the society have voted to build two parsonage-houses on the site whereon the old one now stands, and it appears that the church and congregation, at their meeting on 22d May, 1809, voted and accepted the report of a committee by them appointed to devise ways and means to build two parsonage-houses, which was to appropriate so much of the capital stock as might be found necessary for that purpose; and the church at their meeting, 6th June, 1809, voted that the trustees of the fund be requested to furnish the society with so much from the same as may be required to complete the said houses, upon condition that the interest be punctually paid, and the buildings be insured to secure the said payment; and *whereas* the church and congregation, at their meeting on the 7th June, 1809, voted that the standing committee for the year be the committee to contract for building said houses, and carry the same into effect, — we, therefore, the undersigned, ministers and deacons, trustees as aforesaid, in compliance with the above request, do hereby agree to pay to said committee, or to any person or persons appointed by them to receive the same, a sum out of said funds not exceeding fourteen thousand dollars.

BOSTON, December, 1809.

JOSEPH ECKLEY.<br>JOSHUA HUNTINGTON.<br>WILLIAM PHILLIPS.

Attest,
    E. M. HUNTINGTON.
    JOHN MOREY.

---

To the preceding information two separate answers were, in March, 1860, filed by "The Old South Society, in Boston," and by "The Ministers and Deacons of the Old South Church, in Boston." These answers were as follows: —

THE SEVERAL ANSWER OF THE OLD SOUTH SOCIETY, IN BOSTON.

The Old South Society, in Boston, now and at all times hereafter saving and reserving to themselves all benefit and advantage of exception which can or might be had or taken to the many errors, uncertainties, and other imperfections in said complainant's bill of complaint contained, for answer thereunto, or unto so much and such parts thereof as these defendants are advised is or are material, or necessary for them to make answer unto, these defendants answering say: —

These defendants admit they are a corporation duly established by the laws of this commonwealth; that they were incorporated by an act of the legislature passed in the year eighteen hundred and forty-five, by which Samuel T. Armstrong and others, proprietors of pews in the Old South meeting-house, in Boston, and their successors, were made a body corporate by the name of "The Old South Church, in Boston," and that their name was changed by an act of the legislature passed in the year eighteen hundred and fifty-nine to that of "The Old South Society, in Boston;" and that the ministers and deacons of the Old South Church are, by the laws of this commonwealth, to be deemed a body corporate for the purpose of taking and holding in succession all grants and donations made to them and their successors, or to their church, or to the poor of their church.

And these respondents, further answering, admit, on their information and belief, that Ann Mills, Mary Ireland, Thomas Bromfield, and Captain Armitage gave or bequeathed to the Old South Church, in Boston, the several sums of money set forth in said bill of complaint, at the times therein named, and for the purposes and objects therein set forth, and that said several sums were paid over to said church; and these defendants say, on their information and belief, that these several sums of money were used and appropriated by said church and the ministers and deacons thereof for the purposes and objects designated by said donors; and these respondents, further answering, say, that they have no personal knowledge of the aforesaid facts, but that their belief of them is founded upon the records of said church and society, and upon the fact that they never knew or heard of any complaint ever having been made by any member of said church or society, or of the congregation worshipping in the Old South meeting-house, or by the poor of said church or congregation, or by any one else, that the moneys aforesaid had not been faithfully and rightfully appropriated according to the intention of the donors, except from the relator in the case for some short time before the filing of this bill of complaint.

And these respondents admit, on their information and belief, that divers other persons, named in said bill of complaint, between the year seventeen hundred and the year eighteen hundred, gave or bequeathed different sums of money to the Old South Church, or to the poor of said church, or to the ministers and deacons thereof; but these defendants have no knowledge, information, or belief, how much money was so given or bequeathed, or what portion thereof, if any, was specifically given or bequeathed for the use of the poor of said church; but these defendants say, on their information and belief, that all sums of money so given or bequeathed have been faithfully and scrupulously appropriated and used for the purposes and objects for which they were given or bequeathed, because they never heard of or knew of any complaint having been made in said church or congregation, or among the poor thereof, or by any one else, until by the relator in this case quite recently, that said sums of money were not rightfully and properly appropriated according to the will of the donors thereof, and that they can find no record of any such complaint on the records of said church or society. And these respondents further answering say, that it appears from the records and accounts of said church and society, which they believe to be true and accurate, that large sums of money were from the year seventeen hundred down to the present time yearly appropriated for the poor of said church and congregation under the direction of the ministers and deacons of said church, and they submit said records and accounts for examination in such manner as shall be directed by this Honorable Court.

And these respondents, further answering, admit, that it was formerly the custom in said Old South Church to take up a contribution on communion Sundays; but they deny, on their information and belief, that the proceeds of such contributions were specially and specifically designed for any specific or certain objects and purposes as alleged in the bill of complaint; on the contrary, they say, on their information and belief, that the said contributions were given generally to the Old South Church, to be appropriated to any objects and purposes desired by said church. And these defendants admit, on their information and belief, that from said contributions and former gifts and bequests to the church, or to the ministers and deacons thereof, and from the accumulations of interest thereon, there had gradually accumulated a fund belonging to said church, which was under the direction and management of the ministers and deacons of said church, and of which a separate account was kept; and that, in the year eighteen hundred, said fund amounted to the sum of sixteen thousand and sixty-two dollars and seventy-one cents, as appears by a report of the Old South Society made to said society, May 11, 1800, and which report these defendants believe to be true and accurate, and which is annexed to the bill of complaint, and marked A; and which amount these defendants believe was invested as set forth in said report. And these defendants, further answering, say, on their information and belief, that of said amount of $16,062.71, belonging to said church in the year eighteen hundred, but a small portion thereof was composed and made up of gifts and contributions made specifically for the benefit of poor of said church and congregation and no other purposes, and that the larger part thereof belonged to said church free from all conditions and limitations; said church possessing full power to appropriate and use the same for any useful, charitable, and religious purposes said church might determine upon.

And these defendants say, on their information and belief, that said church, through and by their ministers and deacons, from the first gathering of said church and congregation, appropriated more money to the poor of said church and society than was given them for the poor alone, — so that it could not be used for any other object.

And these defendants, further answering, admit, on their information and belief, that in the year eighteen hundred, or about that time, the Old South Society did borrow of the ministers and deacons of the Old South Church the sum of fourteen thousand dollars to build stores on Washington Street, in acordance with a vote of said society passed May 11, 1800, and that it was voted by said society to pay said ministers and deacons six per cent per annum on the sum they should deliver to the society. And these defendants say, on their information and belief, that the interest on said loan was accounted for and paid to said ministers and deacons; and that it appears by an examination of the books of said society, of the accounts of the treasurer thereof, the Hon. William Phillips, that on the first day of April, A.D. 1807, there was a credit to the ministers, trustees for the church, for compound interest on money loaned to the society as per vote passed May 11, 1800, of twenty-one hundred and ninety-five dollars and twelve cents; and that afterwards, up to April 1, 1810, interest is credited to said ministers and deacons quarterly on said loan, which credits amount to the sum of nine hundred and forty-four dollars and five cents. And these defendants say, on their information and belief, that the whole loan authorized by the vote aforesaid of May 11, 1800, was repaid by the society to the ministers and deacons of the church before the expiration of the year eighteen hundred and ten; and they admit that, partly in pursuance of the agreement annexed to said bill of complaint, marked D, the society borrowed of the ministers and deacons the sum of fifteen thousand nine hundred and twenty dollars and ninety-two cents for the purpose of building two parsonage-houses, of which sum of $15,920.92 the sum of three thousand one hundred and thirty-nine dollars and seventeen cents was the interest on the loan of $14,000.00, made by authority of the vote of May 11, A.D. 1800. And these defendants admit, that a balance of two thousand dollars remained of said fund belonging to said church, and under the control of the ministers and deacons thereof, after the last loan of $15,920.92 to build the two parsonage-houses; but they deny, on their information and belief that the same has been merged in the general funds of the society: on the contrary, they say, on their information and belief, that the same has always been kept separate from the funds of said society, and is now held for the said ministers and deacons of the church, and is invested in four shares of the Massachusetts Bank, the par value of which is $1,000, and a bond of the Massachusetts Hospital Life Insurance Company for $1,000; and the said Old South Society have never taken or meddled with the proceeds of said investments, but they have always been under the control of the ministers and deacons of the church. And these defendants, further answering, say, on their information and belief, that the first loan made in pursuance of the vote of May 11, A.D. 1800, from said ministers and deacons to said society, has been fully paid, both principal and interest, more than forty-five years since; that no claim or complaint has ever been made from any source that it was not paid; and that the great lapse of time ought to be a sufficient bar to any claim now made that it has not been paid.

And these defendants admit, that, instead of paying any interest as such on said last-named loan to build the two parsonage-houses, the Old South Society, by agreement between said society and the Old South Church and the ministers and deacons thereof, paid to the ministers and deacons for the use of the poor the rent of the easterly parsonage-house, — which for the first year was $450.00, for the second year was $500.00, and from the year 1816 to the year 1828 was ranging from $650.00 per year to $775.00 per year, and from 1828 to the year 1845 was $600.00 per year, and since the year 1845 there has been paid the sum of $600.00 per year by virtue of a by-law of these defendants; and these defendants admit that since 1845 no separate account has been kept by them of the interest on the money delivered by the ministers and deacons aforesaid to these defendants by the agreement, a copy of which is annexed to the bill of complaint, marked D, except by paying said rent and said yearly sum of $600.00 as aforesaid. And these defendants admit there are, and always have been, persons answering to the description of the poor of the Old South Church.

And these defendants, further answering, say, on their information and belief, that there has always been since the year eighteen hundred a sum paid over by the Old South Society to the said ministers and deacons for the support of the poor of the church and congregation, and so used and appropriated, fully equal to the interest upon any and all sums which were ever given to the said church, or to the ministers and deacons thereof, for the sole purpose of being used and appropriated for the benefit of the poor. And these defendants further say, that they believe there never has been at any time any misappropriation, either by the ministers and deacons aforesaid or by this defendant corporation, of any funds or moneys given or contributed to either for the support of the poor; and from the best information they can derive from the records of said church and society, and also from the high character and integrity of these persons acting for said church and society in times past, they believe and say that the said society has from time to time paid over to the ministers and deacons, for the support of the poor, all the yearly proceeds of any and all sums given or appropriated solely for the support of the poor, and for no other use.

And the defendants, further answering, say, upon their information and belief, the arrangement herein before set forth by which the said ministers and deacons delivered to the Old South Society the sum of $15,920.71 for the purpose of building two parsonage-houses, and the said society paid over to the ministers and deacons for the use of the poor the rent of the easterly parsonage-house till the year 1845, and since that year the sum of $600.00 per year, has been acquiesced in by all members of both said church and society, and all other persons, and that no complaint or dissatisfaction has ever been expressed with the same from any source until recently by the relator in this case; and therefore these defendants say they believe said arrangement so made was just and fair, and beneficial to the interests of the poor of the church and congregation as any that could be made, and that the same ought not now to be disturbed or set aside.

And these defendants, further answering, say, on their information and belief, that the minister and deacons of said Old South Church have used and appropriated for the relief and support of the poor of said church and congregation all the money that in the exercise of a sound discretion they believed that the wants and needs of said poor required; and that, since the year eighteen hundred and thirty-eight, said ministers and deacons have disbursed for the relief of the poor of said church and congregation, on the average, each year, the sum of $1,048.93; and that large sums have been applied by said ministers and deacons each year, since the year eighteen hundred, for the relief of the poor of said church and congregation, — a large portion of which disbursements has been paid into their hands by this defendant corporation for that purpose. And they annex hereto a statement of the amount so paid by the ministers and deacons for the relief of the poor, as appears by the records and accounts of said society and church, which they believe to be true and correct, from the year 1800 to the present time. And these defendants, further answering, say, on their information and belief, that, for the last four years before the filing of the bill of complaint, the disbursements aforesaid for the relief of the poor have been made by the deacons alone, at the request and by the consent of the ministers, to relieve the latter from that burden, on account of the pressure of other official duties and calls.

And these defendants, further answering, deny, on their information and belief, that there are any funds which should be in the hands of said ministers and deacons, to be applied by them to the use of the poor of the Old South Church, in the possession of these defendants, which are used by these defendants for the other purposes set forth in said bill of complaint; but, on the contrary, they say, on their information and belief, that this defendant corporation are and have been paying yearly to said ministers and deacons, for the support of the poor, all the money they are in law, equity, and good conscience bound to pay, and they believe as much as could have been realized in any way or manner of investment from all gifts and contributions made solely for the use of the poor.

And these defendants, further answering, deny that there is any other matter, cause, or thing, in the said complainant's bill of complaint contained, material or necessary for these defendants to make answer unto, and not herein and hereby well and sufficiently answered, confessed, avoided, or denied, is true to the knowledge, information, or belief of these defendants, all which matters and things these defendants are willing to aver, maintain, and prove as this Honorable Court shall direct, and humbly pray to be hereof discharged and dismissed with their reasonable costs in this behalf sustained.

ZACHARIAH JELLISON.
JABEZ C. HOWE.
GEORGE HOMER.
CHARLES BLAKE.
SIMON G. CHEEVER.
SAMUEL COVERLY.
SAMUEL JOHNSON.
INCREASE S. WITHINGTON.
JOSHUA B. KIMBALL.

COMMONWEALTH OF MASSACHUSETTS.

*Suffolk, ss.* At Boston, in said county, on the 9th day of April, A.D. 1860, personally appeared before me Zachariah Jellison, Jabez C. Howe, George Homer, Charles Blake, Simon G. Cheever, and Samuel Coverly, and on the 10th day of said April personally appeared before me Samuel Johnson, Increase S. Withington, and each made oath that the foregoing answer by them signed respectively is true to the best of their knowledge, information, and belief; and on the first day of May, 1860, personally appeared before me Joshua B. Kimball, and made oath that the foregoing answer by him subscribed is true to the best of his knowledge, information, and belief.

Before me,

JOSIAH W. HUBBARD,
*Justice of the Peace.*

The following sums have been distributed to the poor of the Old South Church from the year 1800 to 1859, as appears from the books of the treasurer, viz. (the year in the society's books closes with March):—

| Year | Amount | Year | Amount |
|---|---|---|---|
| 1800–1 | $747 00 | 1830–1 | $736 04 |
| 1801–2 | 754 00 | 1831–2 | 767 74 |
| 1802–3 | 645 00 | 1832–3 | 715 81 |
| 1803–4 | 575 00 | 1833–4 | 633 21 |
| 1804–5 | 685 00 | 1834–5 | 726 10 |
| 1805–6 | 660 00 | 1835–6 | 752 76 |
| 1806–7 | 635 00 | 1836–7 | 760 48 |
| 1807–8 | 613 00 | 1837–8 | 844 03 |
| 1808–9 | 545 00 | 1838–9 | 887 35 |
| 1809–10 | 630 00 | 1839–40 | 1,100 91 |
| 1810–11 | 497 00 | 1840 | 1,074 47 |
| 1811–12 | 460 00 | 1841 | 1,296 14 |
| 1812–13 | 520 00 | 1842 | 918 68 |
| 1813–14 | 507 00 | 1843 | 895 75 |
| 1814–15 | 532 00 | 1844 | 870 38 |
| 1815–16 | 561 00 | 1845 | 1,001 86 |
| 1816–17 | 510 00 | 1846 | 1,047 45 |
| 1817–18 | 400 00 | 1847 | 1,107 94 |
| 1818–19 | 484 00 | 1848 | 1,114 70 |
| 1819–20 | 723 83 | 1849 | 1,274 70 |
| 1820–21 | 728 87 | 1850 | 1,170 50 |
| 1821–22 | 724 21 | 1851 | 1,136 02 |
| 1822–23 | 696 54 | 1852 | 1,115 87 |
| 1823–24 | 757 38 | 1853 | 985 01 |
| 1824–25 | 929 64 | 1854 | 918 93 |
| 1825–26 | 928 21 | 1855 | 1,019 70 |
| 1826–27 | 975 03 | 1856 | 946 79 |
| 1827–28 | 981 46 | 1857 | 991 04 |
| 1828–29 | 892 69 | 1858–59 | 1,066 77 |
| 1829–30 | 709 17 | 1859–60 | 1,145 48 |

THE SEVERAL ANSWER OF THE MINISTERS AND DEACONS OF THE OLD SOUTH CHURCH, IN BOSTON.

The ministers and deacons of the Old South Church, in Boston, now and at all times hereafter saving and reserving to themselves all benefit and advantage of exception which can or might be taken to the many errors, uncertainties, and other imperfections in said complainant's bill of complaint contained, for answer thereunto, or unto so much and such parts thereof as these defendants are advised is or are material, and necessary for them to make answer unto, these defendants answering say: —

These defendants admit that the Old South Society, in Boston, is a corporation duly established by the laws of this commonwealth; that it was incorporated by an act of the legislature, passed in the year eighteen hundred and forty-five, by which act Samuel T. Armstrong and others, proprietors of pews in the Old South meeting-house, in Boston, and their successors, were made a corporation by the name of the "Old South Church, in Boston," and that the name of said corporation was changed by an act of the legislature, passed in the year eighteen hundred and fifty-nine, to that of "The Old South Society, in Boston;" and that the defendants are, by virtue of the laws of this commonwealth, to be deemed a body corporate for the purpose of taking and holding in succession all grants and donations made to them and their successors, or to their church, or to the poor of their church.

And these defendants, further answering, admit, upon their information and belief, that Ann Mills, Mary Ireland, Thomas Bromfield, and Captain Armitage gave or bequeathed to the Old South Church, in Boston, the several sums of money set forth in the said bill of complaint, at the times therein named, and for the purposes and objects therein set forth, and that said several sums were paid over to said church; and these defendants say, on their information and belief, that the several sums of money aforesaid were used and appropriated by said church and the ministers and deacons thereof, for the purposes and objects designated by said donors. And these defendants, further answering, say, that they have no personal knowledge of the aforesaid facts, but that their belief of them is founded upon the records of said church and society, and upon the fact that they never knew or heard of any complaint ever having been made by any member of said church or society, or of the congregation worshipping in the Old South meeting-house, or by the poor of said church or congregation, or by any one else, that the moneys aforesaid had not been faithfully and rightfully appropriated according to the intention of the donors, except from the relator in this case for some short time before the filing of this bill of complaint. And these defendants admit, on their information and belief, that divers other persons named in said bill of complaint, Mr. John P. Bolt, Nathaniel Cunningham, Daniel Henchman, Elizabeth Loring, Samuel Mores, William Mauley, John Maylem, Benjamin Pemberton, Rev. Dr. Sewall, John Simpson, and John Osborn, between the year seventeen hundred and the year eighteen hundred, gave or bequeathed certain sums of money to the Old South Church, or to the poor of said church, or to the ministers and deacons thereof. And these defendants, further answering, say, on their information and belief, that none of the gifts or bequests of said last-mentioned persons were made to the church or the ministers and deacons thereof to be invested, and the yearly interest thereof expended, for the benefit of the poor; but that, when made for the use of the poor of the church, they were made generally for the use of the poor of the church so that the whole gift or bequest would be used immediately for that purpose. And these defendants say on their information and belief, and from an examination of the records and accounts of said church and society, that said sums, so given for the use of the poor of said church generally, were, very soon after such gifts and bequests, appropriated, used, and expended by the ministers and deacons for that purpose. And these defendants, further answering, say, on their information and belief, that no gifts or bequests were made to said church at any time for the use of the poor, where the yearly interest only of the gifts or bequests were to be so appropriated, except the gifts and bequests before-named of Ann Mills, Mary Ireland, Thomas Bromfield, and Captain Armitage, amounting in all to the sum of £454. 16s. 5½d.; and that all the moneys belonging to the said church at any time, with the exception of said £454. 16s. 5½d., did not arise and were not made up from gifts or bequests to the church, or the ministers and deacons thereof, for the use of the poor; but that all such gifts and bequests were expended, soon after their reception, for the purposes for which they were given; and that all funds held at any time by said church, or the ministers and deacons thereof, except said sum of £454. 16s. 5½d., could be used, appropriated, and disposed of for any charitable or religious use or purpose at the will and discretion of said church. These defendants say, on their information and belief, that all sums of money so given or bequeathed have been faithfully and scrupulously appropriated and used for the purposes and objects for which they were given or bequeathed; because they never knew or heard of any complaint having been made in said church or congregation, or among the poor thereof, or by any one else, until by the relator in this case quite recently, that said sums of money were not rightfully and properly appropriated and used, according to the will of the donors thereof; and that they can find no record of any such complaint on the records of said church or society. And these defendants, further answering, say, it appears from the records and accounts of said church and society that large sums of money were, from the year seventeen hundred down to the present time, yearly appropriated for the poor of said church and congregation, under the direction of the ministers and deacons of said church, which records and accounts these defendants believe to be correct; and they submit said records and accounts to examination in such manner as shall be directed by this Honorable Court. And these defendants, further answering, admit, that it was formerly the custom in said Old South Church to take up a contribution on communion Sundays; but they deny, on their information and belief, that such contributions were specially and specifically designed for any specified or certain objects and purposes as alleged in the bill of complaint; on the contrary, they say, on their information and belief, that the said contributions were given generally to the Old South Church, to be appropriated to any objects and purposes desired by said church. And these defendants admit on their information and belief, that from said contributions and from gifts and bequests to the church or to the ministers and deacons thereof, and from the accumulations of interest thereon, there had gradually accumulated a fund belonging to said church, which was under the management and direction of the ministers and deacons of said church, and of which a separate account was kept; and that, in the year eighteen hundred, said fund amounted to the sum of sixteen thousand and sixty-two dollars and seventy-one cents, as appears by a report of a committee of the Old South Society made to said society, May 11, A. D. 1800, and which report these respondents believe to be true and correct, and which is annexed to the bill of complaint, marked A, and which fund these defendants say, on their belief and information, was invested as set forth in said report. And these defendants, further answering, say, on their information and belief, that of said sum of $16,062.71, in the year eighteen hundred, but a portion thereof was composed and made up of gifts and contributions made specifically for the benefit of the poor of said church and congregation and no other purposes; and that a portion thereof belonged to said church free from all conditions and limitations, said church possessing full power to appropriate the same to any useful, charitable, and religious purpose and use said church might determine upon. And these defendants further say, on their information and belief, that said church, through and by their ministers and deacons, from the first gathering of said church and congregation, appropriated more money to the poor of said church and society than was given them for the poor alone, — so that it could not be used to any other object.

And these defendants, further answering, admit, on their information and belief, that in the year eighteen hundred and one, or very near that time, the Old South Society did borrow of the ministers of the Old South Church the sum of fourteen thousand dollars to build stores on Washington Street, in accordance with a vote of said society passed May 11, A. D. 1800; and that it was voted by said society to pay the ministers and deacons six per cent per annum on the sum they should deliver to the society. And these defendants say, on their information and belief, that the interest on said loan was paid and accounted for to said ministers and deacons; and that it appears by an examination of the books of the treasurer of said society at that time, — the Hon. William Phillips, who also acted as treasurer of the Old South Church, — that April 1, A. D. 1807, there was a credit to the ministers and deacons, trustees for the church, for compound interest on money loaned to the society, as per vote passed May 11, 1800, of $2,195.12; and that afterwards, up to April 1, A. D. 1810, interest is credited to said ministers and deacons regularly and quarterly on said loan, which credits amount to $944.05. And these defendants say, on their information and belief, that the whole loan authorized by the vote of May 11, 1800, was repaid by the society to the ministers and deacons before the expiration of the year eighteen hundred and ten; and they admit, that, partly in pursuance of the agreement annexed to said bill of complaint, marked D, the society borrowed of said ministers and deacons the sum of $15,920.92 for the purpose of building two parsonage-houses, of which sum of $15,920.92 the sum of $3,139.17 was the interest on the loan of $14,000.00, made by authority of the vote of May 11, 1800, as aforesaid. And these defendants admit that a balance of $2,000.00 remains of said fund belonging to the said church, after said money furnished for building the parsonage-houses, but they deny that the same has been merged in the general funds of said Old South Society; on the contrary, they say the same has always been kept separate and apart from the funds of said society, and is now held for said ministers and deacons, and is invested in four shares of the Massachusetts Bank, the par value of which is $1,000.00, and in a bond of the Massachusetts Hospital Life Insurance Company of $1,000.00. And these defendants admit, that, instead of paying any interest as such on said last-named loan, said Old South Society paid to the ministers and deacons, for the use of the poor, the rent of the easterly parsonage-house, which for the first year was $450.00, for the second year was $500.00, and from the year 1816 to the year 1828 was varying from $650.00 to $775.00 per year, and from 1828 to 1845 was regularly $600.00 per year, and since 1845 there has been paid the sum of $600.00 per year by virtue of a by-law of said society. And these defendants admit, that, as far as they know, since 1845, no separate account has been kept of the money delivered by the ministers and deacons to said society to build said parsonage-houses by virtue of the agreement annexed to the bill of complaint marked D, except by paying said rent and said yearly sum of $600.00 as aforesaid. And the defendants admit, that there are and always have been persons answering to the description of " the poor of the Old South Church." And these defendants, further answering, say, on their information and belief, that there has always been, since the year eighteen hundred, a sum paid over by the society aforesaid to the ministers and deacons for the support of the poor of the church and congregation, and so appropriated, fully equal to the interest upon any and all sums which were given to the said church, or the ministers and deacons thereof, for the sole purpose of being appropriated for the benefit of the poor. And the said defendants further say, they believe there never has been at any time any misappropriation, either by the ministers and deacons of the Old South Church, or by the Old South Society, in Boston, or by both, of any funds given or contributed to either for the support of the poor; and from the best information they can derive from the records of said church and society, and also from the high character and integrity of those persons acting for said society and church in times past, they believe and say that the society has from time to time paid over to the ministers and deacons, for the support of the poor, all the yearly proceeds of any and all sums given or appropriated solely for the support of the poor and for no other use.

And these defendants further answering, say, the arrangement herein before set forth by which the ministers and deacons delivered to the Old South Society the sum of $15,920.92 for the purpose of building two parsonage-houses, and the said society paid over to the ministers and deacons the rent of the easterly parsonage-house till the year 1845, for the use of the poor of said church and congregation, and since 1845 the sum of $600.00 per year, has been acquiesced in by all members of both church and society, and all other persons; and that no complaint or dissatisfaction has ever been expressed with the same from any source until recently by the relator in this case; and therefore these defendants say they believe said arrangement so made was just and fair, and as beneficial to the interests of the poor of the church and congregation as any that could be made, and that the same ought not now to be disturbed and set aside.

And these defendants further say, that, upon their personal knowledge since they have occupied their positions as ministers and deacons, and upon their information and belief before, the ministers and deacons have used and appropriated for the relief and support of the poor of the church all the money that in the exercise of a sound discretion they believed that the wants and needs of said poor required; and that, since the year eighteen hundred and thirty-eight, they have disbursed for the use of the poor each year, on the average, the sum of $1,048.93, which money has been derived from the income of the Massachusetts Bank stock aforesaid and the Life Insurance Company's bond, and from payments to them by the Old South Society for the support of the poor; and that large sums have been used each year by the ministers and deacons for the support of the poor since the year 1800, a very large portion of which was paid into their hands for that purpose by the Old South Society; and they annex to the answer a statement of the amounts paid by the ministers and deacons for the use of the poor, as appears by the records and accounts of the society and church, and which they believe to be true and correct, from the year eighteen hundred to this time. And these defendants say, that, for the last four years before the filing of this bill of complaint, the disbursements aforesaid for the poor have been made by the deacons alone, with the approval and consent of the ministers, to relieve the latter from that burden, on account of the pressure of their other official duties and calls. And these defendants, further answering, deny on their information and belief, that there are any funds which should be in the hands of said ministers and deacons, to be applied by them to the use of the poor of the Old South Church, in the possession of the Old South Society, in Boston, and applied and used by them for the purposes such as those set forth in the bill of complaint; but, on the contrary, they say, on their information and belief, that they are and have been receiving yearly from the Old South Society all the sums for the support of the poor which the latter ought to pay, and, as they believe, as much as could have been realized in any way or manner of investment from all gifts and contributions made solely for the support and use of the poor.

And these defendants, further answering, deny, that there is any other matter, cause, or thing, in the said complainant's bill of complaint contained, material or necessary for these respondents to make answer unto, and not herein and hereby well and sufficiently answered, confessed, traversed, avoided, or denied, is true to the knowledge, information, or belief of these defendants, all which matters and things these defendants are willing to aver, maintain, and prove as this Honorable Court shall direct, and humbly pray to be hereof discharged and dismissed with their reasonable costs in this behalf sustained. And these defendants do not affix hereto any corporate seal, because they never have adopted one.

G. W. BLAGDEN, } Ministers.
J. M. MANNING,

CHARLES STODDARD, } Deacons.
LORING LOTHROP,

COMMONWEALTH OF MASSACHUSETTS.

*Suffolk, ss.* At Boston, the fourth day of May, 1860, personally appeared before me the above named G. W. Blagden, Charles Stoddard, and Loring Lothrop, and on the fifth day of May, 1860, personally appeared the above named J. M. Manning, and each severally made oath that the foregoing answer by them severally subscribed is true to the best of their knowledge, information, and belief.

Before me,

CHARLES HOUGHTON,
*Justice of the Peace.*

---

The following sums have been distributed to the poor of the Old South Church from the year 1800 to the present time, as appears from the books of the treasurer (the year in the society's book closes with March): —

| Year | Amount | Year | Amount |
|---|---|---|---|
| 1800—1 | $747 00 | 1830—1 | $736 04 |
| 1801—2 | 754 00 | 1831—2 | 767 74 |
| 1802—3 | 645 00 | 1832—3 | 715 81 |
| 1803—4 | 575 00 | 1833—4 | 633 21 |
| 1804—5 | 685 00 | 1834—5 | 726 10 |
| 1805—6 | 660 00 | 1835—6 | 752 76 |
| 1806—7 | 635 00 | 1836—7 | 760 48 |
| 1807—8 | 613 00 | 1837—8 | 844 03 |
| 1808—9 | 545 00 | 1838—9 | 887 35 |
| 1809–10 | 630 00 | 1839–40 | 1,100 91 |
| 1810–11 | 497 00 | 1840–41 | 1,074 47 |
| 1811–12 | 460 00 | 1841 | 1,296 14 |
| 1812–13 | 520 00 | 1842 | 918 68 |
| 1813–14 | 507 00 | 1843 | 895 75 |
| 1814–15 | 532 00 | 1844 | ‑870 38 |
| 1815–16 | 561 00 | 1845 | 1,001 86 |
| 1816–17 | 510 00 | 1846 | 1,047 45 |
| 1817–18 | 400 00 | 1847 | 1,107 94 |
| 1818–19 | 484 00 | 1848 | 1,114 70 |
| 1819–20 | 723 83 | 1849 | 1,274 70 |
| 1820–21 | 728 87 | 1850 | 1,170 50 |
| 1821–22 | 724 21 | 1851 | 1,136 02 |
| 1822–23 | 696 54 | 1852 | 1,115 87 |
| 1823–24 | 757 38 | 1853 | 985 01 |
| 1824–25 | 929 64 | 1854 | 918 93 |
| 1825–26 | 928 11 | 1855 | 1,019 70 |
| 1826–27 | 975 03 | 1856 | 946 79 |
| 1827–28 | 981 46 | 1857 | 991 04 |
| 1828–29 | 892 69 | 1858–59 | 1,066 77 |
| 1829–30 | 709 17 | 1859–60 | 1,145 48 |

The following statement of account, though not a portion of the answer, is inserted here, in order to show the sources from which the above sums, alleged to have been distributed among the poor, and amounting in all to $49,029.64, were actually derived.

| DR. | | | | |
|---|---|---|---|---|
| | To income received from notes, dividends, &c. | | $8,229 99 | |
| 1800 to 1813, | " contribution acct. | | 691 53 | |
| " " " | candle money | | 38 00 | |
| | | | | $8,959 52 |
| 1813 to 1860, | " rent of house | | 29,232 73 | |
| " " " | Thanksgiving collection | | 132 89 | |
| " " " | rent of cellar | | 50 00 | |
| " " " | candle money | | 150 00 | |
| " " " | notes, dividend, &c., as above | | 4,589 46 | |
| " " " | contribution account | | 3,389 37 | |
| " " " | quarterly charity funds and collection | | 4,505 62 | |
| | | | | 42,050 07 |
| | | | | $51,009 59 |

CR.
| | | | |
|---|---|---|---|
| 1800 to 1813, | By money paid out during this time | $7,966 00 | |
| 1813 to 1860, | By " " | $41,063 64 | |
| | | | $49,029 64 |
| | " house rent 1860 not in | | 600 00 |
| | | | $49,629 64 |
| | Balance on hand not paid | | 1,379 95 |
| | | | $51,009 59 |

In March, 1860, the following decree was entered in the case by agreement: —

### DECREE.

In accordance with an agreement heretofore filed, it is ordered that the above-entitled cause be referred to Henry W. Paine, Esq., as special master, to inquire into and report to the court all matters pertinent to the issues raised on the bill and answers.

By the court,

March 4, 1861. GEORGE C. WILDE, *Clerk.*

In the summer of 1862, the case was argued by counsel before the master, who, after a long and careful examination, presented in March, 1865, the following report: —

MASTER'S REPORT.

The undersigned, having, in pursuance of the order annexed, duly notified the parties, and having heard their evidence, respectfully submits to the Honorable Court the following report: —

He was requested by the complainant to ascertain "the amount of the fund which in law and justice should be in the hands of the ministers and deacons of the Old South Church, in Boston, to be applied by them to the use of the poor of the church;" and this is the only matter pertinent to the issues raised by the bill and answers, to which his attention has been directed.

The evidence introduced consisted principally of records and account-books of the Old South Church, some of which dated back to the early part of the last century. The first statement of the fund claimed as a poor-fund appears in one of these books, entitled, "South Church Booke, Sacramental Contrabutions, 1708." This statement is found under date of 1761, and is headed, "Stock belonging to South Church, in Boston, at interest." A fuller and more exact statement is, however, given in the same book, under date of Jan. 1, 1766; and as after this, though an account of the fund as a whole has been regularly kept down to the present day, there is no other authentic statement of the fund distinguishing the several sources from which it arose, or the relative proportions belonging to each division, it becomes important to examine this statement carefully.

It is as follows: —

"Rise and increase of the church-stock is as follows: —

| | | | | |
|---|---|---|---|---|
| 1. Rev. Mr. Pemberton, | legacy, | . . | £17. 7s. 9d. | |
| 2. Mr. Cunningham, | " | . . | 66 13 4 | |
| 3. Mrs. Mills, | " | . . | 100 19 10 | |
| 4. Mrs. Eliza Loring, | " | . . | 13 6 8 | |
| 5. Capt. Jona. Armitage, | " | . . | 13 6 8 | |
| 6. Mr. Farr Tollman, | " | . . | 40 0 0 | |
| 7. Daniel Henchman, | " | . . | 66 0 0 | |
| 8. Mr. John Simpson, | " | . . | 30 0 0 | |
| 9. Mrs. Mary Ireland, | " | . . | 133 6 8 | |
| 10. Rev. Dr. Sewall, gift, | | . . | 20 0 0 | |
| | | | | £501. 0s. 11d. |
| 11. Pious and Charitable Fund, | | . . | £63. 12s. 6¼d. | |
| 12. Ministers' widows, | | . . | 3 6 8 | |
| | | | | 66 19 2¼ |
| 13. Sacramental stock, | | . . | £186. 19s. 5¼d. | |
| 14. Interest received on the above, | | . . | 119 14 8½ | |
| | | | | 306 14 1¾ |
| | | | | £874. 14s. 3d." |

The Rev. Mr. Pemberton, by his will (proved 26th February, 1716), gave "fifty pounds, to be put out at interest by my executrix and overseers; the interest to be annually distributed to the poor of the town of Boston, according to their good discretion." The first item in the aforesaid statement was undoubtedly paid over to the ministers, under this clause of Mr. Pemberton's will.

Nathaniel Cunningham, by his will (proved 13th December, 1748), "gave unto the poor of the aforesaid meeting-house — i. e., the church and congregation — five hundred pounds in passable bills of credit." Under this clause the second item was received.

Mrs. Ann Mills, by her will, directed "all the rest and residue of her estate to be equally divided as followeth; viz., one-quarter part to the Old, or First Church, in Boston, and one-quarter part to the Old South Church, in Boston, to be improved for the relief of the poor of said churches, at the discretion of the minister, or ministers and deacons." The third item was received from the executors of this will.

No copy of the will of Eliza Loring was produced; but by an entry in the aforesaid book (page 86) it appears that she bequeathed £13. 6s. 8d. for the use of the poor, and that it was received by the ministers and deacons.

Jonathan Armitage, by his will (proved 7th May, 1751), gave "to the Old South Church one hundred pounds, old tenor, or thirteen pounds, six shillings, and eight pence, lawful money of the province, forever, to be put out at interest by the ministers and deacons of the aforesaid church; and the interest of it to be given to the poor members of the aforesaid church, as the ministers and deacons shall think fit."

Mr. Farr Tollman, by his will (proved 22d October, 1751), gave "unto the poor of the church the sum of three hundred pounds, old tenor, or forty pounds lawful money; the same to be paid into the hands of the deacons of said church, to be put out at interest, and said interest to be paid yearly to the poor forever."

Mr. Daniel Henchman, by his will (proved 6th March, 1761), gave "unto the Old South Church the sum of sixty-five pounds, thirteen shillings, and four pence, lawful money; the same to be put out at interest, and the interest thereof to be paid to such of the poor of the said church as the ministers and deacons thereof shall in their prudence judge proper, forever."

Mr. John Simpson, by his will (proved 2d August, 1764), gave "unto the poor of the church the sum of thirty pounds, to be paid to the deacon or deacons of said church, to be by them distributed among said poor."

Mrs. Mary Ireland, by her will (proved 17th October, 1763), gave "unto the Old South Church the sum of one hundred and thirty-three pounds, six shillings, and eight pence, lawful money; to be put out on interest, the interest thereof to be annually paid to such of the poor of said church as the ministers and deacons thereof shall in their prudence judge proper, forever."

By an entry in the aforesaid book (page 43), it appears that Dr. Sewall gave "£20. 0s. 0d., the income of said sum to be distributed to the poor of the Old South Church, in Boston, yearly, by the deacons of said church," and that this sum was received.

It appears by the church records, that at a meeting of the church and congregation in 1738 it was proposed, "that some part of the money, which is or may be collected for charitable and pious uses, should, as we shall find ourselves able from time to time, be made a stated fund; the income of it to be improved for such uses as the brethren of the church and congregation shall from time to time determine." That a committee was raised to consider and report upon this proposal, and also upon another proposal; viz., "to establish a fund for the support of the widows and fatherless children of the pastors of the said South Church from time to time;" that the committee made a report recommending the establishment of such fund, and the mode and manner of perpetuating it; that "said report was read, voted, and established accordingly by the church and congregation."

This report recommended that the pastors and deacons shall, from time to time, be the trustees to manage said fund.

That the principal stock shall be kept entire, without being broken in upon on any occasion.

That it shall be kept at interest, or laid out in real estate, or lent to the church for the improvement of the real estate of the church.

That the money shall always be specified in gold or silver, and, when loaned to individuals, neither the borrower nor either of his two sureties shall be of the church or congregation.

Not long after this vote was passed, a fund was set apart, called the "Pious and Charitable Fund," and another and smaller one for the use of the widows and fatherless children of the pastors.

These two funds, thus created, and appearing in the foregoing statement, are not afterwards to be found, though there are in said book several statements of church stock. They do not appear to have been kept distinct from the other funds in the hands of the ministers and deacons, as was recommended by the committee and ordered by the vote, but were mingled with them; and the presumption is strong that the brethren of the church and congregation who were to control the fund had directed its application to the same uses for which the greater part of the fund was held, though no vote authorizing such application is to be found.

Thomas Hubbard, by his will (proved 23d July, 1773), gave "to the Charitable and Pious Fund of the Old South Church, so-called, in Boston, fifty pounds;" and it appears, by the aforesaid book (page 85), that this sum was received from the executors of Mr. Hubbard's will, in August, 1773, and mingled with the general fund.

The item denominated "Sacramental Stock" is the one which raises questions of the greatest difficulty. The history of this stock may be traced back to the year 1708. The opening entry in the aforesaid book is as follows: —

July 12, 1708. By the last account for the balance brought from the old book, folio 23; viz., a bond of Capt. N. Williams for payment of so much, seventy-eight pounds, . . . . . . . . £78. 0s. 0d.
Cash in sundry bags at Capt. Hill's, . . . . . 17 8 5

Total, . . . . . . . . . £95. 8s. 5d.
This amount was in old tenor.

This account is continued regularly from July 12, 1708, down to the year 1789.

The other credits in this account are sacramental contributions, sums received for the use of the palls, and sums bequeathed for the use of the poor and not required to be put at interest. Of the sacramental contributions, it appeared that, from time to time, certain portions at the time of their contribution were specially designated to be for the poor, or for some poor person named; but the great mass was made without any special appropriation.

On the other side are debited moneys expended for the communion service, expenses incurred by delegates to ordinations and councils, moneys paid to procure and keep in repair the palls, moneys paid for the expenses of conventions of ministers of the neighborhood at the pastor's, and moneys disbursed to the poor.

Much the larger portion of the receipts was from the sacramental contributions, or moneys taken up on communion Sundays; and much the larger part of the disbursements was for the use of the poor.

The balance of this account gradually increased till 1761, when the larger part of it was invested in a treasury note for £134. 0s. 0d. lawful money. This note is not afterwards in any way included or mentioned in the sacramental account, but appears in the above-mentioned statement of 1761, and, with several other small balances that were transferred from the sacramental to the general account, between 1761 and 1766, forms the thirteenth item in the foregoing statement; viz., £186. 19s. 5¼d.

From 1766 to 1789, the date of the latest sacramental account (that has been brought to the knowledge of the master), a balance was almost every year transferred from that account to the general fund, called the church stock; and from 1789 down to the time of the discontinuance of the sacramental collections, in 1849, in the account of the general fund, there is annually, with but few exceptions, a credit to that fund of a balance of sacramental collections transferred.

The general character of the items in the sacramental account has been already stated. The following items of an exceptional character also appear: —

"July, 1708. Paid for catechizing, . . . . . £1. 10s. 0d.
"March, 1771. Paid Rev. Mr. Prentiss for board, and sundry charges on the sickness and death of Dea. Sewall, as per account, . . . . . . . . . 9 13 6
"Dec., 1771. Paid Rev. John Walley for taking catalogue of the library of the late Rev. Dr. Sewall, as per his account, the greatest part of seventeen days, . . . 30 12 0
"Sept., 1764. 100s. 0d. appropriated expressly to the poor, given to sundries, . . . . . . . 5 0 0"

On the debit side of this account, under date of July, 1749, is found this entry: "To cash lent out of this stock, July 6, 1747, to pay off the deficiency of our ministers, as per vote of the church, £192. 0s. 0d." It no where appears that this sum was ever refunded.

In 1798, it appears by the records of the church and congregation, that it was *Voted*, "That the deacons be a committee to obtain an estimate of the expense of repairing the steeple, and such other parts of the building as may be found necessary, and to devise some plan for raising a sum sufficient for said purpose;" that the committee reported "that the repairing of the steeple would cost fifteen hundred dollars, and that it would be proper to open a subscription in the society for raising this money;" and that it was voted " to open a subscription."

It appears by the records of the church, that, at a regular church-meeting in 1849, it was voted to discontinue the collections on communion Sundays, after remarks from Deacons Cutler, Stoddard, and Dimon, showing that the omission of the custom of the church to take a collection at the close of the communion season for the benefit of the poor of the church would not, in the present circumstances of the Old South, in any degree hurt the interests of the poor."

This record purports to be signed by the clerk, who was also at that time the sole pastor.

The general fund, entered on the books as church stock, was increased by legacies for the use of the poor, by balances of sacramental collections, and by accumulations of interest. This sum was invested in bonds and stocks, which, at their par value in 1800, amounted to $16,062.71.

On April 3, 1800, a committee appointed to take into consideration the propriety and right of building a number of stores on the land belonging to the society adjoining the meeting-house reported that it was expedient to erect five brick stores, and recommended borrowing of the society for the purpose; they being of opinion, that, after paying the same interest upon the sum borrowed as it was then producing, there would be a surplus of rents which might be applied towards the support of an additional minister, "providing the society should choose to expend it in that way," "in doing which," they say, "the views of the donor, not only of the land, but those who have left legacies from time to time, will be fully answered, as the poor of said society will have as much as they now receive, and the other will be laid out in pious uses for the support of public worship." This report was accepted.

At the same meeting a committee was raised to examine into the society's funds, and to report the sums of money and their different appropriations.

The following is the report of that committee, made to the church and congregation, April 22: —

BOSTON, 18th April, 1800. Your committee, appointed to examine into the state of the funds of the South Church and Congregation, to endeavor to find from what source they have arisen, and the intentions of the donors, have attended to that business, and beg leave to report that, on examining, they find them to have arisen as follows: —

| | | |
|---|---:|---:|
| Given by sundry persons for the poor of the church, to the care of the deacons of the church | £102. 18s. 4d. | |
| Given by sundry persons for the poor of the church, to the care of the ministers and deacons of the church | 153 6 8 | |
| Given for the poor of the church and congregation, to the care of the ministers and deacons £5. 12s. 0d. | | |
| Given by Mrs. Mills . . . . . . 100 19 10 | | |
| Given by Mr. Cunningham . . . . 66 13 4 | — £173. 5s. 2d. | |
| Collected at sundry times the interest to the use of ministers' widows and children | 66 19 2 | |
| Given to the poor of the church, not mentioned to whose care | 6 0 0 | |
| Given, and not mentioned whether to the use of the church, or church and congregation | 8 0 4 | |
| Collected from 1733 to May, 1757, for the use of the palls | 46 7 6 | |
| Balances arising from the sacramental collections at different times to the year 1766, over and above what paid the expenses | 186 19 5 | |
| We find by the church books, given by sundry persons, which we find no minutes in the papers for what use, but as they are in the church accounts, suppose for their use | 136 14 5 | |
| | £880. 11s. 0d. | |

This was in possession 1766, and at interest, and has been used ever since. The war coming on in about nine years after this time, and the moneys remaining during that period, must have accumulated considerably. After peace came on, the money was generally called in, and invested into public funds, where it now remains, and is as follows, viz.: —

| | |
|---|---:|
| Massachusetts Bank shares, sixteen, at $500.00 each | $8,000 00 |
| Forty-two and one-half Union Bank shares, at $8 | 340 00 |
| Samuel Hinkley & Co. bond | 416 66 |
| Three per cent stock | 4,935 75 |
| Eight per cent stock | 600 00 |
| Five and a half per cent ditto, | 1,000 00 |
| Massachusetts State note, 5 per cent, | 709 37 |
| Deferred stock of the United States | 60 93 |
| | $16,062 71 |

All which is submitted per order.

JOHN WINSLOW, *Chairman.*

At the meeting at which this report was made, it was *Voted*, "That a committee of five, three of the church and two of the congregation, be desired to apply to the trustees, the minister, and deacons for the loan of the sums necessary to defray the expenses of building the stores."

At a meeting of the church and congregation, held May 11, 1800, the following votes were passed: —

"*Voted*, That the committee appointed on the 22d of April last to borrow moneys of the minister and deacons to defray the expenses of erecting stores on the society's land be hereby discharged from that duty. And it is *Voted*, —

"That the minister and deacons be requested, and they are hereby authorized, to pay and deliver from the money of the church and congregation to the committee of contractors appointed on the said 22d April, and to any other committee that may be employed to erect said stores, all such sums of money as may from time to time be found necessary by such committees for building said stores, said committee rendering regular accounts thereof to said minister and deacons, so that it may appear how much of said money shall be transferred and changed from their present situation to the property in said stores. And whatever money shall be so paid and delivered shall be considered as having been duly accounted for by said minister and deacons, the present trustees thereof.

"And the said minister and deacons shall at all times be entitled to receive so much of the rents and income of said stores as shall amount to six per cent per annum upon the moneys they shall pay and deliver as aforesaid, to the end that they may be enabled to appropriate the same in like manner as the interest of said moneys has heretofore been appropriated, according to the pious intentions of the donors thereof.

"And as it is highly probable that the rents and income of said stores will exceed the rate of six per cent per annum upon said moneys, by reason that the value of the land will be added to the value of the stores, it is therefore *Voted*, That whatever rents and income said stores shall produce over and above the legal interest on said moneys shall go into the hands of the treasurer distinct from any other funds of the society, and shall be used and applied for the purposes set forth in the committee's report of the 20th March last, and which was accepted the 3d day of April last, in such manner as the church and congregation shall from time to time vote and determine, or for such other ecclesiastical purposes as they shall order."

In pursuance of this vote, the society received out of the fund fourteen thousand dollars, all of which, except the sum of $5,245.00, was soon after reimbursed.

On a pledge of a portion of the stocks, money was borrowed of a bank; and the interest on the loan was paid in advance out of the fund, until April 1, 1801, when the stock was sold. The interest so paid amounted in the aggregate to $479.46.

The committee raised to examine the treasurer's account reported to the society, at a meeting held April 13, 1807, that "there is due to the Church and Congregation Fund, for the poor thereof, the interest on $5,245.00, which was vested in the five stores, called South Row, as by vote passed by the church and congregation at a meeting held on 11th May, 1800; viz., from first day of April, 1801, to the first day of April, 1807, six years at six per cent, and reckoning compound interest, amounts to $2,195.12, which interest, by a vote passed as aforesaid, was to be paid from the income of the stores to the minister and deacons, trustees for the distribution of the same;" and the committee recommends that a vote be passed requiring the treasurer to pay, and "place under the direction of the trustees, one thousand dollars out of the balance of income from the stores, in part of the above interest."

The report was accepted, and it was thereupon *Voted*, " That the treasurer be desired, and he is hereby authorized, to pay the balance of interest due the church and congregation to the first of October next out of income of the stores when received, and that, at the end of every quarter-year afterwards, he pay to the minister and deacons, trustees for the distribution of said interest money, the quarter's interest, being $78.67½, as the same may become due and payable out of the income accruing from said stores." But it does not appear that any part of this sum, $2,195.12, has been paid.

At a meeting of the church and congregation, held May 22, 1809, " the committee of ways and means for the purpose of building two parish-houses, having considered the subject committed to them," reported, " That there is in the hands of the treasurer of the society certain capital stock, the interest of which only is appropriated to the use of the poor of the church; that, instead of borrowing money of a bank or of any individuals, and depositing this stock as security for payment, it should be disposed of, or so much thereof as may be found necessary, and the proceeds invested permanently in those buildings. The interest appropriated to the use of the poor may always be drawn from the surplus of permanent income, as stated in the schedule annexed: —

Estimate, viz., eighteen bank shares at $500.00 is $9,000.00.

| | |
|---|---:|
| If they should be sold at 25 per cent advance, which is 3 per cent under the price quoted, will produce . . | $11,250 00 |
| Money, when received for pews sold . . . . . | 1,290 00 |
| Money of the church and congregation in the treasurer's hands . . . . . . . . . . | 2,824 49 |
| Twenty pews in the gallery unlet and unsold, if disposed of to workmen in part pay, say . . . . . | 2,000 00 |
| Making the sum of . . . . . . . | $17,364 49 |

This sum, it is supposed, may be sufficient for the purpose of building the two houses. The interest of $11,250.00 is $675.00, for the use of the poor," &c.

This report was accepted.

At a meeting of the church, held June 6, 1809, it was *Voted*, " That the trustees of certain funds placed in their hands be requested to furnish the society with so much from the same as may be required to complete the building of two parsonage-houses, upon conditions that the interest be punctually paid, and that the buildings be insured to secure payment thereof."

In a report of a committee appointed to examine the accounts of the treasurer of the society, made 20th April, 1808, this item appears: "Interest money of the poor of the church and congregation, subject to the direction of the ministers and deacons, trustees for the fund, $2,509.81." An item, similarly entitled, amounting to $2,824.49, is also to to be found in the report of the committee of 1809.

In December, 1809, on application of the standing committee, the minister and deacons gave them a written agreement, of which the following is a copy: —

*Whereas* in times past there have been legacies, bequests, and donations made to the Old South Church, to be placed at interest for the benefit of the poor of said church and of the church and congregation, and the interest arising thereon to be distributed among them according to the direction of the ministers and deacons of said church, trustees for the purpose; and *whereas* the society have voted to build two parsonage-houses on the site whereon the old one now stands, and it appears that the church and congregation at their meeting on 22d May, 1809, voted and accepted the report of a committee by them appointed to devise ways and means to build two parsonage-houses, which was to appropriate so much of the capital stock as might be found necessary for that purpose; and the church, at their meeting on the 6th June, 1809, voted that the trustees of the fund be requested to furnish the society with so much from the same as may be required to complete the building of said houses, upon condition that the interest be punctually paid, and the buildings be insured, to secure the said payment; and *whereas*, the church and congregation, at their meeting on the 7th June, 1809, voted that the standing committee for the year be the committee to contract for building said houses and carry the same into effect, — we therefore, the undersigned, ministers and deacons, trustees as aforesaid, in compliance with the above request, do hereby agree to pay to said committee, or to any person or persons appointed by them to receive the same, a sum out of said funds not exceeding fourteen thousand dollars.

BOSTON, December, 1809.

JOSEPH ECKLEY.<br>JOSHUA HUNTINGTON.<br>WILLIAM PHILLIPS.

Attest,
    E. M. HUNTINGTON.
    JOHN MOREY.

The standing committee say, in their report communicating the result of their application to the minister and deacons, "We embrace this opportunity to communicate to the society, that, by the records, it appears that there was a committee appointed April 3, 1800, to examine into the state of the funds, who reported that the foundation upon which the funds had arisen consisted of certain items as they stood in 1766, the whole of which amounted to £880. 11s. 0d. lawful money; that the funds on 3d April, 1800, consisted of bank shares, specie value $8,000.00, and other securities nominally to $8,062.72. At a meeting of church and congregation,

11th May, 1800, it was voted that the ministers and deacons deliver from the money of the church and congregation, to the committee empowered to erect the stores, such sums as might be necessary for the purpose. This last sum, when reduced to specie value, amounted to $5,221.40 (sold afterwards for $5,245.00), and was then considered to be the property of the church and congregation, leaving the bank shares to belong to the church. By another part of the report of that committee of 3d April, made May 11, 1800, it might seem that the whole $5,221.00 (or $5,245.00) grew out of certain donations from particular persons. That, however, does not appear to have been the fact; but, on the contrary, arose from the four last items, as stated in that report, amounting to £378. 8s. 8d. lawful money. This statement is founded on that of the committee of 3d April, 1800, on the state of the funds. The society will therefore consider whether the ministers and deacons had the disposal of the interest of that part, as was then supposed in said vote. The standing committee are unanimously of opinion they had not that right. If the society concur in the same opinion, it would seem that the $5,221.40 ($5,245.00) vested in the stores, as well as the income that has since arisen on the same, was the property of the church and congregation, and entirely at their disposal. If so, the vote or votes passed May 11, 1800, as respects the control of the interest by the trustees, should be reconsidered." This report was accepted; but no further action was had thereon.

The master has not been able to trace any connection between the £378. 8s. 8d., the sum of the last four items in the statement of 1766, and the sum of $5,245.00 invested in the stores.

The account of the fund now claimed as a poor-fund was kept by the treasurer with the South Church, and the general statements of the fund were entered in the books under the head of church stock down to 1813, when the money had been advanced for the building of the two parsonage-houses. After that time, no general statement of the fund appears; but the account of what remained thereof was kept as before by the treasurer with the South Church. In this account the church was credited with the interest on the remaining fund as received, as well as sacramental contributions, and was charged with the expenses of the church before mentioned, and money disbursed to the poor.

As the sacramental collections were entered with the gifts and legacies made expressly for the use of the poor; as from the earliest account, in 1708, to the final discontinuance of these collections in 1849, all the surplus, after payment of certain church expenses (and a few others, not so clearly of that character, before specified), was made a part of the fund out of which disbursements to the poor were made, which fund consisted mainly of moneys left by will to be kept at interest for the benefit of the poor; as the church, as early as 1747, by borrowing from it to pay their minister, treated it as a fund not subject to their disposal; and as, when discontinuing the collections, they were called collections "for the benefit of the poor," and the discontinuance was voted for the reason assigned, that they were not needed for the poor, — the Master has been forced to the conclusion, that the items of sacramental stock in the statement of 1766, and the balances afterwards transferred, are a part of the poor-fund. From the facts, he infers that these contributions were originally made with the understanding that any surplus remaining, after defraying certain special church expenses, should be applied to the benefit of the poor. If this was not the clear understanding and intention of the contributors, the balances were so mingled with moneys held expressly in trust for the use of the poor that it is not practicable now to separate them, and assign to each its due proportion.

The item in the statement of 1766, called "Interest received on the above," is evidently interest on all the preceding items.

The master is of opinion that the sum of £874. 14s. 3d., appearing at the foot of the statement of 1766, is to be regarded as the poor-fund at that date, excepting items 11 and 12, which he presumes afterwards became a part thereof, as before stated.

After 1766, a separate and regular account was kept of all the income received from, and of all disbursements out of, this fund. This account shows that between that date and the 18th April, 1800, this fund increased largely, so that at the latter date it amounted to the sum of $16,062.71, taking the stocks in which it was invested at their par value. At their market-value the sum would be somewhat larger. This increase arose principally from the rise in the value of the stocks and notes in which the fund was invested, and from accumulations of income, but in part from legacies, one of which was expressly required " to be let out at interest, and the interest applied to the use of the poor;" and from small balances transferred almost every year from the sacramental account. During this period, the payments charged in this account were mainly for the poor. After the discontinuance of the separate sacramental account in 1789, a few charges are made of sacramental expenses; and, in one case, of expenses of a delegate to an installation. This charge is as follows: "30th July, 1789. By cash supplied John Sweetser, Jr., Esq., expenses of journey to New Concord for instalment of the Rev. Mr. Evans, as per memorandum. N. B. — See folios 33 and 34 for presidents of the like kind, £10. 16s. 4d." (Folios 33 and 34 contain the sacramental account from 1746 to 1751.) There is also a charge in January, 1800, of "Paid Mr. J. Pierce, for black cloth and flannel, to put the meeting-house in mourning for General Washington, $40.17." And there is another charge on March 28, 1799: "Paid Jeffrey & Russell, for sperm candles, $43.33." From this date to 1823, sums are charged from time to time for candles; and the other side of the account shows, that from 1809 to 1826, a sum which for the first two years was $9.00, and afterwards $10.00, was annually in December credited as "received at" or "of quarterly meetings, for candles;" though these credits do not equal the amount charged during the same time as paid for candles. Other portions of the book contain accounts of collections taken at meetings held in March, June, September, and December of each year during this period, called Quarterly Charity Meetings, and of the distribution among the poor of the amount so collected.

In 1808, an addition to this fund was made of $650.00, "received," as appears by the books, "of the treasurer of the late Thursday evening Charitable Society, as per vote passed Feb. 3, 1808, the income of which to be applied to the benefit of the poor of that church."

A separate account was kept for a number of years, with several of the legacies which were directed to be put at interest. On the one side, the interest was credited, and on the other the disbursements to the poor were charged. Such an account was kept with one of the legacies down to 1791, when it was discontinued.

In accordance with their agreement before recited, the ministers and deacons, in 1810, furnished to the society on May 3, 1810, $4,524.00; on July 1, $4,364.00; and on Jan. 1, 1811, $3,895,75; in all, $12,783.75.

On Jan. 1, 1811, the society was indebted to the fund as follows: —

| | |
|---|---:|
| For balance unpaid of first loan | $5,245 00 |
| " interest paid the bank to April 1, 1801 | 479 46 |
| " compound interest, as per vote, to April 1, 1807 | 2,195 12 |
| " interest from April 1, 1807, to Jan. 1, 1811 | 1,781 90 |
| " money furnished May 1, 1810 | 4,524 00 |
| " interest on same to Jan. 1, 1811 | 180 96 |
| " money furnished July 1, 1810 | 4,364 00 |
| " interest on same to Jan. 1, 1811 | 130 92 |
| " money furnished Jan. 1, 1811 | 3,895 75 |
| | $22,797 11 |

From the time of its completion down to 1845, the rent of the "easterly parsonage-house," so called, was annually paid over to and received by the ministers and deacons, instead of interest on the loan. This rent for the first year was $450.00; for the second year, $500.00; from 1816 to 1828, it ranged from $650.00 to $775.00 per year; and from 1828 to 1845, it was $600.00 per year. By a by-law passed in 1845, the treasurer of the society was directed to pay annually to the deacons for the use of the poor the sum of six hundred dollars; and this sum since that time has been paid regularly.

The sums of money annually distributed among the poor are correctly stated in the answers; but these sums were derived, in part, from sacramental collections of the year, from the income of so much of the poor-fund as was admitted to be held by the treasurer for the ministers and deacons, and from sources other than the funds of the society.

The total of disbursements to the poor of the society from its own funds, from July 1, 1811, to Jan. 1, 1861, including the aforesaid sums paid to ministers and deacons, is $29,232.73. The total of interest on the sum due from the society to the poor-fund from Jan. 1, 1811, to Jan. 1, 1861, is $62,109.99.

This difference between these two sums, viz., $32,877.26, added to the aforesaid sum of $22,797.11, makes the amount in the hands of the society, Jan. 1, 1861, belonging to and constituting the principal part of the poor-fund, viz., $55,674.37.

The residue of this fund, which in January, 1861, was in the hands of the treasurer of the society, though admitted to be a part of the poor-fund, was invested in four shares Massachusetts Bank stock, $1,000, and in note of Mass. H. & L. I. Co., for $1,000; and the fund was indebted to said treasurer in the sum of $52.50. It was in proof that the wants of the poor of the Old South Church had been liberally supplied, and that no complaint had been made by any one but the relator, and that no complaint had been made by him that the necessities of the poor had not been liberally supplied.

The report sets out the facts in evidence, from which the master has drawn his conclusions.

The respondents except to this report, and file the exceptions which are herewith returned.

March 3, 1865.
H. W. PAINE.

Master's fees, $500.00.

To this report the defendants filed the following exceptions: —

And now the said defendants come and except to the master's report filed in this case, and file the following specifications of their exceptions; viz., —

1. They except to said report because said master has reported the "poor-fund" of said church and society to amount to $55,674.37 on the first of January, 1861, when, upon the facts and evidence, it should have been a much smaller sum.

2. They except to said report because said master has included in, and made a part of, said poor-fund of said church and society, any other sums than those given to said society and church, or the minister and deacons thereof, for the use of the poor, and the interest thereof unexpended for that purpose.

3. They except to the said report because the said master has included in, and made a part of, the poor-fund of said church and society, the sacramental contributions named in said report, and also that fund described as the sacramental stock as well as the interest accruing from said contributions and stock; the said defendants alleging, that, upon the facts and evidence, said contributions and funds formed no part of any fund devoted exclusively to the use of the poor.

J. G. ABBOTT,
*For the Defendants.*

Upon these exceptions, the case finally came up for argument before the full bench of the Supreme Court, in November, 1866. The briefs of the respective counsel were as follows: —

## COMPLAINANT'S BRIEF.

This information was brought to establish a charity for the benefit of the poor of the Old South Church, — that an account of all moneys bequeathed, contributed, and accumulated for such charity might be taken; that the said Old South Society might be decreed to pay over such sum as might be found due from them, upon the taking of such account, to the ministers and deacons of said church, the other respondents, to be by them held and applied to the purposes of such charity; and that such further and other directions as the case might require might be given for the establishment and maintenance of said charity.

The several answers of the two respondents, in substance, admit the existence of a fund as charged; but deny that it is as large as alleged, and assert that there is no ground for the interference of this Court.

Henry W. Paine, Esq., was appointed a special Master, " to inquire into, and report to the Court, all matters pertinent to the issues raised on the bill and answers." The Master has made his report, by which the following facts appear: —

On the 1st January, 1766, there was a certain fund, amounting to the sum of £874. 14s. 3d., which had arisen from several sources, as shown in a statement of that date found in an ancient account-book of the Old South Church. (Master's Report, pp. 1, 2.)

Of this sum of £874. 14s. 3d., more than half, or £510. 0s. 11d. (being the amount of items 1–10 in said statement), had come from legacies and gifts made expressly to the poor, and most of them expressly required to be put at interest, and the *income* only distributed in charity. (pp. 2, 3.)

The sum of £63. 12s. 6¼d. (being item 11 in said statement) was held as a fund "for charitable and pious uses;" "the income of it to be improved for such uses as the brethren of the church and congregation shall from time to time determine." (p. 3.)

The small sum of £3. 6s. 8d. (being item 12 in said statement) was "a fund for the support of the widows and fatherless children of the pastors" of said church. (p. 3.)

The sum of £186. 19s. 5¼d. (being item 13 in said statement) arose principally from the excess of the amount of the collections taken at said church on communion Sundays, during a long series of years, over the amount required to defray the expenses of the communion service and certain other special charges (p. 4). The Master reports (p. 11), that, "from the facts, he infers that these contributions were originally made with the understanding that any surplus remaining, after defraying certain special church expenses, should be applied to the benefit of the poor." The facts from which he draws this inference are as follows: —

That it appears from an account running back to 1708, that, during the time in which this sum of £186. 19s. 5¼d. had been accumulating, there had been entered, promiscuously with the sums received from these collections, many sums received from gifts and legacies made expressly for the use of the poor, but not, as with those before noticed, required to be put at interest. (pp. 4, 10.)

That, during this long period, the payments made out of these communion moneys had, with one trifling exception, been made either to the poor, or to defray the special church expenses before referred to. (pp. 4, 5.)

That the church, as early as 1747, by borrowing of this fund to pay their minister, had treated it as a fund not subject to their disposal. (pp. 5, 10.)

That the same thing is shown by the subsequent history of these sacramental contributions: 1st, from the fact that from this date (1766) until the discontinuance of these collections in 1849, a balance, consisting of the surplus not needed for the special objects above referred to, was annually, with but few exceptions, transferred to form a part of the fund out of which disbursements to the poor were made, and which fund consisted mainly of moneys left by will to be kept at interest for the poor (pp. 5, 10). And 2d, from the fact that from the records of said church, signed by Dr. Blagden, then sole pastor and clerk, it appears that, at a regular church-meeting in 1849, it was voted to discontinue the collections on communion Sundays, "after remarks from Deacons Cutler, Stoddard, and Dimon, showing that the *omission of the custom of the church to take a collection at the close of the communion season for the benefit of the poor of the church would not, in the present circumstances of the Old South, in any degree hurt the interests of the poor.*" (pp. 5. 10.)

The remaining sum of £119. 14s. 8½d. (being item 14 in said statement) consists of interest which had accumulated on all the preceding items, and should be distributed proportionately among them. (p. 11.)

From these facts the Master concludes that the whole of this fund of £874. 14s. 3d., with the exception of items 11 and 12, amounting to £66.-19s. 2¼d., was in 1766 a fund already devoted to charitable purposes, as claimed by the information. (p. 11.)

After 1766, a separate and regular account was kept of all the income received from, and of all disbursements out of, this fund as a whole (p. 11). Separate accounts were also kept for some years with several of the legacies mentioned, but they were finally discontinued (pp. 11, 12). No separate account was kept of the funds mentioned in items 11 and 12. They were not kept distinct from other funds, as it had been voted that they should be when they were established (p. 4), and the Master finds that, "The presumption is strong that the brethren of the church and congregation who were to control these funds had directed their application to the same uses for which the greater part of the fund was held, though no vote authorizing such application is to be found" (p. 4). A legacy of £50. 0s. 0d. given in 1773 to the first of these two special funds, but mingled directly with the large general fund, is of course liable to the effect of the same presumption. Thus the only portions of the fund concerning which there was any question in 1766 are found by the Master to have become shortly afterwards devoted to the same purposes as the remainder of the fund, and the fund became, as a whole, properly a *poor fund*. This conclusion of the Master is stated by him in his Report (page 11).

But, if there be any doubt whether this fund was thus early devoted wholly to the poor, its later history leaves no room to doubt that it has been at some time so devoted.

After 1766, it increased in amount, being in 1800 over $16,000.00 (p. 11)

This increase arose principally from rise in stocks and accumulations of income, but also in part from legacies to the poor, — one of which was, like those before mentioned, expressly required to be let out at interest, and the interest applied to the use of the poor, — and from balances of sacramental collections (pp. 11, 5). In 1808 the sum of $650.00 was added to this fund, having been given by a charitable society expressly that the income might be applied to the benefit of the poor of the church (p. 11). All these moneys were merged undistinguishably in one general fund, the payments out of which, with the exception of the loans to be mentioned hereafter, and of a few insignificant matters mentioned on page 11, have down to the present day been made wholly to the poor or for their use. (p. 11.)

But, if these facts are not sufficient to prove that all this money had been devoted to the poor, we have the fact, as found by the Master (p. 11), that those portions of the fund about which any question can be raised "were so mingled with moneys held expressly in trust for the use of the poor that it is not practicable now to separate them, and assign to each its due proportion."

And now, to preclude all question as to this fund, we have the distinct and repeated admissions of the respondents that it all belonged to the poor.

On 3d April, 1800, a committee of the society recommended borrowing from this fund for the purpose of building stores on the society's land, paying the same interest therefor that it was then producing, "in doing which," they say, "the views of . . . those who have left legacies from time to time will be fully answered, *as the poor of said society* will have as much as they now receive" (pp. 5, 6). This report was accepted, and at a subsequent meeting it was voted that application be made to the ministers and deacons, trustees, for such a loan ; and that they should be paid interest at six per cent upon the amount thereof, " to the end that they may be enabled *to appropriate the same in like manner as the interest of said moneys has heretofore been appropriated, according to the pious intentions of the donors thereof*" (p. 7). The sum of $14,000.00 was accordingly loaned, all of which except $5,245.00 was soon repaid (p. 8). The existence of this indebtedness was acknowledged in the report of a committee made in 1807, which stated that "there is due to the Church and Congregation Fund *for the poor thereof*, the interest on $5,245.00, . . . which interest by a vote," &c., "was to be paid . . . to the minister and deacons, trustees for the distribution of the same." This report was accepted, and the treasurer was ordered to pay interest then due to the amount of $2,195.12, and interest quarterly thereafter (p. 8). Similar recognitions of "*interest money of the poor*" were made by committees in 1808 and 1809, at which last date it amounted to $2.824.49. (p. 9).

The answers of both the respondents (Answers pp. 14, 23) admit such interest as due to the ministers and deacons, and included, to the amount of $3,139.17, in the second loan, which is next to be considered, and which is thus admitted by the respondents to have been larger by the above amount than it is found by the Master to have been. [This amount of $3,139.17 is made up by adding to the sum of $2,195.12, above-mentioned, $944.05, as simple interest on $5,245.00 for the three years from 1st April, 1807, to 1st April, 1810. See Answers, pp. 14, 22.]

In 1809, a committee appointed to consider the means of raising money to build two parsonage-houses reported, that there was "in the hands of the treasurer of the society certain capital stock, the interest of which only is *appropriated to the use of the poor of the church*," and they recommended borrowing this money, recognizing in terms twice afterwards in their report that the interest of the money so borrowed would belong *to the poor* (pp. 8, 9). This report was also accepted, and shortly afterwards the sum of $12,783.75 (p. 12) was loaned for the above-mentioned purpose by the ministers and deacons, trustees, in accordance with a written agreement set forth in full in the Master's Report, and which distinctly acknowledges that the moneys then loaned had arisen from "*legacies, bequests, and donations made to the Old South Church to be placed at interest for the benefit of the poor*" (p. 9). Upon this sum certain amounts in the nature of interest have been paid yearly down to the present time (p. 12). But the principal, as well as the $5,245.00 before mentioned as remaining unpaid of the first loan, has never been repaid. As alleged in the bill (p. 4), and not denied in the answers, the standing committee of the society, as late as 1823, in express terms, acknowledged that certain sums were then paid " to the ministers and deacons for interest of money borrowed by the society for the purpose of building the two parsonage-houses, which money was left by a number of persons at different periods to the ministers and deacons of the Old South Church in trust for the benefit of the poor of said church." It is also admitted in the Answers (pp. 14, 15, 23) that the sum of $15,920.92 was borrowed in 1810 by the society from the ministers and deacons, and that no part of the principal, and only an inadequate sum as interest, has been repaid. The small balance of the fund still remaining after the above loans is still recognized as belonging to the poor (p. 12). (Answers, pp. 14. 23.) But even this amount is asserted by the respondents to be held *for* the ministers and deacons, and not *by* them, as it should be.

By the figures given in the Master's Report at page 12, the amount of the poor fund is thus shown to have been on the 1st January, 1861, $57,621.87.

The only act of the society at all inconsistent with the existence of this indebtedness to the trustees for the poor is to be found in a report of a committee made in 1809 or 1810 (p. 10), which gives the opinion of the committee that the sum of $5,245.00 before-mentioned did not belong to the poor, and which recommends that the votes by which the society agreed to pay them interest therefor should be reconsidered. But, though said report was accepted, *no such reconsideration was had, nor any other action taken upon the subject* (p. 10). But in this report the committee give the reasons for their opinion, and such reasons are evidently invalid, and show moreover that the committee did not proceed upon information as to the origin of the fund so authentic as that now before the Court.

1. The report of the committee of 1800 (p. 6), upon which they say they found their opinion, is on the face of it vague and general, and evidently of

no weight in comparison with the statement on page 2 of the Master's Report, which is taken from the original books of account, containing the full account of this fund, and which gives the items in such a manner that they can almost all be traced to their orginal source in a will or elsewhere.

2. The Master reports that he has not been able to trace any connection, as claimed by the committee as the foundation of their opinion, between the sum of £378. 8s. 8d. and that of $5,425.00, and such connection is evidently wholly arbitrary and unfounded.

Thus, to review the ground we have gone over thus far : the Master's Report shows a fund which in 1766 was almost wholly devoted to the poor, — the small, exceptional items being shortly afterwards so devoted. It shows that, whatever questions may be raised about the beneficial ownership of the fund in 1766, all such questions are removed by its subsequent history, which proves that the only parties who could lay any claim to use it for their own purposes so treated and managed it as to show that they subsequently devoted it to the poor. And it shows still further, that the respondents have repeatedly, and in the most solemn manner, admitted that it was a fund belonging to the poor, and over which they had no control. The Report shows further that the ministers and deacons, who, as a corporation under G. S. c. 31, s. 1, should properly hold this fund in their own hands in trust for the poor, do not in fact so hold any part of it. That a sum of about $2,000.00 is acknowledged to be so held *for* but not *by* them ; that additional sums, amounting with simple interest unpaid to $55,674.37, have been borrowed from the fund by the society, for which the said ministers and deacons hold no evidence of indebtedness, and for which the said society now denies its liability, though it has for more than fifty years paid an inadequate sum towards the interest upon it, — inadequate as interest, but claimed as sufficient as regards the wants of the trustees and their beneficiaries, the poor.

## I.

It seems to us that this case must turn more upon the facts than upon any question of law.

1. The issue seems to be, whether this fund, in regard to the *existence* or *amount* of which there can be no controversy, is held by the defendants as a charitable trust, or in their own right, according to their present claim.

2. The *conceded facts* in the case seem to us to place the character of a charitable trust upon it, beyond all controversy.

1. It is shown we believe to the satisfaction of the court, that the *donors* of every portion of it expressly *devoted* it to a *permanent investment*, the interest to be for the *benefit* of the *poor of the church and congregation*. This constitutes a public charity for the poor designated. Tudor's Charitable Trusts, 6, " A gift to the poor, either indefinitely or of a *particular parish* or place, has been held to be charitable." Attorney General *v.* Peacock, Rep. T. Finch, 245 ; same *v.* Matthews, 2 Lev. 167. But as precisely in point, Attorney General *v.* Clarke, Amb. 422, where the bequest was of the interest of £4,200.-0s. 0d., " to the poor inhabitants of a parish, and held to be a public charity."

This principle is recognized in all the subsequent cases. Attorney General *v.* Bovill, 1 Phill. 762. The *extent* of the *scheme* here for expending the income of the fund is well worthy of note, as well as the history of the charity and the expenditure of the income, and will relieve the defendants from all embarrassment as to applying the *whole* income of the fund in their hands. So gifts to the widows and orphans of a parish are public charities. Attorney General *v.* Comber. 2 Sim. and Stu. 93. And, if the poor be not expressly named, it will be presumed they were intended. Tudor 7. Attorney General *v.* Trinity Church, 9 Allen.

2. The manner in which this fund has been kept by the ministers and deacons shows that they always regarded it as a *permanent fund*, and that the interest was for the poor of the parish, which is the essence of public charity. Tudor, 7.

3. If there were any doubt as to any particular portion of the fund, the trustees, having so mingled them that they cannot be separated, must lose all claim upon any portion of the fund. (And the defendants do not attempt to define the present extent of the "poor fund" in their answers even, but admit, in a general way, that there is or was such a fund, pp. 21, 22.) Hart *v.* Ten Eyck, 2 John, ch. 62, where it is held that if the trustee mingle the trust-fund with his own in such a manner that it cannot be separated, or distinguished, he must lose his own. The same principle is applied to other subjects: where the party withholds or destroys evidence, the presumption will be taken most strongly against him. Amory *v.* Delamirie, 1 Str. 505 : Lupton *v.* White, 15 Vesey, 432; Panton *v.* Panton, *id.* 440.

The same rule exists everywhere in regard to the commixture of property. The party in fault, although not intentionally, must run the risk of separation; and the party thus making the mixture will lose his own, unless he can show what his share is. Ryder *v.* Hathaway, 21 Pick. 298; Pratt *v.* Bryant, 20 Vt. Rep. 333.

## II.

We do not apprehend the defendants can claim any benefit from the long lapse of time in the case.

No statutory or presumptive bar applies to a trust, and especially a public charitable one. Where the trust is express, i.e., declared upon the face of the gift, there is not, and never was, any limitation or restriction as to the extent to which the trustees will be held liable to account for the income. Tudor, 341, 342; Attorney General *v.* the Mayor of Exeter, Jac. 443, 448.

It is here said, that where the trustee has for a long period, "under an innocent mistake, misapplied the fund, from the laches and neglect of others, — that is, from no one of the public setting him right, — when the accounts have in consequence become entangled," the Court will, from the hardship of the case, fix a limit to the account. But that certainly is not this case.

Where the trust is created by the act of the parties, i.e., appears upon the face of the donation, no time is a bar to the relief. Clanricarde *v.* Henning, 30 Beav. 175.

The rule seems to be entirely well settled, that, in all cases of that character, no statute of limitations or presumptive bar will operate; and that there is no limitation as to the extent to which the account may be *carried back.* Attorney General *v.* Brewers Co., 1 Mer. 498.

And even the English Stat. Lim. 3 and 4, Wm. IV. ch. 27, which, in terms, embraces charitable trusts, "leaves the liability of express trustees, to account without any limit, as it was before." Hicks *v.* Sallit, 3 DeG. M. & G. 782, 816.

Each case must rest upon its peculiar circumstances; and "*accounts will be carried back as far as there appears to have been any misappropriation of the funds.*" "Where the trustees admitted possession of the charity estate for two hundred years, and stated that they had always been ready to account for the rents, an account was directed for the whole period." Tudor, 343, where the author states "*the result of the* authorities as above."

1. It will scarcely be denied that the present case is one of express trust.
2. The misapplication of the fund appears clearly, both by the defendants' own books, and by the finding of the Master.
3. The repeated acknowledgments of the trust down to a very recent period, 1849, must remove all question, if the case came within the presumptive bar; which this does not.

### III.

The accepting the $600.00 annually, of the society by the trustees, can be no legal bar to the account, for numerous reasons.

1. The trustees and the society are in the same interest, and not competent therefore to make any contract binding upon the charity.
2. It was never agreed to be, or understood to be, in full of the interest due from the society. It was what the trustees, by arrangement with the society, saw fit to expend and call sufficient for the present necessities of the poor of the parish.
3. The law will not presume a contract, in such a case, contrary both to the facts, and to the duty of the trustees. The law will presume that trustees intend to perform their whole duty, when that is consistent with the facts. *Story* J. in Ricard *v.* Williams, 7 Wheaton, 59.

The recent case of Davies *v.* Hodgson, 25 Beavan, 177, seems to bear upon this point. It was there held, that receiving the income of the fund arising from an improper investment does not legalize the investment, from the acquiescence, but only restricts the claim for income to the difference between what was thus received and what should have been received by a proper investment.

### IV.

The late English cases seem to have a bearing upon the extent of the accountability of the society which has had the money, knowing it to be trust-money.

1. It is settled that they are under the same restrictions and responsibility

as the actual trustees, and cannot any more plead a statute or presumptive bar. Ernest *v.* Croysdill, 6 Jur. N. S. 740.

2. A trustee *de son tort* is held the same as an express trustee, and his accountability is not barred by lapse of time. Cooper *v.* Green, 7 Jur. N. S. 785; Hennessey *v.* Bray, 33 Beav. 93.

3. All the members of a firm to whom trust-money is paid are liable as trustees. Eager *v.* Barnes, 31 Beav. 579.

4. And any release by the *cestui que trust* must be by one clearly having the authority, and must be understandingly made. Farrant *v.* Blanchford, 1 DeG. J. and Sm. 107; 9 Jur. N. S. 423.

5. The language of Lord Justice *Turner*, in Attorney General *v.* Corporation of Rochester, 5 DeG. M. and G. 797, 822, "If the court finds a clear trust expressed on a will, no length of time during which there has been a deviation from it can warrant this Court, as I apprehend, in making a decree in contradiction of such trust," is forcibly applicable here. And the language of the same learned judge, in same *v.* Beverly, 6 *id.* 268, is similar: "If the Court clearly sees what the intention of the testator was, and that there has been a breach of trust in the non-observance of that intention, I apprehend that no argument founded on the length of time can prevail."

In a case in the English Court of Chancery Appeal, decided in July, 1865, Attorney General *v.* St. John's Hospital, 11 Jur. N. S. 629, where a charity for the poor had been misapplied for several centuries, the Court decreed in favor of the restoration of the fund. In this case certain payments had been all along made for the poor, but not the whole their due.

## V.

There is in truth no case, upon the facts, of a claim adverse to that maintained by the information, until within a very recent period.

Both the trustees and the society have all along treated this church-fund, which the Master finds to have been intended both by the donors and the society for the use of the poor, as a trust of so sacred a character that it could not be infringed in any the slightest particular by them.

The Master thus states his own conclusions in regard to the character of this fund, which must be regarded as *entirely conclusive in the matter*, unless contradictory in its own terms, or set aside for some cause (pp. 10, 11.) : —

"As the sacramental collections were entered with the gifts and legacies made expressly for the use of the poor, as from the earliest accounts, in 1708, to the final discontinuance of these collections in 1849, all the surplus, after payment of certain church expenses (and a few others not so clearly of that character, before specified), was made a part of the fund, out of which disbursements to the poor were made, which fund consisted mainly of moneys left by will, to be kept at interest for the benefit of the poor; as the church, as early as 1747, by borrowing from it to pay their minister, treated it as a fund not subject to their disposal; and as, when discontinuing the collections, they were called collections "for the benefit of the poor," and the discontinuance was voted for the reason assigned, that they were not needed for the poor, —

the Master has been forced to the conclusion, that the items of sacramental stock in the statement of 1766, and the balances afterwards transferred, are a part of the poor fund. From the facts, he infers that these contributions were originally made with the understanding, that any surplus remaining, after defraying certain special church expenses, should be applied to the benefit of the poor. If this was not the clear understanding and intention of the contributors, *the balances were so mingled with moneys held expressly in trust for the use of the poor that it is not practicable now to separate them, and assign to each its due proportion.*"

" *The Master is of opinion that the sum of* £847. 14s. 3d., *appearing at the foot of the statement of* 1766, *is to be regarded as the poor fund of that date, excepting items* 11 *and* 12, *which he presumes afterwards became part thereof as before stated.*"

2. There is a statement (page 4, of the information), not contradicted by the answers, and extracted from the report of a committee of the society, recorded upon their books under date of April 28, 1823, stating that the rent of the " easterly parsonage-house," usually amounting to about $600.00, was paid to the " ministers and deacons for interest of money *borrowed by the society* for the purpose of building the two parsonage-houses, which money was left by a number of persons at different periods to the ministers and deacons of the Old South Church, *in trust for the benefit of the poor of said church.*" This is the defendants' own recorded claim in regard to this question, as late as 1823. Could any thing be more decisive in favor of the plaintiffs' present claim ?

3. In every instance where this fund is referred to upon the defendants' books, with the single exception of the report of one committee, never acted upon, this fund is spoken of in the same, or similar, terms.

Thus, on April 3, 1800, on occasion of the first loan, " The poor of said society will have as much as they now receive " (pp. 5, 6). And the loan is upon the express condition, that the trustees " shall at all times be entitled to receive so much of the rents and income of said stores as shall amount to six per cent, &c., that they may be enabled to appropriate the same in like manner as the *interest of said moneys has heretofore been appropriated, according to the pious intentions of the donors*" (p. 7).

And on May 22, 1809, on occasion of the loan for " parsonage-houses," the committee say, " that there is in the hands of the treasurer of the society *certain capital stock, the interest of which only is appropriated to the use of the poor of the church*," and they propose a permanent investment in the parsonage-houses, and " the interest *appropriated to the use of the poor may always be drawn from the surplus of permanent income*" (p. 8).

And June 6, 1809, the loan is asked " *upon conditions, that the interest be punctually paid, and the buildings be insured to secure payment thereof* " (p. 9).

And the act of borrowing (page 9) recites, " Whereas in times past there have been *legacies, bequests, and donations made to the Old South Church, to be placed at interest for the benefit of the poor of said church* and of the church and congregation, *and the interest arising thence to be distributed among them according to the direction of the ministers and deacons of said church, trustees for that purpose.*"

And as to the $650.00 (page 11) received from another charitable society in 1808, by the very vote of donation, recorded in the defendants' books, it is provided, " the income of which to be applied to the benefit of the poor of that church."

Judging therefore from the defendants' own recorded declarations, it will be impossible to do them the discredit of allowing, that they have ever, until the present suit, repudiated, or attempted to evade, the full responsibility of the trusts upon which they hold this fund.

The effect of the lapse of time therefore must be to confirm the claim which we assert, the acquiescence being all in that direction.

The defendants, in their answers (pp. 15, 23) admit they were liable for interest upon this fund to the trustees, and that the interest has not been formally accounted for.

### VI.

And in regard to the only portion of this fund as to which there was ever any question, the sacramental collections, — and that is now removed by the finding of the Master, — 2 Daniels's Ch. Pr. 1475, 1490, — these repeated acts and declarations of the defendants through so long a period of time would otherwise have been important. Thus in Attorney General v. Rochester, *supra*, Lord Justice *Turner* said, " Undoubtedly, if an instrument, or any act of donation, be doubtful in its terms, contemporaneous usage may be referred to; and, if there has been a long usage in the application of funds to purposes which may be warranted upon one construction of the instrument, but which may not be warranted upon another construction of the instrument, the Court will lean to that construction of that instrument, provided it be doubtful, which will best correspond with the mode in which the funds have been for so long a time applied; but that is the case where the trust is doubtful in its terms and interpretation." This is all that we could desire to have the Court do in the present case, if all questions of doubt were not conclusively settled by the finding of the Master.

The cases are very numerous where similar doctrines have been declared. Lord *Eldon* in Attorney General v. Bristol, 2 Jac. & W. 321; same v. Catherine Hall, Jac. 381. Lord *Cranworth* in same v. Deans and Canons of Windsor, 6 Jur. N. S. 833, 843, " I feel that such a continual usage is not to be overlooked, when we *are trying to discover what was the intention of those who founded the charity.*" If defendants' conduct had all along been consistent with their present claim, no doubt, as to the sacramental collections, it would before the Master have been of great weight. But the character of that fund is now clearly established, both by the defendants' recorded acts and declarations and by the finding of the Master.

### VII.

There can be no question that the accumulation of this fund must now be treated as part of the corpus of the charity; for the Courts sometimes direct an accumulation. Attorney General *v.* Bovill, 1 Phill. 762. They will therefore adopt accumulations already made, and not expend them at once.

We think therefore that we are fully justified in saying that the Master's Report has established the fact, beyond all controversy, that the whole of this fund, with its present accumulations, is held by the Old South Society as a *charitable trust, the income of which is for the use of the poor of the church and congregation in all future time.*

And that this finding is confirmed both by the books and the acts and declarations of the society. It is fair to say, that there is not one entry in the account of this fund upon these books, nor one act of the society in relation to it, so far as it has any bearing upon the issue, for the period of a hundred years and more, which does not confirm the finding of the Master, and contradict the defendants' present claim to appropriate this fund, in their own discretion, the same as any other of their private estate.

The history of this fund during all this long period is that of a sacred trust, to be kept inviolate from all ordinary uses of the society. If they used any portion of it except for the poor, they borrowed it of the trustees, upon express stipulation to pay six per cent interest, as they would of any stranger; and they repaid portions of it with interest, or gave recognizance to pay with "compound interest;" and until within the last few years have always acknowledged the character and extent of the trust.

## VIII.

We therefore ask the Court for a decree establishing this charity, and directing the money paid over to the trustees according to the stipulations of the society when they borrowed it, and that it be referred to the Master to settle a *proper scheme* for the expenditure of the income.

Isaac F. Redfield and Tuxbury & Crocker,
*Counsel.*

### DEFENDANTS' POINTS AND AUTHORITIES.

This is a bill in equity, to compel the defendants to account for certain funds alleged to have been given to the ministers and deacons of the Old South Church for the benefit of the poor of said church and society, and loaned by the ministers and deacons to the Old South Society, and misappropriated. There is no allegation that the ministers and deacons have refused to supply the wants of the poor, or that those wants have not been amply supplied. The complaint is, that the funds alleged to have been given for the poor have been permitted to remain in the hands of the Old South Society, and that no separate account of them has been kept (Bill, p. 4).

The answers admit that certain sums were given to the church, or the ministers and deacons, the interest of which was to be appropriated for the poor of the church; and also certain other sums which were to be used for the poor of the church without restricting such use to the interest (Answers, p. 20). They also allege that they have appropriated all funds given them for the poor to that purpose; that certain sums were loaned to the society, but that the society have always paid yearly a sum for the poor more than equivalent to meet the interest of any sums given for that purpose. That the arrangement between the church and society by which at first the society paid the annual rent of one house, and afterwards six hundred dollars per year, for the use of the poor, had subsisted more than half a century, and been acquiesced in by all parties, and ought not now to be disturbed. The case was submitted to a Special Master to report to the Court all matters pertinent to the issues raised on the bill and answers. This report has been made, to the conclusions of which exceptions were taken; and the case now comes before the Court on the bill, minus report and exceptions.

## I.

No case is made for the action of the Court upon the information of the Attorney General.

The allegation is, that the ministers and deacons of the Old South held for the church a fund for the poor of the church, which has been permitted to be misappropriated, by not keeping it separate and apart from all other funds.

Suppose that all the requisites necessary for to make a public charity, and to justify the interference of the Attorney General, exist, still it is a charity to be managed according to the discretion of the ministers and deacons and church. They are a corporation to take, hold, and manage the fund, and use it at their discretion for the poor. The whole power is with them. No one else has any right to interfere in the exercise of that discretion, while it is admitted they have exercised their discretion and judgment in reference to the objects and purposes for which the fund was given them.

Parker v. May, 5 Cush. 351. Attorney General v. Foundling Hospital, 2 Vesey, jun. p. 42.

It is also submitted that a fund held " for the poor of the church " is not a public charity in the sense of the law. The persons for whose benefit the charity was established were certain and well-defined. There was no uncertainty or indefiniteness as to the objects of the charity. They were the poor of the church; and those of the church who were poor were to be ascertained by the ministers and deacons.

Attorney General v. Federal-street Meeting-house, 3 Gray, 1.

## II.

On the facts alleged in the bill and answers, and found in the Master's Report, the bill cannot be maintained certainly against the Old South Society. The bill seeks to set aside an arrangement made between the church and society in reference to the fund in question half a century ago, and which has been acted upon, and acquiesced in by all parties, up to the time of bringing this bill.

The statute of limitations need not be pleaded. It is quite sufficient, upon the authorities and on principle, that all the facts upon which the application of the statute must depend should be set forth in the answer. A demurrer may be taken, even where the bill itself makes a case within the statute. In this case, all the facts upon which the application of the statute depends appear by the bill and are set forth in the answers, and the defendants both claim that the state of affairs so long settled and acquiesced in should not be disturbed (Monroe, pp. 15, 16, 23, 24).

Bogardus v. Trinity Church, 4 Paige, 197. Mit. Eq. Pl. 259. Harpending v. Dutch Church, 16 Pet. 486. Hubert v. Trinity Church, 24 Bent, 595. Dunlap v. Gill, 4 Yerger, 96. Forster v. Hodgson, 2 Vesey, 183.

Here the bill and answers both set forth the fact, that, in 1800, a part of the fund was loaned by the church to the society, which the bill claims has not been repaid, or no interest paid since 1807. The report of the Master also finds the same fact; nor is it claimed that there has been any promise or undertaking on the part of the society which would take the case out of the statute, during the half-century that has elapsed since the loan. Now, clearly, in reference to the society, they cannot be called on at this time to pay this debt, if one existed. No trust attaches to this money in their hands, as between the church and society it is but an ordinary loan of money.

Attorney General v. Rochester, 5 DeG. M. & S. 797. Same v. Beverly, 6 DeG. M. & S. 268. Same v. Bristol, 2 Jacob & W. S. 321. Same v. Payne, 27 Beavan, 168. Marjoran v. Attorney General, 5 H. of Lord's cases, 1.

So in reference to the loan of 1811, nothing is ever alleged to have been paid upon it as a loan since it was made. An arrangement was made by which the rent of a house was paid over, and afterwards six hundred dollars per year, which arrangement we claim cannot now be set aside, after so long an acquiescence.

But at any rate, as to the balance found to be unpaid by the Master on the first loan of five thousand two hundred and forty-five dollars, and the three items of interest therein, amounting to four thousand four hundred and fifty-six dollars and forty-eight cents in 1811, it is not claimed that since 1811 any thing has ever been done to revive that debt; and the society cannot now be called on to repay it with interest upon the ground that the church held it for certain charitable purposes.

### III.

Upon the facts stated in the bill, and found by the Master, we claim that after an acquiescence of all parties in interest for nearly half a century, and without any complaint that the alleged objects of the charity, the poor, are injured, the Court will not interfere with and disturb the arrangement made by the church and the society in reference to the administration of the fund in their hands. The bill claims that the poor-fund in the hands of the ministers and deacons included all that was called " church stock," and which was made up, not only from legacies for the poor, but also from sacramental contributions, and sums received for the use of the palls. The answers deny that the portion arising from the two last sources formed any part of a poor-fund, or that they were given for that purpose. The Master has reported a large number of facts bearing upon that question, from which he has arrived at the conclusion that the sacramental contributions, and sums received for the use of the palls, became a part of the poor-fund; but certainly it appears to be a matter of doubt, and very difficult to be ascertained at this time, whether the poor-fund included the whole of the church stock from 1800 to 1811. Now it is admitted that an arrangement was made by which at first the society were to pay the ministers and deacons the rent of one house, more or less, as an equivalent for the interest of the fund that belonged to the poor, and that this was done from 1811 till 1845, when the fixed sum of six hundred dollars per year was substituted for the rent.

In view of the fact that the parties to the transaction then knew what the poor-fund was better than any one can now determine it, and that no bad faith or fraud is alleged or pretended, we claim with entire confidence that the arrangement so made between the ministers and deacons and society cannot now be inquired into and set aside; because it was an arrangement competent to be made by the first party as trustees, in the exercise of their discretion in behalf of the church; and because it is to be presumed, in the absence of all testimony to control such conclusion, that they made the best arrangement they could make under the circumstances.

The ministers and deacons for the church had full power to invest the fund in their hands, granting it was all a poor-fund, according to their judgment and discretion. They do so, by placing it so that they are to receive the rent of a house, instead of interest from a corporation whose credit was undoubted; they receive this rent, everybody acquiescing, for thirty-four or five years, and then, instead thereof, a yearly sum equal to the average rent of the house, for twelve or thirteen years more. Can it now be claimed that this arrangement, so long acted on, can now be set aside?

From aught that appears, this was the best arrangement in reference to an investment of the fund that could be made. It is very doubtful whether, if an attempt had been made by the ministers and deacons to keep the fund in their own hands, they could have realized so much for the forty-seven years; or whether, at the end of that time, the fund might not have been mostly lost by the great fluctuations in business and values.

Therefore we claim on the admitted facts in this case, without now discussing the question whether the whole or what part of the fund called "church stock" was a poor-fund, and however that may be decided, that the Court will not interfere with and open an arrangement made and acted on for nearly half a century without interference or objection from any one.

Authorities cited to the second point. The Dublin case, 38 New Hamp. R. 459.

## IV.

But upon the bill, answer, and the facts reported by the Master, the poor-fund as reported by him is too large, and includes sums that form no part of it.

This fund is called the "church stock" until after eighteen hundred. It is nowhere intimated up to that time that it is a "poor-fund;" on the contrary, the name given it, and the report made in that year, show it was a fund where all the moneys belonging to the church were kept. The report finds that certain sums were given to the church the interest of which was to be expended for the poor, and certain other sums without any such restriction; which last were undoubtedly disbursed at about the time of their reception. Those sums given the interest only of which was to be expended formed a part of the church stock, the interest of which, or a part of which, was disbursed (Report, pp. 11 and 12).

Down to the present century, then, no expression is used to indicate an exclusive appropriation for the poor. On the contrary, the statements of 1761 and 1766 indicate what portions are for the poor, and what for other purposes. So the report of the committee of April 18, 1800 (Report, p. 6), to "*inquire into the state of the church funds, and to endeavor to find from what source they have arisen, and the intention of the donors,*" clearly indicates, that at that time there had been no appropriation of the whole fund to the poor, or that it was so understood; as they were appointed to find out from *whence it had arisen*, and also the *intention of its donors*. They report its sources, making it in 1766 £880. 11s. 0d., of which £429. 10s. 2d. was given for the poor, and £451. 0s. 10d. was derived from sacramental contributions, use of the palls, and gifts to the church, without any object being designated; that is, in 1766, *over half of the fund was not given for or appropriated to the poor.*

In the vote of May 11, 1800, just after this report had been made and accepted, these funds are not alluded to in any way as appropriated to the poor exclusively; on the contrary, taken in connection with the report just made, the contrary is recognized. Six per cent interest is ordered to be paid to the ministers and deacons, so that they may appropriate it, *not to the poor exclusively*, but as *it had been appropriated theretofore, according to the pious intentions of the donors;* that is, a part for the poor, and a part for general church and religious uses.

The vote of April 13, 1807, was the first one speaking of this fund as one for the poor; and the terms used in that vote are not inconsistent with the fact, that the fund in question was for other church purposes, as well as for the poor exclusively. As we have seen before, a large portion of it was for the poor; and it might, as a designation, be called the "church's fund for the poor thereof," without excluding, necessarily, the fact that it was also a fund for other purposes.

At any rate that vote does not, and does not purport to, make any appropriation of the fund; it merely describes a fund then existing, and we have seen that up to that time there had been no recognition or appropriation of it as exclusively a poor-fund. Besides, this was the vote merely of the *society*, and not of the *church*; and they could not, even if they had attempted it, without the assent of the church, have altered the legal character of the fund.

The vote also of May 22, 1809, is open to the same criticism; it speaks of a fund in the hands of the treasurer, the interest only of which is devoted to the poor. Now, this again is but a description of a fund by reference to the main purpose for which it was used, and is by no means inconsistent with the fact that a portion of it might be used for other purposes; and, what is more important, it was a vote of the society in reference to a fund *not belonging to themselves*, but the *church*. It is to be remarked also, that by this vote they recognize the fund the interest of which belongs to the poor as but eleven thousand two hundred and fifty dollars, the interest being six hundred and seventy-five dollars. It seemed, then, to have been ascertained that the other part of the fund had not been appropriated for that purpose.

The only vote of the church upon this subject is that of June 6, 1809 (Report, p. 9), where no intimation is given that the church considered this fund *exclusively as a poor-fund;* on the contrary, they request *the trustees of certain funds placed in their hands* to furnish a certain amount to the society.

In the December following, the ministers and deacons agree with the society to furnish fourteen thousand dollars to build two parsonage-houses. They recite the fact, that there have been legacies and donations to the church, to be placed at interest for the benefit of the poor, and the interest to be distributed among them, which was strictly true, as appears by the statements of 1761 and 1766, and the report of 1800; but it also appeared by the same statements and report, that but half the church stock arose from such legacies and gifts. This recital certainly does not give the whole fund any exclusive character as a poor-fund, nor does it attempt to do so. Even if it did, the ministers and deacons could not alter or change the legal character of the fund in their hands.

These are substantially all the facts, except that the church funds were all kept together as "church stock;" from which it is claimed that the whole church stock was a poor-fund.

If it was all a poor-fund, then it must have become so either because the sums of which it was composed had been given for that purpose, or because those to whom the whole fund belonged appropriated it to that use.

In this case, less than half the fund in 1766 was given for the poor; the rest was under the control of, and belonged to, the church, — for, as we shall see hereafter, it cannot be claimed that the sacramental contributions were devoted to any one object.

That portion of the fund, then, arising from other sources than gifts for the poor, more than half in amount, in order to become a poor-fund must have become so by the action of the church, to whom it belonged.

Now, there is not offered a single vote of the church making any such appropriation; on the contrary, all their acts are inconsistent with such an appropriation. They have, for nearly half a century, acted upon the ground that there was no such appropriation by them.

The votes of the society, of 1807 and 1809, even if they had undertaken, which they do not, to make such an appropriation, could have no such effect; because the society — the congregation — had not a particle of authority to act in the matter.

So of the recital of the ministers and deacons. If they had undertaken to fix the legal character of the fund, and devote it to the poor, instead of reciting how a large part of it was obtained, it would not have had the slightest effect, for the reason that they had no power to do it; the church only had that power.

There is not claimed to be the slightest evidence that the church ever voted or acted in reference to such an appropriation.

On the contrary, it is evident the church never intended to make such an appropriation, and never supposed they had, for these reasons: —

*First,* They caused separate accounts to be kept of several of the legacies given them for the poor, of the interest received, and the persons to whom it was distributed, long after 1766; one being kept up till 1791. This certainly is inconsistent with the church considering the whole fund a poor-fund, for then no separate accounts would be necessary.

*Second,* The church used this fund for general church purposes and objects other than supplying the poor, at their discretion; they loaned the society, which was never repaid, £192. 0s. 0d., to help pay the salary of the minister. After the discontinuance of the sacramental account in 1789, sacramental expenses, expenses of a delegate, cost of putting the church in mourning, candles for lighting the house, were charged to this fund; which facts are inconsistent with its being exclusively a poor-fund.

*Third,* The inquiry made by the committee to ascertain the sources of the fund, and their report, are utterly inconsistent with the claim that the fund was then a poor-fund exclusively.

*Fourth,* The subsequent action of the church and the ministers and deacons, in permitting the whole fund to go into the hands of the society upon the payment of interest, or about one-half of it, for the poor, which has continued for nearly half a century, is inconsistent with the whole fund being a poor-fund.

*Fifth,* The action of the committee of the society in their report of December, 1809, which was accepted, sets forth the fact that the whole of the "church stock" did not originate from the donations of certain persons, and was not therefore a "poor-fund." That report sets forth the fact, that the five thousand two hundred and forty-five dollars and twenty-one cents, before advanced for the stores, was not a poor-fund, but arose from other sources than gifts for that object; and so, that there was no indebtment to the ministers and deacons on that account. From the fact, that from this time all traces of the five thousand two hundred and forty-five dollars and twenty-one cents, and the item of interest, disappear from the accounts, no payments for either principal or interest being paid or demanded, and no account being kept of it, — and this having been acquiesced in for nearly half a century, — shows that the church and society both accepted the result arrived at by the committee, and acted upon it (Report, p. 10).

It certainly cannot be claimed here, that the sacramental contributions, or sums received from the use of the palls, were originally contributed for the poor exclusively, or that they were made with any condition attached. The answer denies such fact, and alleges that they were made for the benefit of the church, to be disposed of as the church saw fit. Nor does the report find that they were made originally for that object (Report, p. 11). They can only be made a poor-fund, then, by the action of the church; that is, the church, having the exclusive control of the sacramental gifts, with the right to appropriate them as they pleased, could appropriate them for supplying the wants of the poor. And, for the sake of the argument, suppose such had been the appropriation by the church, — and that is as strongly as it can be stated for the complainant, — the money still remains in their hands. It is not the case of their passing it out of their hands into those of trustees, when it would be beyond their control; but, while the money remains in their own possession, they can change the appropriation of it at their discretion, and no one can interfere.

The case is no stronger than would be that of a rational person who established a certain fund for the poor, in his hands, keeping it separate from his other property, and applying all its income, except what was needed for the poor, to add to it. Very clearly, such a fund would at all times be within the control of such person, to discontinue it, and apply it to any other use. So in this case, if the sacramental gifts were ever set aside as a poor-fund by the church, they still remained in the possession of the church, and they could apply them to other purposes, as they very clearly have in this case, more than half a century since. This would seem to be a perfect answer to the attempt after this lapse of time to set aside the last appropriation, and compel the church to adhere to their first application of the funds.

## V.

The conclusion of the Master was clearly wrong in including the sacramental stock, and sums received for the use of the palls, in the poor-fund, upon the facts found.

In the first place the answer expressly denies that the sacramental contributions are expressly for the use of the poor; but, on the contrary, claims them to be gifts to the church, without conditions.

Then there is no proof offered of any custom or rule among Congregational churches to that effect; and the facts reported here, so far from justifying the conclusion, establish the fact of its incorrectness.

It is admitted that there was no act of the church expressly appropriating the sacramental contributions to the poor, but it is inferred from the conduct of the parties.

In the first place, the fact that all church expenses were paid out of the fund. as well as the expenses of conventions and delegates; then that other payments were made, like those appearing on page 5 of the report, — show that the church had the most absolute control of the fund.

The fact, too, that occasionally a part of the contribution was expressly designated by the contributor to be for the poor is irreconcilable with the conclusion that the contributions without such designation were not made free of all conditions.

The vote of the church in 1849 to discontinue the collections, because such discontinuance would not hurt the interests of the poor, is no evidence to prove that they were not entirely at the disposal of the church. They were undoubtedly applied for the benefit of the poor, but no such use was made the condition of the gift.

Nor does the borrowing from the fund to pay the clergymen's salary lead to any such result. The salary was paid by the society, and not out of this fund; the vote only indicates that those whose duty it was to pay the clergymen's salary should repay this sum.

This case is no stronger in favor of the claim of the complainants than one which has been passed on by this Court. In the case referred to, many of the facts upon which it was claimed that the sacramental gifts were devoted to a poor-fund were almost exactly like those upon which the same claim is made here; but the claim was disallowed by the Court.

Parker v. May, 5 Cush. 357.

Nor is there any trouble in separating what was given for the poor from what was not so devoted; accurate accounts are kept of the disbursements to the poor, and separate accounts kept of the interest received from certain of the legacies, and paid out on their account, down to 1791, so that an account substantially correct can be arrived at. Besides, the committee of the society say in 1809 that they had made such separation, and that the five thousand two hundred and forty-five dollars loaned to the society in 1801, with the interest thereon, arose from funds not given to the poor. This report has been acted upon and acquiesced in for more than forty years by both parties.

If that separation thus made and acted on is adopted and adhered to, the matter becomes one of easy solution.

The ministers and deacons loaned in 1811, as appears by the report, twelve thousand seven hundred and eighty-three dollars and seventy-five cents; the Master has added to that sum the amount loaned in 1801, and interest on it, amounting to nine thousand seven hundred and one dollars and forty-eight cents; and this has swelled up the sum due the poor-fund to twenty-two thousand seven hundred and ninety-seven dollars and eleven cents on the 1st of January, 1811.

If the sum then advanced is taken as the poor-fund, — viz., twelve thousand seven hundred and eighty-five dollars and seventy-five cents, which is certainly giving all to it that can be asked, — it becomes easy to ascertain the amount of that fund to the present day. If the arrangement made is to be set aside, — which we claim ought not to be done, — taking that sum with the amount of interest, and deducting the payments made by the church to the poor, you have the present amount of the fund.

And a sum so found, it is submitted with great confidence, is the largest sum that can under any circumstances, after an acquiescence by all parties for nearly half a century, be decreed to the poor-fund.

J. G. ABBOTT, *for Defendants.*

The Master's Report makes the Old South Society indebted to the poor-fund on the 1st of January, 1861, for the sum of $55,674.37; which result is accounted for in the following manner: —

Certain stocks and obligations were loaned the society (under special conditions) by the trustees of the poor-fund, for the erection of five stores upon a portion of the land held in trust from Mrs. Norton, as follows: —

| | |
|---|---:|
| 3 per cent stock | $2,406 00 |
| Hinkley's bond | 135 56 |
| Deferred United States stock | 53 41 |
| Massachusetts State notes | 617 40 |
| 5½ United States stock | 850 00 |
| 40½ shares in Union Bank | 412 00 |
| 3 per cent United States stock | 102 03 |
| 8 per cent United States stock | 645 00 |
| | $5,221 40 |

The above when sold realized to the society $5,245.00. These assets came into possession of the society as an investment of a part of the funds of the poor-fund, precisely in the same manner as that of the Massachusetts Bank stock.

| | |
|---|---:|
| | $5,245 00 |
| For prepaid interest on moneys borrowed of Massachusetts Bank, and charged to poor-fund, and not repaid | 479 46 |
| " amount paid for building parsonage-houses | 12,133 75 |
| " " of United States stock | 650 00 |
| " compound interest on $5,245.00 as per vote Nov. 17, 1807. Jan. 1, 1811. | 2,195 12 |
| For interest on $5.245.00 and $479.46 equals $5,724.46 from April 1, 1807, to date | 1,781 90 |
| " interest on 7 bank shares sold May, 1810, to date | 180 96 |
| " " " 7 " " " July 1, 1810, to date | 130 92 |
| " " " whole sum, principal and interest, from Jan. 1, 1807, to Jan. 1, 1864 | 62,109 99 |
| | $84,907 10 |

Cr.

1860.

| | |
|---|---:|
| By amount of rent received from 1830 to 1860 from parsonage-houses, when vacant by death of Dr. Eckley, as per books, | $29,232 73 |
| | $55,674 37 |
| To which is to be added, to make up the present amount of the fund which should be in the hands of the ministers and deacons, trustees: — | |
| 4 shares Massachusetts Bank $1,000 00 | |
| Loan to Massachusetts Life Insurance Company  1,000 00 | 2,000 00 |
| Cash balance on hand Jan. 1, 1861 | $57,674 37 |

It will in the above account be seen, that, after the conscientious restoration of the compound interest on the amount of $5,245.00, intending to carry out in a degree the bargain entered into when the money was borrowed in 1800, then earning nine per cent, no more than lawful interest is calculated, and yet to what a large sum it comes in 1861! Assuming therefore that this had continued at nine per cent, to what a sum would it have amounted! Add to this the amount received by the society under their management, and the riddle is at once solved why the property now in their possession, including the meeting-house, is estimated at seven hundred thousand dollars.

In this answer it is stated, that there has been distributed to the poor of the Old South Church (the poor of the congregation not being mentioned as recipients), from 1800 to 1860, as appears from the books of the treasurer, an amount, set forth in sixty items, of $49,029.64. A reference to the treasurer's book will show that there was received during the same time $51,009.59, credited to the following sources, viz.: —

| | |
|---|---:|
| To income received from 1800 to 1813, from bank stock and notes | $8,229 99 |
| " balance of sacramental account for same time | 691 53 |
| For lighting Old South Charity Lectures. | |
| To candle money taken out of quarterly charity | 38 00 |
| " amount Thanksgiving collection | 132 89 |
| " rent of meeting-house cellar | 50 00 |
| " candle money received from Charity Sacramental Lectures, sundry items | 150 00 |
| " interest from bank stock and notes | 4,589 46 |
| " contributions received from sacramental celebrations | 3,389 37 |
| " quarterly charity contributions, and interest on fund belonging to that charity | 4,505 62 |
| " rent of parsonage-house received from 1813 to 1860, paid as interest for money borrowed of poor-fund | 29,232 73 |
| | $51,009 59 |

In the above statement, the only items of money not directly belonging to the poor were the rent of the parsonage-house (which, in reality, as far as it sufficed to pay interest, was theirs), the rent of the cellar, and that proportion of the light-money paid by other associated societies belonging to the Charity Lecture for their part of the expense incurred by the Old South Society in lighting the meeting-house on charity-lecture nights, as well as the monthly preparatory ones. In fact, therefore, nearly the whole of it belonged justly to the poor, and it became the duty of the Old South Society to distribute it to them.

## CHAPTER X.

### Rescript and Final Decree.

In January, 1867, the Court made their decision in the case, and filed a rescript of their reasons therefor, a copy of which is as follows: —

"The gift of Dr. Sewall, and the various bequests stated in the Master's Reports for the poor of the town, or of the parish, or of the church, were clearly public charities, to be appropriated by the ministers and deacons, according to the intention of the donors. But the contributions are not shown to have been so exclusively and absolutely devoted to the poor as to be impressed with the character of a public charity. The appropriation, from time to time, out of such contributions, for the expenses of administering the sacrament, of the expenses of delegates of the church, &c., were according to common usage. These payments, as well as those for lighting the church, and towards the salary of the ministers in 1747 (which does not appear to have been refunded), tend to show that these contributions were not considered or treated as having been made or devoted exclusively for the relief or benefit of the poor. The reasons assigned by the decision in 1849 for discontinuing such collections only tend to show that the sums so collected had been annually given to the poor. It is to be presumed that the small portion of them specially designated by the donors at the time of contribution as intended for the poor were immediately so applied. The mingling of the fund for the poor with the other funds of the church does not entitle the trustees of the poor to the whole of the church fund, there being evidence by which the amount of each fund can be approximately ascertained. Assuming, as most favorable to the claim made in behalf of the attorney general, that the "Poor and Charitable Fund," and the fund for the support of the widows and fatherless children of the ministers of the church (amounting together to £66. 19s. $2\frac{1}{4}d$.), are to be included in the fund for the poor derived from bequests and gifts, and amounting to £501. 0s. $11\frac{1}{2}d$.; the statement on the church books in 1766 of the "church stock," shows that at that time the charity was entitled to the sum of £568. 0s. $1\frac{1}{4}d$.; and this, the "sacramental stock" (£186. 19s. $5\frac{1}{4}d$.), and the interest accrued thereon, amounted to the sum of £306. 14s. $1\frac{3}{4}d$., and the whole church stock £874. 14s. 3d. This last sum was therefore to be divided between the two funds in the proportion of those sums, £568. 0s. $1\frac{1}{4}d$. and £306. 14s. $1\frac{3}{4}d$. The statement of 1766 shows a larger proportion to the charity than the report of the committee in 1800. In the latter year the whole church stock, estimated at the par value of the securities in which it was thus invested, amounted to the sum of $16,062.71, and of this the market value was something more. Even if we assume its whole value in 1800 to have been nearly $20,000, the poor-fund appears to have received about its proportion in the sum of $12,783; this was invested in the parsonage-houses erected on the land of the society in Milk Street, under the agreement of the ministers and deacons of the society. If the transaction in reference to the funds between 1800 and 1809 are followed out, the result would be substantially the same. This sum of $12,783.75 must therefore be taken as the principal sum belonging to the charity, and invested in said estate at that time. The payments by the society, and the receipt by the ministers and deacons, in lieu of the interest on this sum, of the rent of the easterly parsonage-house from this time annually to 1845, although for a greater part of this time less than such interest computed at six per cent would have been, must, after so long a lapse of time, and in the absence of any evidence of bad faith or unreasonableness in the arrangements, be deemed a substitute for, and a satisfaction of, such interests. From 1845, when the payment and receipts of such rent ceased, the charity is entitled, to the time of filing this bill in 1859 and since, to annual interest at the rate of six per cent annually, deducting therefrom the annual payments of $600.00 made by the society to the ministers and deacons since 1845. The principal sum of $12,783.75, with so much of the interest thereon as remains unpaid, together with the further principal sum of $1,947.50 belonging to the charity, admitted to have been in the hands of the treasurer in January, 1801, with interest thereon to date of the decree, will constitute the amount due to the charity.

"A decree may be entered for the payment of this sum, when computed, by the society to the ministers and deacons of the church, to be held by them for the use of the poor. Inasmuch as the intermingling by the defendants of the funds of the charity into these funds has afforded grounds for the information, and the information is sustained in part, the costs incurred in support of it, taxed as between counsel and client, are to be paid out of the 'charity,' and the defendants will bear their own costs."

In accordance with the foregoing rescript, the following decree was entered in January, 1867, finally disposing of this case, which had then been pending for seven years and a half.

### Final Decree.

This case came on to be heard before the Court upon the Bill, Answers, and Master's Report, and was argued by counsel; and thereupon, upon consideration, it was finally ordered, adjudged, and decreed as follows: —

That there is a public charitable trust of the character described in the information, to the amount of $18,291.27; and that the same is hereby established for a perpetual public charity for the benefit of the poor of the church and congregation connected with the Old South Society in Boston, under the direction and control of the ministers and deacons of the Old South Church in Boston.

That $2,000.00 of said fund is now held by the treasurer of said Old South Society for said ministers and deacons of said Old South Church; that the balance of said trust fund, viz., $16,291.27, is now in the hands of the Old South Society in Boston, one of the defendants, said sum being the amount loaned by the ministers and deacons to said society under the agreement of said ministers and deacons with said society, of the date of December, A.D. 1809, set forth in the Information and Master's Report, together with the interest thereon which has not been paid by said society heretofore; and that said sum of $16,291.27, in the hands of said Old South Society, and said sum of $2,000.00, held by the treasurer of said society for said ministers and deacons, be forthwith delivered and paid over to the ministers and deacons of the Old South Church, the lawful trustees of the same, to be administered by them according to the terms of the trust as above stated. That the sum of $739.40, taxable costs in this suit, and the sum of $1,750.00, for counsel fees, in behalf of the plaintiff, be paid out of said fund by the said trustees; and that the said defendants bear their own costs.

## CHAPTER XI.

Poor-fund as a Public Charity. — Regret at Small Amount awarded. — Deacons' Book Account. — Accounts from 1708 to 1755. — General Accounts. — Extracts from Old Accounts of the Church. — Ministers' Pay. — Collections and Assessments on Pews. — £192 Loan to Ministers. — Pious and Charitable Fund. — Thomas Hubbard and William Phillips, Sen. — Discontinuance of Sacramental Collections. — Mingling of Funds. — Old South Stores. — Eckley and Huntington Parsonage-houses. — Mrs. Norton's Real Estate Gift. — Accounts of Pious and Charitable Fund. — Church Stock of 1761–1766. — Particular Account of the £186. 19s. 8½d., " Sacramental Balance," and also of the " Interest, £119. 14s. 8½d., Account." — General History of the Poor-fund. — Parsonage-house Rent. — Responsibility of the Old South for the Whole Fund. — Utter Uselessness of the Decision as to the True Amount due the Poor.

The permanent establishment of this institution as a public charity is a source of much gratification to its friends, for the reason that it places it more immediately under the guardianship of the public at large than it has been heretofore; while, at the same time, it cannot but be regretted that the whole, or a larger part, of the amount of property claimed under the award of the Master, Henry W. Paine, Esq., could not have been consistently awarded. The great difference in amount existing between this award and the one finally received by the trustees induced a desire to respectfully examine into the presumptive evidence which had so much weight in forming the character of this decision. Believing therefore that one of the surest means of arriving at the true intent and meaning of the acts of those of a by-gone age is to be derived from their own records of them, to those records we have resorted, and have found the following results: —

The Old South deacons' book of accounts, commencing 1708, contains a record of the monthly collections received from that portion of the sacramental celebration called the offertory for the poor, and appears to have invariably been the record, also, of all collections which were marked by the donors for special destination, as well as all sums of money bequeathed by will or otherwise for the present or future use of the poor. These sums, together with the balance of what remained of the monthly collections after the expenses attending the ordinance were paid, were devoted to the relief of the poor whose names were recorded. This account continued from 1708 to 1755, — for forty-seven years, — when it was settled with a committee appointed for the purpose. The following analysis of it is presented, for its curiosity as well as usefulness in the present case: —

| 1708, | £. | s. | d. | 1749, | £. | s. | d. |
|---|---|---|---|---|---|---|---|
| July 12, A bond of Capt. Williams, and cash in sundry bags at Capt. Hull's, | 95 | 8 | 5 | July. Cash distributed to poor, | 2,813 | 19 | 11 |
| | | | | Cash paid for wine, | 3,508 | 16 | 10 |
| | | | | Cash paid for bread, | 112 | 3 | 4 |
| Cash received for sundry contributions, | 7,543 | 1 | 0 | Cash for small repairs, | 2 | 8 | 0 |
| | | | | Cash, ordination of ministers | 137 | 3 | 0 |
| Cash received for special contributions, | 19 | 0 | 0 | Cash lent out of this stock to July 6, 1747, to pay off the deficiency of our ministers as per the vote of the church, | 192 | 0 | 0 |
| Cash received from legacies of eight persons, | 183 | 3 | 0 | | | | |
| Cash, exchanging silver for paper, | 7 | 7 | 0 | | | | |
| | | | | Cash for old tenor bills, note, | 360 | 0 | 0 |
| Cash received for wine furnished for other than sacrament, | 12 | 14 | 8 | Cash for sundries, | 6 | 5 | 7 |
| | | | | Cash for silver tankard under S. More's will, | 30 | 8 | 0 |
| Cash received for old tenor note, | 20 | 0 | 0 | Amount of error in account 1711, | 1 | 0 | 0 |
| | | | | Balance of account on hand, | 716 | 9 | 5 |
| Old tenor, | £7,880. | 14s. | 1d. | Old tenor, | £7,880. | 14s. | 1d. |

Contemporary with the sacramental accounts was the church stock account, wherein the legacies and other gifts to the poor were registered, and the balances of the sacramental collections carried to the credit of the poor-account. Also, another account of the expense of building the meeting-house, and raising the funds, as well as a general parish-account of the moneys raised by collection for salaries of ministers, repairs of their houses, wood, and all other parish expenses, until 1745, when a tax was laid on the pews, to defray the salaries assessed and to pay for the repairs. A reference is here made to some extracts from the oldest church records, to explain the mode in which the business of that day was done: —.

"1705. Subscription taken for new parsonage-house.

1719. It is just and reasonable that such persons as enjoy the privileges of the pews and best seats in the meeting-house do contribute agreeably to support the worship of God there.

1725. Collections on Fasts and Thanksgivings for pious uses among the poor.

1728. Subscription for a new meeting-house.

1733. Subscription to pay balance £469. 18s. 7d. due on new meeting-house, wood for pastors, and paving and posts round the meeting-house.

1735. Contributions to enlarge ye ministers' pay, their allowance made by the church falling short.

1737. Treasurer Osborn received at sundry times £13,029. 18s. 9d., of which he has paid £12,987. 7s. 8d., balance £42. 11s. 1d. Received £30.-0s. 0d., for cellar rent of Capt. Williams.

1737. Collected for Revs. Mr. Bass £1. 0d. 0s., Torry £4. 19s. 0d., Cotton £3. 0s. 0d.

1738. Pious and Charitable Fund established.

1738. Collection to be taken to be divided equally between the pastors.

1738. Widow and Fatherless Children of the Pastors' Fund proposed.

1738. Collections for Widows' and Ministers' Children Fund.

1738. Collected for Messrs. Bass £1. 0s. 0d., Torry £1. 0s. 0d., Carpenter £1. 0s. 0d., Callender £6. 0s. 0d.

1738. Collection Fast £85. 2s. 2d.

1738. Gave out of the Pious and Charitable Fund to Cotton and Torry for preaching, £20. 0s. 0d.

1739. Appropriated to Ministers' Widows Charity Fund,     £5. 0s. 0d.
" Pious and Charitable "     5 0 0
" Bass and Torry,     2 0 0
" Nurse Kenny,     1 0 0

1740. Weekly contribution for ministers' support.

1740. Collection, charitable and pious uses,     5 0 0

1741. Collection for sufferers by fire at Charleston, S.C.

1742. Collected for charitable and pious uses,     5 0 0

1743. Collected " " "     4 0 0

1744. Collected " " "     5 0 0

1745. Collected " " "     5 0 0

1745. Collected for sufferers taking Cape Breton; contributors to mark who the money is for.

1745. Pews to be assessed a weekly tax, and the owners obliged to pay pro-rata assessments for repairs.

1747. Collection for Pious and Charitable Fund.

1748. Pew-tax altered by committee.

1748. Collected for Charitable and Pious Fund,     £15. 0s. 0d.

1749. Collection to repair Dr. Sewall's house and meeting-house.

1749. Collected to pay debts and salaries.

1749. Collected for Pious and Charitable Fund,     10 0 0

1750. Collected " "     10 0 0

1751. That ye contributors be requested to mark the donations for the purposes intended.

1754. Coll. Ch. and Pious Fund, £5. 0s. 0d. 1757. Coll. do. £10. 0s. 0d.
1754. " " 4 10 0 1758. " " 15 0 0
1755. " " 7 10 0 1759. " " 15·0 0
1756. " " 10 0 0 1761. " " 15 0 0

1759. " for fire in Boston.

1761. Assessment on pews, and subscription to rough-cast the minister's house.

1762. Coll. Ch. and Pious Fund, £15. 0s. 0d. 1765. Coll. do. £15. 0s. 0d.
1763. " " 19 19 0 1766. " " 2 5 0
1764. " " 17 5 0

1766. Pew-assessment and subscription asked for payment meeting-house repairs.

By the analysis of the long account from 1708 to 1755, forty-seven years, we are enabled to obtain the exact amount of all expenditures that do not generally come under the head of sacramental expenses. After this time the net balance alone was paid to the poor.

In the examination of this portion of the "rescript," the £192.-0s. 0d. loan for payment towards the salaries of the ministers, bears conspicuously upon the question whether "the collections were so exclusively and absolutely devoted to the poor as to be impressed with the character of a public charity." There are certainly strong proofs in affirmation of such an opinion, among which is that the "church stock," "sacramental stock," and Pious and Charitable Fund accounts, and numerous side accounts of the legacies, their investments, and expenditures for the poor, are invariably kept exclusively free (with few slight exceptions) from all other parish matters until 1800. And more especially do the accounts of Thomas Hubbard and the elder William Phillips, treasurers of the Old South, show in every line a large amount of property belonging exclusively to the poor. A glance at the extracts here furnished for inspection will, it is thought, show that the omission of refunding the £192. 0s. 0d. borrowed money was a matter of necessity rather than right, especially that in 1745, two years before this money was obtained, a regular plan of weekly pew-taxes was established, adjusted again in 1766, and continued until near or after 1800, when the present mode of quarterly payments took place. The extracts also show that the financial concerns of the parish, amid such an avalanche of benevolent contributions at that period, were at a very low ebb.

It is reasonably conceived, in view of the evidence on this point, that the discontinuance of taking the sacramental collections presents something more than the mere fact that they were monthly (not annually) given to the poor, in itself a circumstance of ordinary importance. But when it is taken in connection with the universal custom of other religious institutions of that period, it shows that in a close adherence to this general duty they were not only practising for nearly a hundred and fifty years the universal example of other churches, but were fully sustaining the cardinal principles of their own; whose corner-stone was, metaphorically speaking, founded upon Christian charity. "We will give as we are able," says one of the ancient reports; and the present act of incorporation of the Old South is "for charitable purposes." There is no doubt also but the money received at the collections for special purposes was so assigned; a large portion of the Pious and Charitable Fund was so received. No mingling of the poor-fund with other funds of the church could possibly take place before 1800, for they never until that time possessed a dollar. Then, it was, they borrowed the poor-fund to build the Old South Block of five stores, for the express purpose of obtaining money enough to support another minister as colleague with Dr. Eckley. For be it remembered in support of these facts (and "are they not written in the chronicles" of the Old South also), that the property bequeathed by Mrs. Norton to the Old South was all in real estate, in trust, for special purposes, and for "no other use whatsoever." One portion was for the erecting of a meeting-house, and another for pastors' and teachers' dwelling-houses. No provision whatever was made for the expense of erecting these edifices, or defraying the expenses attending their use: all this was done by private efforts (in the manner of other parishes) until 1800, a period of a century and a quarter.

The assumption that the amount of £66. 19s. 2½d. lawful " is most favorable to the claim made in the behalf of the attorney general" proves to be a most unfortunate mistake, being much less than one-half the sum, exclusive of interest justly due that portion of the poor-fund denominated the Pious and Charitable Fund, of which the Ministers' Widows' and Children's Fund was the branch or offshoot, founded in 1738, and which received this £66. 19s. 2½d. by collections, as per record before noted, the fundamental principle avowed at its organization being "that the principal stock of said fund, together with all additions that shall be made to said principal by persons disposed thereto, either by contribution, presents, deeds, or otherwise, shall be kept perpetually entire, without being broken into on any occasion; but the principal moneys shall either constantly be let out to interest, or laid out in real estate bringing in some income. When Treasurer Hubbard made up his accounts in 1766, preparatory to his resignation of his office as treasurer, he credited this fund with £9. 11s. 11d. as the balance of interest due the Pious and Charitable Fund. The principal, £66. 19s. 2½d., he charged to Mr. Phillips, his successor. Mr. Phillips, in crediting £874. 14s. 3d. as church stock, has specifically itemized the £66. 19s. 2½d. while the £9. 11s. 11d. is credited in the £119. 14s. 8½d., balance of interest in favor of the poor-fund received by Mr. Phillips, the £186. 19s. 5½d. with this £119. 14s. 8½d. being together £306. 14s. 1¾d., the sum the rescript calls the "other funds of the church." In 1771, Treasurer Phillips credits as interest received for Pious and Charitable Fund £1. 6s. 8d., and, in 1773, also received from the executors of Treasurer Hubbard a legacy bequeathed by him of £50. 0s. 0d., which was immediately put out at interest, until it amounted in 1782 to £64. 12s. 9d., when it was invested in a State note of that amount until the interest was £10. 13s. 3d.; from which time it was lost sight of, it having been swallowed up in the general fund, together with £66. 19s. 2½d., the first sum. These various amounts added make £143. 11s. 10½d. lawful money, or $478\frac{64}{100}$ dollars, due this fund in 1782; with interest to 1861, $2,500.00.

For the purpose of presenting a correct statement of the account of church stock of 1766, which bears so strongly upon the decision in this case, it will be proper to go back to Treasurer Hubbard's church-stock account made up to 1761, which was duly audited and accepted by the church, and is really the foundation of the account of 1766, the latter being only a continuation of it. The account of 1761 contains eight items of different amounts of treasurer's notes, wherein was invested all the legacies, with the names of the donors of the separate sums belonging to the poor-fund or "sacramental stock," to the amount of . . . £379. 14s. 3d.
And a treasury note of . . . . . 134 0 0

Making in the whole, in 1761 . . . . £513. 14s. 3d.

In the analysis of the long account settled in 1755, it will be seen that, in 1752, a charge was made for an unexpended balance of moneys arising from the legacies, gifts, and collections at that time, to the amount of £360. 0s. 0d. "It was" (so says the record in the deacons' book) "for old bills burnt, and interest received from Treasurer Foye in dollars, and was vested in committee notes to draw interest from the province, being 160 dollars, amounting to £360. 0s. 0d. as above." When Treasurer Hubbard made up his "sacramental account," in 1761, it stands in the deacons' book as follows: —

| 1761. | | £. | s. | d. | 1758. | | £. | s. | d. |
|---|---|---|---|---|---|---|---|---|---|
| Oct. 31. To South stock invested in a note of this date | . | 134 | 0 | 9 | June 1. By acct. of the stock let out 1752 . . 360 0 0 "interest to this day . . . 150 6 0 " more money let out 1755 . . 225 0 0 " interest on same 29 14 0 ——————— 765 0 0 lawful. " £765. 0s. 0d., old tenor, £. s. d. invested in province note . . . . 102 0 0 " a note for one year, invested 1760 . . . 6 2 4 " a note for one year, invested 1760 . . . 8 5 1 " interest received on £116. 7s. 5d. to Oct. 31, 1761 . 16 13 11 | | | | |
| 1761. Oct. 31. " the sacramental stock to make an even balance, | | | | | | | 18 | 8 | |
| | | 134 | 0 | 0 | | | 134 | 0 | 0 |

Mr. Hubbard's 1761 account not being settled until 1763, this £134. 0s. 0d. will be found indirectly to compose an item in a general account embracing other matters (being the only one in the deacons' book, evidently placed there for explanatory purposes only), wherein this £513. 14s. 3d. account is balanced, and the treasury note, £134. 0s. 0d., paid over to Mr. Jeffries for Treasurer Phillips among treasury notes amounting to £418. 0s. 0d.

When this same sacramental stock again appears, it is in the stock account of 1766, amounting to £874. 14s. 3d., which Mr. Phillips as treasurer charged to himself, and credited Mr. Hubbard with. In this account we find the sacramental stock increased to £186. 19s. 5½d., being £52. 19s. 5½d. over the amount of £134. 0s. 0d., £42. 1s. 4½d. of which was the balance of the sacramental stock. £315. 10s. 0d. old tenor, or £42. 1s. 4½d. lawful, paid Nov. 1, 1763, according to Treasurer Hubbard's general account of that date, and the balance, £10. 18s. 1d., is credited on his account as received by Treasurer Phillips. It is thought the above statement, sustained by the evidence which has been offered, conclusively proves that this sacramental stock or balance was and is a part and parcel of the trust-fund or poor-fund, and neither more nor less than a portion of unexpended assets, — which in ordinary bookkeeping would be called balance, or profit and loss.

The most extraordinary part of this rescript is now to be considered, — that is, the interest, £119. 14s. 8½d., allowed upon £186. 19s.

5½$d$., the time which elapsed between the two accounts being about three years; and the balance of the advance, £52. 19$s$. 5½$d$., with the £134. 0$s$. 0$d$., being nearly all invested already in treasury notes paying interest. In point of fact, therefore, there was no interest ever calculated or intended upon any such sum. But to set this matter both of principal and interest forever at rest, the following account of interest, sustained by evidence from the deacons' book, will be offered. The occasion of this interest account was as follows: —

When Treasurer Hubbard passed over the assets of the church-stock account or poor-fund, amounting to £874. 14$s$. 3$d$. lawful, to his successor Mr. Phillips, they were all invested in securities of different amounts and dates, making it expedient to calculate the interest upon each item pro and con, for the purpose of effecting a just and equal settlement of their respective accounts. These identical calculations, copied from the treasurer's accounts in the deacons' book, are here added, presenting the following important result: —

Balance of interest received from Hubbard by Jeffries and Phillips, £9. 11$s$.-11$d$. of which belongs to Pious and Ch. Fund . . £35. 9$s$. 0¾$d$.
Interest received on Whitney's bond . . . . . 8 13 4¾
"    "    Merrick's " . . . . 1 0 11
"    "    McKnight's note . . . . . 0 4 9
"    "    treasurer's note to June . . . 21 1 10
"    "    " . . . . 6 0 0
"    "    " . . . . 19 4 10
"    "    Gould's note, . . . . . 0 4 9
"    "    treasurer's note . . . . . 0 6 8
"    "    " notes . . . . 46 14 9½
"    "    Merrick's bond . . . . . 1 0 11
"    "    Simpson's note . . . . . 1 6 0

Amount received by Mr. Phillips . . . . £141. 18$s$. 6$d$.

Interest allowed Mr. Hubbard on treasurer's
note, £49 . . . . £0. 11$s$. 6½$d$.
"    "    Gould's note . . 0 9 0
"    "    treas. note to Oliver 4 12 4
"    "    " " £730 16 10 11
Deduct amount allowed Mr. Hubbard . . . £22. 3$s$. 9½$d$.

£119. 14$s$. 8½$d$.

Being the precise sum received and credited to the poor-fund by Mr. Phillips in the £874. 14s. 1¾d. account, which proves beyond a doubt that both the £186. 19s. 5¼d., as well as this sum £119. 14s.-8½d., making together £306. 14s. 1¼d., was a part of the church stock or poor-fund.

With such incontrovertible evidence as to the misapprehensions of this rescript, it seems quite unnecessary as well as useless to examine any calculations based upon so unreliable a foundation.

There is also no "absence of complete evidence by lapse of time," or any other cause why any transaction whatever bearing upon the great question at issue (this claim) cannot be as clearly elucidated as any event which has taken place within a few years. The accounts are kept with great accuracy, free almost entirely from mistake or error, easily investigated and understood. The far greater part of the transactions are recorded by Thomas Hubbard and William Phillips, who must both have been practical bookkeepers.

The first transaction between the poor-fund and the society occurred in 1800, when a plan was conceived to erect five stores to rent, for the purpose of obtaining means to support another minister. The society, not having any property themselves which they could use or borrow upon, were compelled to resort for aid to the trustees of the poor-fund then invested in securities, realizing nine per cent per annum. The consent of the society to this measure being questionably obtained (not without the opposition of a large number, who thought the title to the real estate held in strict trust might be imperilled thereby), an agreement was made by which, in addition to the legal interest, they should receive a certain portion of the rents, so that the poor-fund should be protected from any loss in changing the investment. The assets of the fund borrowed were in Massachusetts Bank stock $8,000.00, with Union Bank and other securities which were sold for $5,245.00; which, with money borrowed on note at the bank, whose prepaid interest stands still undischarged, was taken from the poor-fund, — the whole being used for the payment for the stores. The probable reason why the bank shares were not directly turned into cash was, that their dividends were necessary to satisfy the wants of the poor. The money borrowed of the bank being repaid out of the income of the stores, and the bank stock returned, an order was passed that the treasurer should set apart from the rents of the stores a certain part, — which appears never to have been done. All this time there was no mention made of the $5,245.00 amount used in building the stores. When, six years after, the new parsonage-house began to be talked about, it was discovered that the bargain made when the stocks were borrowed that realized $5,245.00 had never been fulfilled on the society's part; and being desirous at once, without the least hesitation, to make all the reparation in their power, the society voted that compound interest on $5,245.00 should be paid up to that time, and directed the treasurer to pay quarterly the interest on $5,245.00 to the trustees of the poor-fund, which directions were followed for some time. No credit was given by the society for this sum, or obligation taken by the trustees. A few years after, when the two parsonage-houses were proposed to be erected, another application to the poor-fund for ways and means became necessary. It was then discovered without any proper examination (for the "opinion" was founded upon a fraud in 1800), that the ownership of the $5,245.00 amount of stocks was questionable.

The committee of ways and means for building the two parsonage-houses for the use of Dr. Eckley and Rev. Joshua Huntington reported, that, there being in the hands of the ministers and deacons certain funds belonging to the poor, it would be better to borrow the amount required of them than of the bank, as it would "simplify" matters, and be less troublesome to manage than it would to take the stocks and borrow upon them. This cool proposition to commit such a breach of trust now stands recorded upon the books of the society. Another bargain was then made to borrow these poor-funds (which at that time, the rescript says, were $12,783.75) of the ministers and deacons, to "an amount not exceeding fourteen thousand dollars." A written agreement between the parties, made at the time, says "that the interest should be punctually paid, and the buildings insured to secure payment." A copy of this agreement is upon record, signed by Joseph Eckley, Joshua Huntington, and William Phillips the treasurer; the latter gentleman probably knowing enough about the amount of the funds to be loaned, as to his engagement, not falling short in that particular. The only reason for building the houses was for the accommodation of the ministers. They being both living made it a manifest absurdity, in the face of a written agreement also, to suppose any such contract could be entered into as to borrow money to build a house for rent, to be received in lieu of the interest on the money borrowed.

At the decease of Dr. Eckley, the vacant house was leased for many years, at various prices, falling some short of the interest on the borrowed funds for the same time. The memorandums on the standing-committees' records, adduced to support the idea of a bargain as to rent and interest, are nothing more than allusions in estimating ways and means from time to time without the slightest connection in the way they have been brought forward in this case. If there had been any such bargain, why, when the houses were removed to make way for the enormously profitable stores, was there no provision made to insure the poor their just part of it, or provide security against the hasty repeal of the six hundred dollars by law annually granted, which could have at any time, before as well as after the promulgation of this "rescript," been effected?

For more than a hundred and twenty years the Old South has been responsible for the funds, — a larger part of them in amount being placed directly in their charge, and the whole indirectly so, the Pious and Charitable Fund and Mrs. Ireland's legacy being held under particular directions.

## CHAPTER XII.

Result of Examination. — Trustees' Obligation.— Regret of Lawsuit.— Conduct of Members of the Old South. — Extraordinary Preaching by one of the Ministers. — More Extraordinary Records of the Standing Committee. — Remarks on the Trial. — Removal of the Poor-fund. — Gratitude to the Memory of its Founders. — Duties devolving upon each Member of the Society. — Spiritual Interests of the Church. — Advantages and Dangers in Example. — Public Charities of McLean and Peabody. — Committees for Examination of Public Charities in England. — Their Success. — Necessity of similar Examination here.

A careful and thorough examination of the books of the society furnishes the following results: —

That the society, from its foundation to 1800, never possessed any property in its own right.

That Mary Norton gave certain real estate to them, on conditions that there should be erected upon it a meeting-house and parsonages for their teachers or ministers, and for "no other purpose whatsoever."

That the society did erect two meeting-houses and a parsonage-house upon said land, and maintain and pay for them, and all other expenses in supporting ministers, parish expenses, &c., &c., for more than a hundred years, by collections, subscriptions, and taxes upon pews.

That, until 1849, a sacramental collection was received monthly, the net amount of which, after customary expenses were deducted, was devoted to the poor.

That certain legacies were placed in the hands of the ministers, "in trust," for the relief of the poor, and an account of them kept in the deacons' books, exclusively distinct from all other accounts of the society.

That the stock account of the poor-fund of 1766, amounting to £874. 14s. 3d., which Treasurer Phillips charged himself with, is a true state of the assets belonging to the poor-fund at that time.

That the sums £186. 19s. 5¼d. and £119. 14s. 8½d., making £306. 14s. 1¾d., which, in the rescript, is assigned to the society, are indubitably, the one a balance of stock, and the other a balance of interest belonging to the poor-fund.

That, consequently, any calculation made upon a basis such as this is proved to be, as to the amount of the poor-fund claimed, is altogether unreliable, and, in justice, should be of non-effect.

That the trustees never agreed to receive the rent of the parsonage for interest on money borrowed of the poor-fund at sundry times.

That there is now due from the society to the fund, not only the sum borrowed to pay off the minister's salary, but other sums, with interest, borrowed at various times and not repaid.

That all the accounts relating to this fund are clearly recorded in the deacons' account and other account books, easily comprehended and elucidated.

Still, under the unfortunate termination as regards the amount awarded, there is much gained in having this institution pronounced a "public charity;" for it relieves it from that close-corporation incubus which well-nigh strangled it. Now the trustees are constrained by legal obligations to thoroughly examine into the true state of the fund committed to their charge, and, irrespective of consequences to others, do their duty at all hazards, in exposing any injustice past, or feared in the future.

Being declared a public charity, they, the trustees, are thereby placed in an anomalous position; for it becomes them as such, under the new construction of things, to examine into the whole matter, and, should they be assured that the late decision has failed in making a just award, it would be their duty to inaugurate proper measures at once to obtain one. This, as church officials, would be proceeding against themselves; while, upon the other hand, any dereliction of duty as trustees, without good and sufficient reason, would be both reprehensible and unjust.

That this affair should have ever been brought into Court is sincerely regretted. It should have been (under the circumstances) the very last place to be resorted to for a settlement of such a subject. In addition to the inquiry resolutions, before the suit at law was commenced, an ineffectual application was made to many prominent members of the society, with the hope of inviting their attention to the subject, and having it fairly investigated, believing, if any wrong had been practised towards the poor, as soon as it was manifested, the church and society would at once make every possible reparation within their power. In some few instances those thus invited to inspect the accounts made promises so to do, which never were fulfilled, but, as a general thing, the faith in the infallibility of the church prevailed, and the attempt was treated with scorn and contempt. So intense was this impression that even the pulpit, on the Sabbath, was desecrated by the preacher proclaiming in his sermon, that the person who had undertaken to disturb the affairs of the Old South had better direct his attention to looking after the legacy which Deacon Henchman left to Harvard College, at the same time irreligiously assuring his hearers that God would protect the Old South against all sacrilegious attempts of the kind. Had this reverend gentleman been but ordinarily "posted up" in this division of his sermon, "deacons' book, article Hubbard, date October, 1761; article Phillips, date January, 1766. Suffolk Probate Records, lib. 58, fol. 104, he would there find that this Deacon Daniel Henchman of the Old South gave in trust to that church a sum of money amounting to £65. 13s. 0d., lawful, which money he directed to be put out at interest, to be paid to the poor of said church as the ministers and deacons thereof in their prudence judge proper, forever; he would also have discovered that, until the year 1800, the ministers and deacons, in their respective times, religiously and honestly executed the duties of their sacred trust, invoking blessings from the widow and the orphan, the poor and the needy. He might also, for the first time perhaps, learn that this benevolent donor, from a confidence inspired by the exalted characters of a Sewall and a Prince, directed that the executive part of the duties appertaining to this trust, should be performed by their successors, the pastors of the Old South. How little did this benevolent donor to this fund imagine that one of these reverend trustees should prove so recreant to the duties of his high office as to direct the fulminations of the pulpit against the bare thought of an inquiry into its welfare!

To also show the state of feeling existing in the few members who exclusively administered the prudential affairs of the society, the following extracts from the records of the standing committees' reports of 1864, 1865, and 1866, are offered, to show that this is the only instance in which this medium is used as a means of church discipline, and the only one wherein the alleged offender had not the opportunity of making a defence: —

*Report of 12th April,* 1864. — "In reference to the suit in equity, prosecuted in the name of Joseph Ballard against the Old South Society, a hearing has been had before the Master in Chancery to whom the case was referred, and a report been made. That report has been recommitted for the purpose of reporting the facts more fully. A new report has not been made by the Master; but our counsel, Judge Abbott, informs us it will no doubt be made in the course of this spring, or early in summer; but the case cannot be heard before the Court until next November, or perhaps not until March, 1865. In the mean time, the committee have no anxiety or fear as to the final result of this suit, — a suit, be it remembered, brought by one of the oldest pew-proprietors in the Old South, and for several years a member of our standing committee."

*Report of 11th April,* 1865. — "The suit in equity, prosecuted in the name of the Attorney-General, at the relation, or instance, of Joseph Ballard, against the Old South Society, a hearing was had last year before the Master to whom the case was referred, and a report made. That report, as stated in your committee's of last year, was recommitted for the purpose of reporting the facts more fully. Our counsel, Judge Abbott, has recently informed your committee the Master's new report will be filed within a few days, so that the matter will probably be determined at the next November session of the full Court. He says, further, he has no doubt the new amended report will contain all the facts in the case which ought to be before the Court. In the mean time, the committee repeat the declaration of last year, that they have no anxiety or fear as to the final result of this suit. Let it be remembered that the complainant in this case, Mr. Ballard, has been a member of the Old South Society for fifty years or more, and for several years a member of our standing committee. Our only regret is, that the party who brought this action, and those few who have sympathized and co-operated with him in causing all this expense and trouble, cannot be made to pay all the costs which have been incurred, or may hereafter be incurred, in prosecuting this uncalled-for and unnecessary suit."

*Report of 9th April,* 1866. — "The suit in equity, prosecuted in the name of the State Attorney-General, at the relation of Joseph Ballard, against the Old South Society, which has been dragging its slow length along for several years past, the committee regret to say is not yet terminated. Judge Abbott, our counsel, at our annual meeting last April, informed the committee that the new revised report of Commissioner Paine, to whom the case was referred by the Court, would be ready for argument before the full Court in April of this year, and a final decision reached. A note from Judge Abbott to the chairman of this committee, received a few days since, informs us, that, in consequence of his own severe illness, and in press of other professional labors, he was unable to argue the case this present April term, and the case has been again postponed until next October term of the Court. The committee regret exceedingly these repeated postponements, but there is no remedy within their power."

"'The law's delay,' of which Shakspeare complained more than three centuries ago, has come down to us as an inheritance of evil and vexation. In the mean time, the committee have only to repeat their full confidence in the justice of their cause, and that the final decision, whenever reached, will be in our favor. Even should the report, in its present form, be accepted by the Court, which we do not anticipate, the committee believe an appeal to another tribunal must result in favor of our society. The printed report of the commissioner referred to accompanies this report, and will be read, if required by the pew-proprietors."

In "The Daily Advertiser" of Feb. 22, 1867, appeared the following article, furnished by an officer of the church. The name of the "person" therein referred to did not, however, appear in the "Advertiser," but was inserted in the manner shown below, when this statement was incorporated in a report of the standing committee as hereinafter stated: —

THE OLD SOUTH CHURCH. — As various contradictory statements have been made relative to a recent decision in our Courts, affecting certain funds belonging to the Old South Church, we have obtained a statement of the facts in the case, and lay them before our readers, as the subject is one of interest to many of our citizens.

About sixty years ago, the Old South Society borrowed of the Old South Church a sum of money with which to build two parish houses, on land owned by the society. For the use of this money, the parish agreed to give the church the annual rent of one of these houses. The rent was thus given quarterly, until the house was taken down in 1845. As the rent then ceased, the society agreed to pay the church, annually, a sum equivalent to the annual rent for the fifteen previous years, and, to make the matter permanent, incorporated the provision in their by-laws. These payments have been made regularly up to the close of the last year. The arrangement was considered by those interested as advantageous to the church, and reasonable for the society; and the loan was regarded as a permanent investment in safe hands.

Nearly seven years ago, a person [Joseph Ballard], a member of the parish, but not of the church, and for some years not a regular worshipper at the Old South, brought a suit in equity against both the church and parish, in the Supreme Judicial Court; and a decision was reached in December last. The Court confirmed the original contract, and the payment of rent from 1809 to 1845, when the houses were taken down. After that time, they directed that the society should pay the church the additional sum of $167.00 yearly, to make the amount equal to six per cent per annum. The whole cost to which the church and society have been subjected in this suit is about $5,000.00, and one-half of this sum is, by order of the Court, taken out of the poor-fund.

With very few exceptions, all the church, and all the society now worshipping at the Old South, were grieved with the whole proceeding from the beginning, while the *poor*, certainly, are not benefited by the change. The decree of the Court is that the money loaned be now paid back to the ministers and deacons of the church. It has never been demanded of the society by the church before this, and consequently they have never refused to pay it, or to acknowledge the debt.

To the above statement the following answer was made, and published in "The Daily Advertiser," Feb. 27, 1867: —

### THE OLD SOUTH POOR-FUND.

*To the Editors of the Boston Daily Advertiser: —*

I notice in your paper of yesterday a statement relative to the recent suit concerning the poor-fund of the Old South Church. As I find myself referred to in that article in a rather uncomplimentary manner, and as I conceive that it gives an erroneous view of the facts, I must ask you to favor me by publishing the following statement: —

In the year 1858, having at that time been a pew proprietor in the Old South for thirty-four years, and having been a regular attendant at that church for over sixty years, certain circumstances directed my attention to the fact, that, at the beginning of this century, there had been in the hands of the ministers and deacons of the church a fund for the benefit of the poor, the greater part of which had been loaned to the society in 1809. On further inquiry I found, not only that this loan had never been repaid, but that the ministers and deacons held no note of the society, or other evidence of indebtedness for the amount loaned, — it is true, as stated in your article, that, in 1845, a by-law of the society made it one of the duties of the treasurer to "pay annually to the deacons for the use of the poor the sum of $600.00;" but it was not recognized in the by-law, or in any other way, that this was to be paid as interest upon money borrowed, or that it was any thing other than a free gift made to the poor by a rich corporation out of its ample funds. The sum of $600.00 did not correspond to the amount of the interest on the above-mentioned loan, which, reckoned at six per cent, would be about $767.00, instead of $600.00; and this by-law was of course subject any day to repeal, or to an amendment diminishing the amount to be paid.

Thinking for these reasons that this fund for the poor — the greater part of which had arisen from legacies given to the ministers and deacons of the Old South, in the last century, by persons who had expressly directed in their wills that it should be forever put out at interest for the benefit of the poor — was likely to be entirely lost sight of, and the money perhaps diverted to other purposes, I offered, at a meeting of the pew proprietors, held in June, 1858, a vote for the appointment of a committee to investigate, among other things, "all matters which might seem in any degree to be a departure from a strictly lawful administration of the valuable property held in trust for religious and charitable purposes." This vote so offered was rejected; and shortly afterwards I published a pamphlet, stating the facts relative to this and other subjects, and distributed it widely among all persons interested in Old South affairs. As the officials of the Old South — including the ministers and deacons, and the standing committee of the pew proprietors — still refused to move in the matter, and as the majority of the pew proprietors had refused even to appoint a committee to investigate it, I was finally compelled to lay the subject before the Attorney-General, and at my suggestion the suit recently decided was commenced by him, in July, 1859. To this suit answer was made, in substance, that every thing was as it should be, and that there was no cause for the interference of the Court; but the Court thought otherwise, and have finally done what I claimed should be done, — they have established and set apart a fund for the poor of the Old South Church and congregation, and have fixed its present amount at $18,291.27; they have decreed that the Old South Society shall repay to the ministers and deacons the amount which they borrowed of them in 1809, with the balance of interest remaining due; and, as showing their judgment as to the propriety and justice of my proceedings, they further decreed that my costs in the matter, taxed as between counsel and client, shall be paid out of the fund which I have been instrumental in saving, and that the respondents, the Old South Society, and the ministers and deacons of the Old South Church, who united in opposing the suit, shall bear their own costs. In your article you say, that "the whole cost to which the church and society have been subjected in this suit is about $5,000.00, and one-half of this sum is, by order of the Court, taken out of the poor-fund." This sentence would seem to be written with a view to give the impression that the Court ordered half the costs of the respondents to be paid out of the poor-fund; while the fact is, as above stated, that the costs of the complainant only, as the prevailing party, were allowed out of the fund, and the respondents were ordered to bear their own costs.

With regard to the grief said to be felt by the Old South Church and Society, I have no doubt that they have reason to feel grieved that they have been involved in the position of formally denying and resisting the just rights of the poor. And with regard to the poor not being benefited by the result of the suit, I can only say that to ordinary minds it would seem that they were benefited when they gained an increased annual sum to be distributed among them, and when the principal of the sum which belonged to them was transferred, together with the arrears of interest, into the hands of its proper custodians, from the keeping of those who, having borrowed it, promising to pay six per cent interest, had through a long series of years failed to keep their promise, and who, when finally called upon to do so, refused to acknowledge that they owed either principal or interest.

I have no desire to become involved in a newspaper controversy on this subject, or to re-argue matters already decided by the highest judicial tribunal of the State. I would, however, say in closing, that I intend at an early day to publish in pamphlet form a full statement of all the facts relating to the origin and administration of the large trust property now held by the Old South Church. Yours, &c.,

JOSEPH BALLARD.

BOSTON, Feb. 23, 1867.

Nearly two months after the appearance of these articles in "The Advertiser," the standing committee of the Old South incorporated the first of them in their Annual Report to the pew proprietors, inserting, in the manner shown above, the name of the "person" therein referred to. At this time, after my reply had pointed out its misrepresentations, and with the final decree before them, it would seem that the committee must have known that the statement which they thus perpetuated on the records of the Old South was a false and unfair one, most especially in its allegation that "the poor certainly are not benefited by the change."

To prevent in future any interference with their affairs, a vote was passed on April 12, 1867, and is now on the records of the standing committee, that the clerk of the society shall not make a copy of any record, or portion of one, or suffer any pew-holder to do so, without first having a vote of permission from the standing committee.

This abortive attempt to suppress the truth, by depriving "the proprietors" of their legal rights of "inspecting" the records, proves, if any further proof is wanted beyond what these pages furnish, that the true position in which the society stands is well understood by the few persons who are suffered so exclusively and secretly to conduct its affairs.

The suit in chancery was commenced July, 1859, nearly four years before the society at large was thus officially informed of its existence. Its progressive stages were only noticed in the same way. Meanwhile the society, in the same happy reposedness to the last in the bland representations of a successful termination, regrets of innocuous vengeance, poetical quotations, and determined appeals, were constrained at last to believe, by a decree of Court, in the reality of their position. Of the majority, who, on two occasions defeated the motion for the appointment of a committee of inquiry, it is believed a larger portion had no motive for it other than an indifference towards a measure not particularly interesting to themselves, and which might prove troublesome, while at the same time it is easy to imagine that there might be *some* more conversant in the affairs of the society who might have objections to a too intimate scrutiny into affairs. If the purpose for which the measure was sought had been designed to remove the property into private hands for other uses than those for which it was intended, it would have fully vindicated the zeal shown in its defence; but, being designed only to restore their rights to an unfortunate and helpless class, it would have been generally supposed that the slightest intimation of such a wrong would have induced an anxiety in those (especially in this case) having charge of affairs to have investigated the matter at once. It cannot justly be supposed that those who from time to time have administered the prudential affairs of this institution are, in the least degree, accountable for these irregularities. They, believing every thing had been done rightly and in order, followed in the steps of their predecessors.

The poor-fund is, by the order of Court, to be paid over to the trustees, thereby relieving the society of any further responsibility of its management or preservation. But this is plainly wrong, as a large portion of the money bequeathed was conditionally given, and so accepted, as is shown in the case of Mrs. Ireland, who expressly required her money to be invested in a particular manner, and an annual account of proceedings relative thereto to be laid before the society; and in that of Mr. Cunningham, where the principal received was ordered by the society to be put out at interest forever, which interest was to be paid to the poor; as well as that of the Pious and Charitable, and Ministers' Widows' and Children's Fund, where the capital stock was ordered by the society "never to be lent to either member of the church or congregation." In fact, all the legacies, without a single exception, were considered as being under the express charge of the Old South Church, and were always so managed until the year 1800. And here, while recording these events, let us retain a grateful remembrance of the labors of those eminent Christians — Sewall, Prince, Hubbard, Jeffries, Phillips, and Mason — who, by their wise and judicious administration of this charity for more than a hundred years, were enabled to afford a generous and ample relief to the poor and afflicted, as well as to leave a large increase of funds to their successors in 1800. Upon whom, by this removal of the funds, does the responsibility of not only the minor duty of distribution of the income, or the far more important one of the security of the principal rest? Are the ever-changing trustees individually or collectively held answerable for any dereliction of duty, or to whom, or when, are they obliged to report their acts, other than through a long protracted course of legal proceedings instituted in the name of the Attorney-General, — which, in reality, is all that official has to do with it? With due deference, it is apprehended, that, had the true position of this matter been understood by the Court, a different decision upon this point would have been made. Should the evidence pointed out in this document prove the amount awarded to be wrong, will the society, should the trustees be so regardless of their duty in demanding redress, fail to commence such proceedings as will insure a restoration of what is due to this fund, even to the last farthing? Can a mere legal escape from such obligations justify a retention of property so manifestly intended for other purposes than those to which it is now devoted? Necessity does not demand it. The property bestowed by Mrs. Norton prevents that, in abundantly providing accommodations for society purposes, which to other institutions are often a source of anxiety and embarrassment.

All the expenses of the church and society having been for years paid from the common stock relieves proportionally, as far as the poor-fund is concerned in that common stock, each pew proprietor from pecuniary responsibilities as a tax-payer. And is it not quite apparent also, that it induces in many instances a free and liberal appropriation of both means and credit of the society, regardless of that wise economy which under even the most favorable circumstances should always be practised as an example to others less favorably situated? Above all other considerations, in due solemnity, it is believed an honest restoration of these funds would prove highly beneficial to the spiritual interests of this church, in relieving it from the " care of where we should bestow our goods," "for where our riches are, there will be our hearts also;" besides, "should we not be concerned that nothing of other men's goods stick to us? for, if we do not shake it off as a burning coal from our flesh, it will spiritually destroy us; it will carry a curse, and leave a curse behind."

Incorporated as the Old South Church is expressly for "charitable purposes," are there not more than ordinary obligations resting upon each individual member of this institution in this matter to "let their light so shine before men that they may see their good works"? Upon their action in this case may depend the welfare of this as well as that of other charities founded, as this was, in good faith. If this, in so short a time comparatively from its beginning, should have been nearly forgotten, and suffered to fall into dilapidation, it may be fearfully apprehended that other charitable gifts of this benevolent age may in the course of time share a like fate. Sad indeed is it even to imagine that the sequel to the Old South poor-fund should ever become just cause of impairing men's confidence in the perpetuity of the benevolent gifts of the present age, or that the munificent charitable foundations of a McLean and a Peabody can ever be forgotten.

Following the example of their ancestors abroad, the first settlers of New England, "as they were able," liberally founded many institutions for the support of churches, as well as relief for the poor. Of these, it is believed, not a few fell into disusage from causes somewhat akin to those mentioned in this relation. To such a degree did this prevail in England some years ago, that the British Parliament took the matter in hand, and appointed a committee to investigate the subject of all the "public charities." They were eminently successful in their labors in re-establishing many charities which were lost, corrected misusage in others, and recovered large sums not for many years thought of. It seems to be a great pity that such an example could not be followed by our Massachusetts Legislature. Its results might prove beneficial in keeping trustees of public charities up to their duty, and afford a substantial pledge to the beneficent that their gifts in that direction will not be uncared for, or misapplied.

For the purpose of placing the subject more understandingly before the reader, so far as the deacons' book is concerned, a perfect copy of it will be appended to this work, with the exception that the names of the recipients of the poor-fund will be omitted; and, for convenience, the accounts are placed in order, they having been transposed in the original book. In April, 1798, this book was closed, and a new one opened by William Phillips (Governor Phillips), the successor of Treasurer Mason; from which time this history is compiled from original documents from various sources, — the early church records, standing committees' records, &c.

Having now fulfilled my promise of February, 1867, that I would publish a full statement of all the facts relating to the origin and administration of the trust property held by the Old South Society, I take my leave of the subject with a sincere hope that the labor bestowed upon it will not be in vain; and that the public, who are now the guardians of this excellent charity, will, in default of suitable action in the premises on the part of its present trustees, inaugurate proper measures to have the same thoroughly examined, with a view of placing it upon its original foundation, and protecting it from further wrong.

JOSEPH BALLARD,<br>
73 years a member of the Old South Society.

BOSTON, May, 1868.

# APPENDIX No. 1.

While the purpose of this history hitherto has been for the restoration and preservation of the poor-fund, many other objects not directly connected with that important question have not passed unnoticed. One among these is that of pews and pew-holders' rights, which demands a more deliberate consideration than could appropriately have been given before.

Mrs. Norton, in 1669, gave to certain persons and their successors forever a piece of land, on the condition that they should erect a meeting-house " publiquely to worship God, and for noe other purpose whatever." The grantees accepted the conditions, and erected a meeting-house at their own cost, which is supposed, in the absence of any plan, to conform in the seating to other similar places of worship at that period of time; as to pews and seats, these being allotted under the principle, that " it is just and reasonable that such persons as enjoy the privilege of the pews and best seats in the meeting-house do contribute agreeably to support the worship of God therein."

As early as 1685, it appears that many difficulties occurred in defining the rights of pews belonging to the estates of persons deceased, which led to the following action on the part of the society : —

October 16th, 1685. — Voted at a church-meeting some propositions presented to the church about regulations of seats in the meeting-house, especially pews.

1st. They are not to be counted (though built at private men's charges) to be an inheritance in fee simple, because not so intended by the grantor, nor any record or evidence for it by the grantees, but many living witnesses to the contrary.

2d. It is equal that they who built the seats should enjoy them as long as they ordinarily attend the assembly in public worship, and their children after them, or any of them as they shall leave their interest to, or shall, in case they have not determined it, and there be need of it, be appointed by the order of the overseers of the seats, deputed by the church.

3d. If such parents die in the infancy of their children, the overseers shall no further give liberty to any of sitting in their seat than will condition to relinquish it again when such children are come to age and demand their right.

4th. It is both illegal, unequal, and contrary to ye true intention of ye grant of ye pews for an owner, when he removes, or shall have no more use of his seat to set in himself, to sell or give his right to whom he seem meet, without the approbation of ye overseers ; both because it was contrary to ye intendment of ye first grant, and opens a door to confusion, and so the most unworthy may be preferred before the most deserving.

5th. If such builder, leaving the house, require his charge, ye overseers shall order his reimbursement by ye church; which they shall either receive again for the church of such whom they again grant it to, or reserve it to ye church's distress as they in prudence see meet.

6th. Where two families are equally interested in one seat, and there fall out a difference between them about their seat or sitting, the said overseers are empowered to issue the controversy; and if the parties concerned will not submit to their determination, they shall, if church-members, be liable to answer it to the church; if otherwise, to civil authority.

7th. For the further managing this affair we commend to the overseers.

1st. That they take an inventory of the pews and ye present proprietors, who have themselves built, or are the children of such, in lawful possession.

2d. That when any seat so considered is vacant, they do not presently dispose of it, but they first enquire whether there be not some person or persons to whom on ye aforesaid grounds there may be some reasons to determine it.

3d. That they be desired to grant no more pews without the approbation of ye church.

Many of the principles embodied in the above were applicable only to the seats and pews of the first meeting-house, although they were the foundation afterwards of the pew regulations established for the present meeting-house, which was built forty-five years after. These principles, partaking more of the nature of police regulations than of any legal authority, held by the society as grantees under the very broad and liberal conditions by which Mrs. Norton's bequest was given, made it very difficult, it seems, to determine any general rule which could be in all cases enforced, and at last obliged them to resort to civil authority.

1727. At a church-meeting it was voted that a new meeting-house should be built.

1728. Voted it should be built by subscription.

1729. Voted that the old pew-holders bring in their claims for pews taken.

1730. Worshipped in the new meeting-house, April 30th.

The present house, according to a plan now extant, was divided upon the lower floor into ninety pews, and fourteen long seats fronting the pulpit, which in churches at that time were devoted to the use of aged and infirm persons, more especially to those whose hearing was impaired. There were four side galleries with similar seats, the two upper ones being occupied by persons of African race; many of whom were very aged, and had passed their lives so far in the service of the best families in Boston. Upon sacrament days, those belonging to the church took their seats in the two windows at each end of the aisles, east and west of the pulpit, and partook with the rest of the worshippers.

These good old practices of ancient days, enabling the aged, infirm, and lowly to enjoy in common with their more fortunate fellow-worshippers church services, were handed down from their English ancestors, where, to the present time, especially in the provincial churches, "rich and poor meet together," for "the Lord is the Maker of them all." There are seen the poor charity-children, with the lame, halt, and blind, worshipping at the same altar with the nobility and gentry, — as far as eligibility is concerned, often having the best seats for their accommodation.

Until 1745 the old mode of payment from collections for seats and pews was continued, when in 1748 a weekly rent for pews and a *pro rata* assessment for repairs was adopted. In 1761 the pew-tax was altered again.

1762. Voted that the hindermost of the long seats be made into pews for the accommodation of strangers.

April, 1801, the standing committee were directed to sell all the society's pews. Nov. 7, 1801, they reported they had sold a number.

November, 1808. A motion was made and seconded that the pews above and below shall be valued, and then sold by auction to the highest bidder, who shall bid for choice, and that the tax be fixed upon each pew per Sabbath before sale; which was voted unanimously, — the standing committee to carry this into effect, and the committee be directed to advertise the above pews for sale.

May 22, 1809. Estimate of pews belonging to the society: —

|  |  |
|---|---|
| Pews to be sold | $1,290 |
| Pews in the gallery | 2,000 |
|  | $3,290 |

1815. Received rent for gallery pews, $300. Received 1818, $459.67.
1833. Ten pews belonging to the society not occupied.
1836. Rent of gallery pews, $368.47.
1845. The society own eight pews on the lower floor and fifty pews in the gallery.

Rent received from the gallery pews, $209.

1853. The Committee on Pews reported, "Upon the subject of pews No. 56 and No. 87, that pew 56 belonged to John Kent, and No. 87 to Samuel Johnson, and that the two pews only pay one pew rent." Upon the subject of the rights of owners of pews who are represented by administrators, executors, and attorneys, it says, —

It is not denied that such pews have the right to be represented at all meetings of the proprietors, in the same manner that shares in a joint-stock corporation are represented; but it is clear that such claimants are not eligible to office, and that the right to vote may be questioned at any time and refused, unless documentary evidence is furnished of such right. In this respect it stands as the right to vote by proxy in other corporations, the administrator or executor being the proxy or attorney of the deceased; and holding the property, not in fee, but in trust, he is not eligible to office. The committee also recommend that the forfeited pews be sold at auction; and voted that the standing committee be authorized to carry into effect the recommendation contained in this report in regard to the sale of pews for taxes, and that the treasurer be authorised to purchase said pews, when sold, in behalf of said society. Signed to the report as Committee on Pews.

URIEL CROCKER.<br>
JOSEPH BALLARD.<br>
GEORGE HOMER.

April 30, 1853. — Report accepted.

Before this report was agreed upon in committee, great care was taken to consult competent authority as to the legal principles there pronounced. If there has been no alteration in the law in relation to corporate property since that time, it may seem that the acceptance of this report would make any action in regard to the pews at present inexpedient.

The extracts from the records, and the foregoing report, prove that the pews were never sold without the special direction of the society until 1858, when the celebrated sale of five pews was expressly made, without that authority, for the purpose of obtaining a majority of votes against having a committee of investigation into the money affairs of the old South. *

The restrictive clauses in the pew deeds were introduced to prevent improper persons from becoming pew-owners, as well as to prevent a class of persons becoming such, who in former days were inadmissible to seats and pews in common with the general congregation; although they were treated in other respects with all Christian kindness, and welcomed to the brotherhood of the church. At the time this feeling prevailed, a pew-holder in a sister church transferred a pew to a person of the proscribed race, who held it in despite of a conditional restriction in the deed; and the society were obliged to settle the matter in an amicable manner. By change of circumstances, this restriction is at the present time become inoperative; and that class of persons are placed upon a par with all others, and choose their pews and seats wherever their ability and convenience may lead them.

Whenever a pew was deemed forfeited, it was invariably for unpaid taxes, or run out; and the reason why such pews were sold at public auction was to legalize their ownership. It is believed that there is not upon record a single case where the forfeiture was caused by the non-attendance at public worship of the pew-owner, or his removal from the society. The *class* to which such property belongs makes it impossible that such restrictions could ever be effectual.

These remarks about pews, and the rights of pew-holders, have been called for by some extraordinary proceedings on the part of the society concerning that species of property. At the annual meeting for choice of officers and business purposes, April, 1867, a pew-proprietor wishing to address the meeting was prevented from so doing by a vote taken at the time, whereby his pew, standing in his own name, was confiscated, and consequently, not being an owner, he had no right to speak, or take any part in the meeting. The next day several applications were made to purchase the mulct pew, the vote

---

* And it is not impertinent to the subject under consideration to say, that it is believed that Messrs. Ames, Learned, Bigelow, Johnson, jr., and Hubbard, who purchased these pews, have never occupied them for a single Sabbath since they owned them.

to the contrary notwithstanding; neither has the control of its ownership ever been assumed by the society. Such a procedure can only be accounted for on two reasons, — one, in having effected their gagging purpose, a measure not by any means for the first time resorted to on such occasions; the other, a latent doubt of its legality. Did it never occur to the members of the society that such practices may invalidate important business transactions, and open claims for damages for private wrong? The next movement in this direction was the sending the following circular to the owners, heirs, administrators, and pew-holders, not omitting the owner of this forfeited pew: —

BOSTON, Oct. 29, 1867.

SIR, — At a meeting of the proprietors of the old South Church, a committee was appointed to call attention to owners of pews, and parties interested in pews, the titles of which stand in the names of deceased persons, to the clause in the deed of grant; viz., "If the said ——— ———, or his legal representatives, upon his or their leaving the said meeting-house, shall neglect to offer the said pew as aforesaid, then he or they shall forfeit the same to the said corporation." The committee was not appointed to enforce the legal rights of the corporation, but to ascertain if some amicable arrangement cannot be made so as to have the titles to the several pews stand in the names of those who actually attend service regularly at the old South Church.

(Signed)   LINUS M. CHILD.
               CHARLES STODDARD.
               LORING LOTHROP.

If this committee, who are so anxious to have the pews filled, are really sincere in the desire to obtain that object only, would it not be a more sure and respectable way for them to recommend that the society should dispose of some of the large number of pews which they own, and first have them filled, before any further measures are taken which may interfere with the rights of individuals or families?

Just before the settlement of the junior pastor, the pews in the west gallery were appropriately fitted up, for the purpose of making them free seats; an invitation was posted up, and in a short time the sitters were doubled in number. Soon a new arrangement was made, appropriating indiscriminately the seats of private pews without the owners' leave; which, naturally, gave some cause of dissatisfaction, more particularly among those who from their childhood clung to their love for the "old family pew" with its many endeared recollections of parents, kindred, and friends, who often in imagination again filled their seats, — seats now to be occupied by the unknown multitude of a populous city.

The society cannot possibly now have any reason of a prudential kind against the disposal of a part of these pews; inasmuch as it was decided in the New South Church case, that the value of a pew for any purpose beyond its legitimate one was next to nothing, and that the ownership of a pew does not carry with it any right whatever in the funds belonging to the society.

An application was recently made in the proper quarter, in behalf of a highly respectable lady, for a regular transfer of a family pew to her. It was denied on the ground that no female could hold a pew in her own name; while at this time there are pews standing in the names of several ladies, and it is well known that in other societies no such distinction exists. Even had it been so, the Old South Church should have been the last to have adopted it, for a grateful remembrance to the memories of Mary Norton, and other "mothers in Israel" who worshipped at the altars which she raised, would forbid such heartless ingratitude.

Under these circumstances, it is not strange that there should be an exodus of some of our oldest worshippers to other places of worship, and that their vacant seats are not filled up with younger persons; neither can it be reasonably expected that this evil can be remedied by any measures contemplated in this pew arrangement. For the time is past when ecclesiastical government rules in these matters. They now can only be permanently settled by reference to "civil authority;" which, in this particular case, seems to be of no consideration whatever with the authorities of this corporation, who, regardless of both common and statute law have ingrafted in their by-law, Art. v., that "no person shall vote by proxy," instead of directing "the mode" by which that act can be performed, as expressed in the statutes under which this society is incorporated.

Should these transactions be considered as a specimen of the business qualities of the small number of persons into whose hands the important matters of this corporation have fallen, it is quite time that the society at large should insist upon an entire change in so ridiculous a condition of affairs, and that all matters of consequence whatever should be submitted to the consideration of a special committee, and reported by them to the society (at a future meeting) to decide upon.

Subsequently, it was thought best by the authorities of the society to give a deed to the lady who owned the pew in question. At the annual meeting for choice of officers and other business purposes, April 14, 1868, this pew question formed no inconsiderable part of the proceedings; and it was clearly demonstrated, in despite of the gag which was freely applied to the forfeited pew-member especially, that the society were determined not to accept such puerile and vague action upon a subject which had been settled as far as it could be by the accepted report of a select committee charged with the subject, in 1853, a copy of which is heretofore given. The present committee — re-organized out of the last year's one — were instructed to purchase pews, instead of seizing them. In the course of the debate, great fears were expressed by some, lest the broad and liberal conditions by which a pew-holder held his pew from Mary Norton as an heir or successor of Messrs. Savage, Davis, Upshur, Rawson, Hull, Scottow, Trewsdale, Raynsford, and Elliott inadvertently imperilled the control of the ownership of the vast property now in possession of the Old South Society; and, unless some obligatory measures were taken to compel the pew-owners to a personal attendance on worship in their own pews, there was nothing to prevent even the Spiritualists from becoming dominant. It was not stated at this time, whether the pew-holders were obliged to believe in the religious, moral, and political opinions preached when this millennial security for the property is reached, or practise "our revolutionary principles," whatever they may prove to be.

# APPENDIX No. 2.

## DEACONS' BOOK.

A copy of this book is published for the purpose of establishing the fact, that the sacramental collections, after paying the expenses attending the celebration of that ordinance and other matters belonging to it, were especially devoted to the poor; and that the accounts of the poor-fund were kept separately, by themselves, — the ordinary parish accounts being kept elsewhere. The number of communicants, during the period covered by this account, was from eight hundred to a thousand.

SOUTH CHURCH

BOOK FOR SACRAMENTAL CONTRIBUTION.

1708.

## Boston, New England, June 22, 1708.

| 1708. | | South Church is Dr. | £ | s. | d. |
|---|---|---|---|---|---|
| July | 12 | To Cash paid for a Book | | 5 | 6 |
| | | " a Box for the Church, &c. | | 2 | 6 |
| | | " Cash to sundry poor* | 2 | 15 | 0 |
| Aug. | 9 | " Hornes for Catechizing [horn books] | 1 | 10 | 0 |
| | 13 | " Sundry poor | 2 | 5 | 0 |
| Oct. | 9 | " Widow Harlow | 1 | 0 | 0 |
| | 28 | " 25 Galls. Canary @ 5s. a gall. | 6 | 5 | 0 |
| | | " Cooperage and porterage | | 1 | 2 |
| Nov. | 5 | " Repairing Glass | | 10 | 0 |
| | 22 | " Sundry poor, 21 persons | 8 | 4 | 0 |
| Dec. | 5 | "    "    "   3   " | 1 | 12 | 0 |
| | 10 | " 31 Galls. Wine @ 5s. | 7 | 15 | 0 |
| | | " Cooperage and porterage | | 1 | 2 |
| 1709. | | | | | |
| Jan. | 24 | " Sundry poor, 6 persons | 2 | 16 | 0 |
| April | 17 | "    "    "  to date, 6 persons | 3 | 19 | 0 |
| May | 16 | "    "    "    11   " | 4 | 4 | 0 |
| | | " 1 Cord of Wood to poor | | 13 | 0 |
| June | 10 | " 21 galls. of Wine @ 5s. | 5 | 5 | 0 |
| | | " Cooperage and porterage | | 1 | 2 |
| | 13 | " Cash for the poor | 3 | 7 | 4 |
| July | 2 | " 31 Galls. Wine, 5s. 3d., £8. 2s. 9d.; Cooperage, &c., 1s. 2d. | 8 | 3 | 11 |
| | 11 | " John Pell's wife | | 10 | 0 |
| | | " Jos. Biscoe for Bread for Sacrament to June 1709 | 3 | 0 | 8 |
| Aug. | 30 | " 21 Galls. Wine, 5s., £5. 5s.; Cooperage, &c., 1s. 2d. | 5 | 6 | 2 |
| Oct. | 31 | " Sundry poor, 15 persons | 13 | 10 | 0 |
| Nov. | 3 | " 2 quarter casks Wine, and porterage | 10 | 11 | 0 |
| | | " 25 galls. Wine, and porterage | 6 | 5 | 8 |
| | 10 | " Andrew Walker | | 8 | 0 |
| | 23 | " Sundry poor at Thanksgiving, 13 persons | 3 | 18 | 0 |
| Dec. | 26 | " Sundry poor, 4 persons | 1 | 11 | 0 |
| | | " Sundry poor, 5 persons | 3 | 4 | 0 |
| 1710. | | | | | |
| Jan. | 23 | " Cash paid for cleaning Plate and Linen 2 years | 2 | 0 | 0 |
| March | 20 | " Sundry poor to date, 20 persons | 8 | 11 | 0 |
| | 26 | " Balance carried to New Account. | 101 | 19 | 7 |
| | | | £221 | 10 | 10 |

* Whose names are mentioned.

## Boston, New England, June 22, 1708.

| 1708. | | Per Contra is Cr. | | | £ | s. | d. |
|---|---|---|---|---|---|---|---|
| | | By Balance brought from Old Book, folio 23; viz.,— | | | | | |
| | | " A Bond of Capt. N. Williams, for payment of South Funds . . £78. 0s. 0d. | | | | | |
| | | " Cash in sundry Bags at Capt. Hills  17 8 5 | | | 95 | 8 | 5 |
| July | 12 | " Cash Recd. of the Sacramental Contribution | | | 5 | 4 | 5 |
| Aug. | 9 | "   "   "   "   " | | | 6 | 17 | 6 |
| Sept. | 5 | "   "   "   "   " | | | 4 | 18 | 6 |
| Oct. | 4 | "   "   "   "   " | | | 5 | 4 | 3 |
| Nov. | 1 | "   "   "   "   " | | | 5 | 6 | 6 |
| | 29 | "   "   "   "   " | | | 5 | 6 | 1 |
| Dec. | 26 | "   "   "   "   " | | | 4 | 6 | 7 |
| 1709. | | | | | | | |
| Jan. | 24 | "   "   "   "   " | | | 6 | 2 | 6 |
| Feb. | 21 | "   "   "   "   " | | | 5 | 10 | 7 |
| March | 21 | "   "   "   "   " | | | 5 | 14 | 11 |
| April | 17 | "   "   "   "   " | | | 5 | 11 | 7 |
| May | 16 | "   "   "   "   " | | | 5 | 2 | 0 |
| June | 13 | "   "   "   "   " | | | 6 | 0 | 6 |
| July | 11 | "   "   "   "   " | | | 5 | 15 | 0 |
| Aug. | 8 | "   "   "   "   " | | | 5 | 9 | 6 |
| Sept. | 5 | "   "   "   "   " | | | 5 | 14 | 9 |
| Oct. | 3 | "   "   "   "   " | | | 5 | 7 | 5 |
| | 31 | "   "   "   "   " | | | 5 | 12 | 5 |
| Nov. | 28 | "   "   "   "   " | | | 6 | 2 | 0 |
| Dec. | 26 | "   "   "   "   " | | | 5 | 1 | 8 |
| 1710. | | | | | | | |
| Jan. | 23 | "   "   "   "   " | | | 5 | 7 | 8 |
| Feb. | 20 | "   "   "   "   " | | | 5 | 4 | 1 |
| March | 20 | "   "   "   "   " | | | 5 | 2 | 0 |

£221 10 10

|  |  |  | £ | s. | d. |
|---|---|---|---|---|---|
| 1710. |  |  |  |  |  |
| April 17 | To Sundry poor, 4 persons | | 1 | 4 | 0 |
| May 29 | " " " 8 " | | 3 | 18 | 6 |
| 30 | " 44 Galls. Wine, and porterage | | 11 | 13 | 2 |
| June 19 | " Joseph Briscoe for Bread for Sacrament past year | | 3 | 0 | 8 |
| July 10 | " Sundry poor, 3 persons | | 1 | 2 | 0 |
| Aug. 8 | " Sundry poor against Thanksgiving, 11 persons | | 3 | 1 | 6 |
| Oct. 2 | " Sundry poor, 12 persons | | 7 | 10 | 0 |
| 17 | " 46 Galls. of Wine, and porterage | | 12 | 12 | 5 |
| Nov. 13 | " Sundry poor at Thanksgiving | | 5 | 16 | 0 |
|  | " Cash pd. for cleaning Plate and Linen past year | | 1 | 0 | 0 |
|  | " Two poor Widows | |  | 14 | 0 |
| 1711. |  |  |  |  |  |
| Jan. 18 | " Cash paid for mending Plate | |  | 6 | 0 |
| 29 | " Sundry poor, 9 persons | | 4 | 10 | 0 |
| Feb. 19 | " Sundry poor, 2 " | | 1 | 10 | 0 |
| March 19 | " Sundry poor, 3 " | | 2 | 0 | 0 |
| 21 | " Widow Moss and Mary Glass | | 1 | 0 | 0 |
| April | " 25½ Galls. Wine, and porterage | | 5 | 19 | 5 |
| 30 | " Mrs. Ball, her husband being sick | | 1 | 0 | 0 |
| May 14 | " Sundry poor, 6 persons | | 4 | 0 | 0 |
|  | " Error in addition of original acct., to agree | | 1 | 0 | 0 |
|  | " Balance carried to New Acct. | | 110 | 7 | 4 |
|  |  |  | £183 | 5 | 0 |

|  |  |  |  |  |  |  |  | £ | s. | d. |
|---|---|---|---|---|---|---|---|---|---|---|
| 1710. | | | | | | | | | | |
| March 28 | By Balance from last Acct. | | . | . | . | . | . | 101 | 19 | 7 |
| April 17 | " | Contribution | . | . | . | . | . | 5 | 2 | 4 |
| May 15 | " | " | . | . | . | . | . | 5 | 3 | 10 |
| June 12 | " | " | . | . | . | . | . | 5 | 11 | 9 |
| July 1 | " | " | . | . | . | . | . | 6 | 3 | 2 |
| Aug. 8 | " | " | . | . | . | . | . | 5 | 5 | 9 |
| Sept. 4 | " | " | . | . | . | . | . | 5 | 5 | 6 |
| Oct. 2 | " | " | . | . | . | . | . | 5 | 12 | 0 |
| 30 | " | " | . | . | . | . | . | 4 | 17 | 0 |
| Nov. 27 | " | " | . | . | . | . | . | 4 | 18 | 0 |
| Dec. 25 | " | " | . | . | . | . | . | 4 | 5 | 0 |
| 1711. | | | | | | | | | | |
| Jan. 22 | " | " | . | . | . | . | . | 5 | 18 | 4 |
| Feb. 19 | " | " | . | . | . | . | . | 6 | 0 | 2 |
| March 19 | " | " | . | . | . | . | . | 6 | 10 | 10 |
| April 16 | " | " | . | . | . | . | . | 5 | 4 | 5 |
| May 14 | " | " | . | . | . | . | . | 5 | 7 | 4 |

£183  5  0

|  |  |  |  |  |  | £ | s. | d. |
|---|---|---|---|---|---|---|---|---|
| 1711. |  |  |  |  |  |  |  |  |
| May | 21 | To Cash for 21 Galls. Canary |  |  |  | 5 | 15 | 6 |
| June | 11 | " Cash for curing " |  |  |  |  | 10 | 0 |
| Aug. | 6 | " Sundry poor, 9 persons |  |  |  | 4 | 15 | 0 |
|  |  | " a poor person |  |  |  | 1 | 0 | 0 |
|  | 13 | " Cash paid Mr. Briscoe for Bread |  |  |  | 3 | 0 | 8 |
|  |  | " Cash paid for altering Plate |  |  |  | 1 | 10 | 10 |
| Sept. | 4 | " the Poor |  |  |  | 1 | 0 | 0 |
|  | 10 | " 25 galls. Canary, 7s. 6d. | £9. | 7s. | 6d. |  |  |  |
|  |  | " 21½ " Wine, 5s. | 5 | 7 | 6 |  |  |  |
|  |  | " Cartage, &c. | 2 | 0 |  | 14 | 17 | 0 |
| Oct. | 2 | " Sundry poor, 2 Persons |  |  |  | 1 | 2 | 0 |
|  | 29 | " Mary Lambert, being sick |  |  |  | 1 | 0 | 0 |
| Nov. | 4 | " 21½ Galls. Wine, and porterage |  |  |  | 8 | 2 | 3 |
|  | 19 | " Sundry poor, 11 persons |  |  |  | 9 | 12 | 0 |
|  | 29 | " Sundry poor at Thanksgiving, 16 persons |  |  |  | 8 | 12 | 0 |
|  |  | " 53 Galls. Wine, cooperage, porterage, &c. |  |  |  | 15 | 8 | 4 |
|  |  | " Sundries |  |  |  | 1 | 14 | 5 |
| 1712. |  |  |  |  |  |  |  |  |
| Jan. | 21 | " Sundry poor, 11 persons |  |  |  | 10 | 5 | 0 |
| Feb. | 11 | " Sundry poor, 3 persons |  |  |  | 2 | 10 | 0 |
| March | 3 | " Sundry poor, 3 persons |  |  |  | 1 | 10 | 0 |
|  | 24 | " Sundry poor, 14 persons |  |  |  | 11 | 0 | 0 |
| April | 12 | " 46½ galls. Canary, porterage, &c. |  |  |  | 14 | 1 | 0 |
|  |  | " Balance carried to New Acct. |  |  |  | 84 | 11 | 6 |
|  |  |  |  |  |  | £201 | 17 | 6· |

|          |    |                                                                                      | £   | s. | d. |
|----------|----|--------------------------------------------------------------------------------------|-----|----|----|
| 1711.    |    | By Balance of Old Acct.                                                              | 110 | 7  | 4  |
| June     | 11 | " Contribution                                                                       | 5   | 7  | 0  |
| July     | 9  | "    "                                                                               | 5   | 10 | 6  |
| Aug.     | 6  | "    "                                                                               | 4   | 17 | 10 |
| Sept.    | 3  | "    "                                                                               | 4   | 10 | 3  |
| Oct.     | 1  | "    "                                                                               | 5   | 2  | 5  |
|          | 29 | "    "                                                                               | 7   | 14 | 0  |
| Nov.     | 26 | "    "                                                                               | 7   | 6  | 6  |
| Dec.     | 24 | "    "                                                                               | 6   | 4  | 10 |
| 1712.    |    |                                                                                      |     |    |    |
| Jan.     | 21 | "    "                                                                               | 5   | 15 | 3  |
|          |    | "    "                                                                               | 6   | 5  | 3  |
| Feb.     | 25 | " Cash Recd. of Dea. Jno. Cutler, Administrator to Mr. John Botts's estate, for a legacy he left for the poor communicants | 12 | 0 | 0 |
| March 17 |    | " Contribution                                                                       | 6   | 19 | 8  |
| April 14 |    |                                                                                      | 6   | 10 | 4  |
| May 12   |    |                                                                                      | 7   | 6  | 4  |

£201 17 6

|  |  |  |  | £ | s. | d. |
|---|---|---|---|---|---|---|
| 1712. |  |  |  |  |  |  |
| May | 20 | To Cash paid for Wine, and porterage | | 2 | 5 | 6 |
| June | 26 | " Sundry poor | | 2 | 12 | 0 |
| | | " 21½ Galls. Wine, and porterage | | 5 | 19 | 5 |
| July | 8 | " Goody Brown | | | 10 | 0 |
| | | " Briscoe for Bread to June last | | 3 | 16 | 0 |
| | 14 | " Dea. Miriam for Poor | | 2 | 0 | 0 |
| | | " Sundry poor, 6 persons | | 3 | 12 | 0 |
| Aug. | 5 | " 25½ Galls. Wine, and porterage | | 2 | 9 | 6 |
| Sept. | 1 | " Poor | | | 15 | 0 |
| | | " 21½ Galls. Wine, and porterage | | 6 | 9 | 8 |
| | 29 | " Henry Wright's wife | | | 14 | 0 |
| Oct. | | " 26½ Galls. Wine, and porterage | | 3 | 7 | 5 |
| | | " Cash paid for cleaning Linen and Plate | | 2 | 0 | 0 |
| | | " Sundry poor, 14 persons | | 10 | 10 | 0 |
| | | " 25 Galls. Wine, and porterage | | 7 | 10 | 8 |
| | 17 | " Sundry poor, for Thanksgiving | | 7 | 15 | 0 |
| Nov. | 19 | " Sundry poor, 4 persons | | | 14 | 0 |
| 1713. |  |  |  |  |  |  |
| Jan. | 2 | " Cash pd. for 21½ Galls. Wine, and porterage | | 5 | 8 | 8 |
| | 28 | " 25 Galls. Wine, and porterage | | 9 | 1 | 11 |
| Feb. | 2 | " a poor woman of the church | | | 11 | 0 |
| | 6 | " 21½ Galls. Wine, and porterage | | 3 | 19 | 6 |
| | 16 | " Sundry poor | | 11 | 10 | 0 |
| May | 11 | " Sundry poor, to date | | 12 | 10 | 6 |
| | | " Balance carried forward to New Acct. | | 69 | 15 | 5 |
| | | | | £175 | 17 | 2 |

|  |  |  |  |  |  |  |  | £ | s. | d. |
|---|---|---|---|---|---|---|---|---|---|---|
| 1712. |  |  |  |  |  |  |  |  |  |  |
|  |  | By Balance brought from Old Account |  |  |  | . | . | 84 | 11 | 6 |
| May | 17 | " Contribution | . | . | . | . | . | 7 | 6 | 1 |
| July | 8 | " " | . | . | . | . | . | 7 | 9 | 0 |
| Aug. | 4 | " " | . | . | . | . | . | 6 | 12 | 4 |
| Sept. | 3 | " " | . | . | . | . | . | 7 | 4 | 0 |
|  | 29 | " " | . | . | . | . | . | 6 | 2 | 0 |
| Oct. |  | " " | . | . | . | . | . | 7 | 6 | 6 |
| Nov. | 24 | " " | . | . | . | . | . | 7 | 8 | 0 |
| Dec. | 22 | " " | . | . | . | . | . | 7 | 3 | 4 |
| 1713. |  |  |  |  |  |  |  |  |  |  |
| Jan. | 19 | " " | . | . | . | . | . | 7 | 18 | 3 |
| Feb. | 16 | " " | . | . | . | . | . | 7 | 1 | 9 |
| March | 16 | " " | . | . | . | . | . | 8 | 0 | 0 |
| April | 13 | " " | . | . | . | . | . | 6 | 17 | 0 |
| May | 11 | " " | . | . | . | . | . | 4 | 17 | 5 |

£175 17 2

|  |  |  |  | £ | s. | d. |
|---|---|---|---|---|---|---|
| 1713. |  | To Cash paid for curing Wine |  |  | 10 | 0 |
| June | 15 | " Cash paid Mr. Briscoe for Bread to this time |  | 3 | 15 | 10 |
| July | 2 | " Cash for 21 Galls. Wine, and porterage |  | 6 | 2 | 6 |
|  |  | " a poor person |  |  | 10 | 0 |
|  | 10 | " 32 Galls. Wine, and porterage |  | 5 | 7 | 2 |
| Sept. | 14 | " Sundry poor, 13 persons |  | 10 | 15 | 0 |
| Oct. | 19 | " Ruth Knight |  |  | 10 | 0 |
|  | 29 | " 51 Galls. Wine, and porterage |  | 14 | 15 | 0 |
| Nov. | 10 | " Sundry poor at Thanksgiving |  | 6 | 0 | 6 |
| Dec. | 7 | " Widow Wormwood and Samuel Grisse |  | 1 | 0 | 0 |
| 1714. |  |  |  |  |  |  |
| Jan. | 18 | " 22½ Galls Wine, and porterage |  | 4 | 3 | 0 |
|  |  | " Cash, Sundries |  |  | 6 | 2 |
| March | 29 | " Sundries at Thanksgiving |  | 3 | 15 | 0 |
| July | 22 | " Mr. Briscoe for Bread |  | 3 | 0 | 8 |
|  |  | " Cash paid for cleaning Linen and Plate for 2 years, ending October next |  | 2 | 0 | 0 |
|  |  | " 2 Brass Cocks for Wine |  |  | 7 | 0 |
| Nov. | 23 | " Sundry poor |  | 8 | 19 | 0 |
|  |  | " 2 Casks and 23 galls. Wine |  | 19 | 13 | 0 |
| 1715. |  |  |  |  |  |  |
| Jan. | 18 | " Sundry poor |  | 6 | 10 | 6 |
| April | 21 | " Jonathan Williams for Wine |  | 9 | 14 | 9 |
|  |  | " 32 Galls. Canary |  | 13 | 0 | 0 |
| June | 5 | " Sundry poor |  | 16 | 0 | 8 |
| July | 8 | " Sundry poor |  | 2 | 0 | 0 |
| Aug. | 5 | " 21½ Galls. Canary, 23 Galls. Sherry |  | 13 | 4 | 9 |
| Nov. | 14 | " Sundry poor |  | 8 | 17 | 0 |
|  | 21 | " Cleaning Plate and Linen |  | 1 | 0 | 0 |
| 1716. |  |  |  |  |  |  |
| Jan. | 26 | " Cash paid J. Williams for Wine |  | 9 | 8 | 0 |
|  |  | " Sundry poor |  |  | 15 | 0 |

*Amount carried forward* . . . £172 0 6

| 1713. | | | | | | | £ | s. | d. |
|---|---|---|---|---|---|---|---|---|---|
| | | By Balance brought from Old Acct. | | | | | 69 | 15 | 5 |
| June | | " Contribution | . | . | . | . | 4 | 18 | 10 |
| July | 6 | " " | | | | | 4 | 16 | 5 |
| Aug. | 3 | " " | . | . | . | . | 4 | 18 | 6 |
| | 31 | " " | . | . | . | . | 4 | 16 | 6 |
| | 28 | " " | . | . | . | . | 4 | 8 | 8 |
| Oct. | 26 | " " | . | . | . | . | 4 | 8 | 5 |
| Nov. | 23 | " " | . | . | . | . | 3 | 0 | 4 |
| Dec. | 21 | " " | . | . | . | . | 4 | 2 | 3 |
| 1714. | | | | | | | | | |
| Jan. | 18 | " " | . | . | . | . | 4 | 6 | 0 |
| Feb. | 15 | " " | . | . | . | . | 4 | 18 | 3 |
| March | 15 | " " | . | . | . | . | 3 | 18 | 11 |
| April | 12 | " " | . | . | . | . | 4 | 6 | 9 |
| May | 10 | " " | . | . | . | . | 5 | 4 | 1 |
| June | 7 | " " | . | . | . | . | 4 | 15 | 7 |
| July | 5 | " " | . | . | . | . | 4 | 5 | 8 |
| Aug. | 2 | " " | . | . | . | . | 4 | 10 | 0 |
| | 30 | " " | . | . | . | . | 4 | 4 | 10 |
| Sept. | 27 | " " | . | . | . | . | 4 | 5 | 0 |
| Oct. | 25 | " " | . | . | . | . | 4 | 6 | 2 |
| Nov. | 22 | " " | . | . | . | . | 4 | 5 | 7 |
| | | " Exchanging of Money for Bills | . | . | . | | 2 | 0 | 0 |
| | 20 | " Contributions | . | | . | . | 4 | 12 | 6 |
| 1715. | | | | | | | | | |
| Jan. | 17 | " " | . | . | . | . | 4 | 8 | 6 |
| | | " Cash for poor, from an unknown hand | | | . | | 3 | 0 | 0 |
| Feb. | 14 | " Contributions | . | . | . | . | 4 | 1 | 5 |
| March | 14 | " " | . | . | . | . | 4 | 8 | 2 |
| April | 11 | " " | . | . | . | . | 4 | 8 | 6 |
| May | 9 | " " | . | . | . | . | 4 | 9 | 2 |
| | | " Cash for Wine | . | . | . | . | | 11 | 0 |
| June | 6 | " Contribution | . | . | . | . | 5 | 6 | 8 |
| | 13 | " Cash for Poor | . | . | . | . | 5 | 0 | 0 |
| July | 4 | " Contribution | . | . | . | . | 5 | 0 | 6 |
| Aug. | 1 | " " | . | . | . | . | 5 | 6 | 2 |
| | | " Exchange of Silver | . | . | . | . | 2 | 8 | 6 |
| | 29 | " Contribution | . | . | . | . | 4 | 17 | 5 |
| Sept. | 26 | " " | . | . | . | . | 4 | 14 | 1 |
| | | " Exchange of Silver | . | . | . | . | 1 | 2 | 6 |
| Oct. | 24 | " Contribution | . | . | . | . | 4 | 17 | 0 |
| | | *Amount carried forward* | | . | . | . | £229 | 4 | 3 |

|  |  |  | £ | s. | d. |
|---|---|---|---|---|---|
| 1716. | | | | | |
| | *Amount brought forward* . . . | | 172 | 0 | 6 |
| Jan. 26 | To Balance carried to New Acct. . . . | | 70 | 7 | 8 |
| | | | £242 | 8 | 2 |

| | | | £ | s. | d. |
|---|---|---|---|---|---|
| 1716. | | | | | |
| March 5 | To Sundry poor . . . . . | | 13 | 18 | 0 |
| April 9 | " 23 Galls. Canary . . . . . | | 9 | 12 | 8 |
| July 7 | " Cash paid Col. Townsend for Wine . | | 15 | 4 | 8 |
| | " " " for Widow George Funeral . | | 1 | 0 | 0 |
| | " Wm. Briscoe for Bread . . . | | 3 | 0 | 0 |
| Aug. 21 | " Sundry poor . . . . | | 6 | 10 | 0 |
| Oct. 8 | " 21½ Galls. Wine . . . . | | 4 | 6 | 0 |
| 26 | " 50 Galls. Canary, bought at Vendue . | | 11 | 13 | 6 |
| Nov. 5 | " Cash towards Mr. Batt's funeral . . | | 1 | 0 | 0 |
| 1717. | | | | | |
| Jan. 29 | " Sundry poor . . . . | | 9 | 10 | 0 |
| May 13 | " " " . . . . | | 11 | 5 | 0 |
| April 8 | " Cash paid cleaning Linen and Plate . | | 1 | 0 | 0 |
| May 20 | " Sundry poor . . . . | | 2 | 0 | 0 |
| June 17 | " Wm. Briscoe for Bread . . . | | 3 | 0 | 8 |
| Aug. 9 | " Sundry poor . . . . | | 8 | 10 | 0 |
| 20 | " 32 galls. Canary, 23½ galls. Green Wine . | | 12 | 0 | 2 |
| Sept. 9 | " Cash paid cleaning Linen and Plate . | | 1 | 0 | 0 |
| 16 | " a poor person . . . . | | | 10 | 0 |
| 20 | " 53½ Galls. Canary . . . | | 8 | 19 | 8 |
| 1718. | | | | | |
| Jan. 15 | " Sundry poor . . . . | | 22 | 13 | 0 |
| Feb. 5 | " Sundry poor . . . . | | 3 | 0 | 0 |
| | " Two new Tankards, made of Wm. More's legacy | | 30 | 8 | 0 |
| | " Balance carried to New Acct. . . | | 64 | 2 | 1 |
| 1716. | | | | | |
| May 29 | " Sundry poor, omitted above . . | | 6 | 15 | 0 |
| | | | £250 | 18 | 5 |

|  |  |  |  |  |  |  |  | £ | s. | d. |
|---|---|---|---|---|---|---|---|---|---|---|
| 1715. | | | | | | | | | | |
| | | *Amount brought forward* | | . | . | . | . | 229 | 4 | 3 |
| Nov. | 21 | By Contributions | . | . | . | . | . | 4 | 8 | 8 |
| Dec. | 19 | " " | . | . | . | . | . | 5 | 3 | 6 |
| 1716. | | | | | | | | | | |
| Jan. | 16 | " " | . | . | . | . | . | 3 | 11 | 9 |
| | | | | | | | | £242 | 8 | 2 |

| | | | | | | | | £ | s. | d. |
|---|---|---|---|---|---|---|---|---|---|---|
| 1716. | | | | | | | | | | |
| | | By Balance brought from Old Acct.. | | | . | . | . | 70 | 7 | 8 |
| Feb. | 13 | " Contribution | . | . | . | . | . | 5 | 9 | 2 |
| | | " Cash for poor | . | . | . | . | . | 3 | 0 | 0 |
| March 12 | | " Contribution | . | . | . | . | . | 5 | 11 | 8 |
| April | 9 | " " | . | . | . | . | . | 5 | 7 | 5 |
| May | 7 | " " | . | . | . | . | . | 4 | 15 | 1 |
| June | 4 | " " | . | . | . | . | . | 5 | 18 | 10 |
| | | " Cash for Wine for the Elders | . | . | . | | | 18 | 0 |
| July | 2 | " Contribution | . | . | . | . | . | 5 | 9 | 10 |
| | 30 | " " | . | . | . | . | . | 5 | 8 | 2 |
| | | " Cash | . | . | . | . | . | | 11 | 3 |
| Aug. | 27 | " Contribution | . | . | . | . | . | 4 | 5 | 6 |
| Sept. | 24 | " " | . | . | . | . | . | 5 | 8 | 4 |
| Oct. | 22 | " " | . | . | . | . | . | 5 | 1 | 8 |
| | 29 | " Exchange of Silver for Bills | . | . | . | | | 1 | 16 | 0 |
| Nov. | 19 | " Contribution | . | . | . | . | . | 5 | 14 | 0 |
| | | " Cash for Wine | . | . | . | . | | 8 | 7 |
| Dec. | 17 | " Contribution | . | . | . | . | . | 4 | 15 | 8 |
| 1717. | | | | | | | | | | |
| Jan. | 14 | " " | . | . | . | . | . | 5 | 8 | 0 |
| | | " Cash for the poor . | | . | . | . | . | 3 | 0 | 0 |
| Feb. | 11 | " Contribution | . | . | . | . | . | 4 | 16 | 9 |
| May | 6 | " " at several times | . | . | . | . | 10 | 14 | 0 |
| July | 29 | " " " " | . | . | . | . | 15 | 6 | 0 |
| 1718. | | | | | | | | | | |
| Jan. | 13 | " " " " | . | . | . | . | 29 | 16 | 0 |
| | | " Saml. More's legacy Recd. of Mr. Hill and Mr. Foreland, 30 oz. of plate, and Bills of credit . | | | | | | 36 | 3 | 0 |
| | | " Contribution | . | . | . | . | . | 5 | 7 | 0 |
| | | | | | | | | £250 | 18 | 5 |

| | | | £ | s. | d. |
|---|---|---|---|---|---|
| 1718. | | | | | |
| March 16 | To 32 Galls. Green, 21½ Galls. Canary Wine | . | 9 | 9 | 1 |
| June 27 | " Sundry poor . . . . . | . | 13 | 5 | 0 |
| | " Mr. Briscoe for Bread . . . . | . | 3 | 0 | 8 |
| Aug. 1 | " Sundry poor . . . . | . | 2 | 15 | 0 |
| 19 | " 32 Galls. Possada, 32 Galls. Green Wine | . | 11 | 6 | 0 |
| Sept. 24 | " 21½ Galls. Canary, 16 Galls. Medera Wine | . | 9 | 9 | 7½ |
| Oct. 20 | " Sundry poor . . . . | . | 1 | 15 | 0 |
| | " Cash paid for cleaning Linen and Plate | . | 1 | 0 | 0 |
| Nov. 6 | " 32 Galls. Canary, 22 Galls. Green Wine | . | 13 | 5 | 3 |
| Dec. 9 | " Sundry poor . . . . | . | 19 | 2 | 6 |
| 1719. | | | | | |
| April 28 | " Sundry poor at various times . . | . | 17 | 0 | 0 |
| | " 32 Galls. Canary, 32 Galls. Green Wine | . | 16 | 18 | 6 |
| May 18 | " Sundry poor . . . . | . | 1 | 8 | 0 |
| June 2 | " Mr. Briscoe for Bread . . . . | . | 3 | 9 | 4 |
| Aug. 18 | " Sundry poor . . . . | . | 2 | 10 | 0 |
| 21 | " 31½ Galls. Canary, 32 Galls. Green Wine | . | 17 | 18 | 4 |
| 25 | " Cash paid for cleaning Linen and Plate | . | 1 | 0 | 0 |
| 1720. | | | | | |
| Jan. 11 | " Sundry poor at various times . . | . | 17 | 5 | 0 |
| | " 6 Galls. Green Wine . . . | . | 1 | 4 | 0 |
| Feb. 4 | " 23 Galls. Sweet Wine . . . | . | 7 | 3 | 0 |
| May 3 | " Sundry poor . . . . | . | 10 | 10 | 0 |
| | " 23 Galls. Possada, 22 Galls. Green Wine | . | 13 | 2 | 0 |
| Aug. 12 | " Sundry poor . . . . | . | 8 | 15 | 0 |
| | " 31 Galls. Wine . . . . | . | 7 | 3 | 3 |
| 22 | " 3 Galls. Sweet Wine . . . | . | | 18 | 0 |
| Sept. 19 | " Cash paid for cleaning Linen and Plate | . | 1 | 0 | 0 |
| 22 | " 17½ Galls. Possada Wine . . | ; | 6 | 3 | 0 |
| Oct. 20 | " Sundry poor . . . . | . | 5 | 10 | 0 |
| | " paid Col. Townsend 32 Galls. Canary . | . | 12 | 17 | 0 |
| | " Balance carried to New Acct. . . | . | 24 | 15 | 9 |

£260 18 3

|  |  |  |  |  |  |  |  | £ | s. | d. |
|---|---|---|---|---|---|---|---|---|---|---|
| 1718. |  |  |  |  |  |  |  |  |  |  |
|  |  | By Balance brought from Old Acct. . |  |  |  | . | . | 64 | 2 | 1 |
| March 10 |  | " Contribution | . | . | . | . | . | 5 | 8 | 0 |
|  |  | " Cash for the poor . | . | . | . | . | . | 3 | 0 | 0 |
| April | 7 | " Contribution | . | . | . | . | . | 4 | 17 | 10 |
| May | 5 | " " | . | . | . | . | . | 5 | 3 | 2 |
| June | 2 | " " | . | . | . | . | . | 5 | 12 | 6 |
|  | 30 | " " | . | . | . | . | . | 5 | 17 | 8 |
| July | 28 | " " | . | . | . | . | . | 4 | 13 | 10 |
| Aug. | 25 | " " | . | . | . | . | . | 4 | 11 | 10 |
| Sept. | 22 | " " | . | . | . | . | . | 5 | 6 | 0 |
| Oct. | 20 | " " | . | . | . | . | . | 5 | 14 | 2 |
|  |  | " Cash out of the other contributions for wine at Mr. Prince's ordination, the whole being charged then . | | | | . | . | 5 | 17 | 3 |
| Nov. | 17 | " Contribution | . | . | . | . | . | 5 | 6 | 6 |
| Dec. | 15 | " " | . | . | . | . | . | 4 | 19 | 4 |
| 1719. |  |  |  |  |  |  |  |  |  |  |
| Jan. | 12 | " " | . | . | . | . | . | 5 | 3 | 6 |
| Feb. | 9 | " " | . | . | . | . | . | 5 | 0 | 0 |
| March | 9 | " " | . | . | . | . | . | 5 | 14 | 6 |
| April | 6 | " " | . | . | . | . | . | 5 | 9 | 0 |
| May | 4 | " " | . | . | . | . | . | 5 | 7 | 1 |
| June | 2 | " " | . | . | . | . | . | 5 | 9 | 0 |
|  | 29 | " " | . | . | . | . | . | 5 | 13 | 4 |
| July | 27 | " " | . | . | . | . | . | 4 | 6 | 4 |
| Aug. | 24 | " " | . | . | . | . | . | 5 | 0 | 0 |
| Sept. | 21 | " " | . | . | £5. | 0s. | 9d. |  |  |  |
| Oct. | 19 | " " | . | . | . | 4 | 19 | 11 |  |  |
| Nov. | 16 | " " | . | . | . | 5 | 14 | 7 |  |  |
| Dec. | 14 | " " | . | . | . | 4 | 16 | 11 |  |  |
|  |  | " " | to be given some of poor | | | 2 | 0 | 0 | 22 12 2 |  |
| 1720. |  |  |  |  |  |  |  |  |  |  |
| Jan. | 11 | " " | . | . | . | . | . | 4 | 16 | 3 |
| Feb. | 8 | " " | . | . | . | . | . | 4 | 18 | 6 |
| March | 7 | " " | . | . | . | . | . | 5 | 6 | 11 |
| April | 4 | " " | . | . | . | . | . | 5 | 13 | 8 |
| May | 2 | " " | . | . | . | . | . | 5 | 8 | 0 |
|  | 29 | " " | . | . | . | . | . | 6 | 1 | 8 |
| June | 27 | " " | . | . | . | . | . | 5 | 8 | 8 |
| July | 25 | " " | . | . | . | . | . | 5 | 8 | 0 |
| Aug. | 22 | " " | . | . | . | . | . | 5 | 8 | 3 |
| Sept. | 19 | " " | . | . | . | • | . | 5 | 8 | 3 |
| Oct. | 17 | " " | . | . | . | . | . | 6 | 15 | 0 |
|  |  |  |  |  |  |  | £260 | 18 | 3 |  |

|  |  |  |  | £ | s. | d. |
|---|---|---|---|---:|---:|---:|
| 1720. |  |  |  |  |  |  |
| Oct. & Nov. |  | To Sundry poor. | | 7 | 5 | 0 |
| 1721. Jan. | 19 | " Townsend, 31½ Galls. Wine | | 7 | 3 | 3 |
|  |  | " Mending 2 Flaggons. | |  | 1 | 0 |
| Feb. | 8 | " Sundry poor. | | 7 | 15 | 0 |
| May | 1 | " Col. Townsend, 31 Galls. Canary | | 4 | 10 | 0 |
|  |  | " | | 12 | 16 | 0 |
|  |  | " Briscoe for Bread | | 6 | 18 | 8 |
| Oct. | 23 | " Sundry poor. | | 5 | 10 | 0 |
| Nov. | 13 | " Col. Townsend, 31 Galls. Canary, 32 Galls. Fayal | 16 | 17 | 6 |
| 1722. |  |  |  |  |  |  |
| Jan. June & J'ly. |  | " Sundry poor. | | 28 | 5 | 10 |
|  |  | " Balance carried to New Acct. | | 58 | 15 | 8 |
|  |  |  |  | £155 | 17 | 11 |
| 1722. |  |  |  |  |  |  |
| Sept. |  | " Paid Col. Townsend 31½ Galls. Canary | | 11 | 0 | 0 |
| Oct. Nov. & Dec. |  | " Sundry poor. | | 33 | 12 | 0 |
| 1723. April |  | " Mrs. Cook scouring Pewter and washing Linen | £0. 5s. 6d. |  |  |  |
|  | 20 | " 3 Galls. Posada | 19  6 |  |  |  |
| June | 10 | " Briscoe for Bread | 3 17  6 |  |  |  |
|  |  | " Townsend Note for Wine | 12  4  6 |  |  |  |
|  |  | " Mrs. Cooke scouring Pewter, &c. | 9  0 | 17 | 16 | 0 |
| July |  | " Poor. | | 3 | 0 | 2 |
| Aug. | 2 | " paid James Townsend exchanging 21 Galls. prickt Wine for Canary | | 18 | 6 | 6 |
| Nov. | 21 | " Sundry poor. | | 7 | 15 | 0 |
| 1724. Jan. |  | " pd. cleaning Linen, Plate, and Pewter | |  | 7 | 0 |
| March |  | " pd. Col. Townsend 23 Galls. Canary | | 8 | 13 | 2 |
|  |  | " pd. Widow Nicholson after the death of her husband | | 1 | 0 | 0 |
| May |  | " pd. Jas. Townsend for 53 Galls. Canary | | 16 | 0 | 3 |
| June to Nov. |  | " Sundry poor and small charges | | 31 | 9 | 9 |
| 1725. Jan. | 12 | " Sundry poor. | | 17 | 7 | 0 |
| June | 1 | " Cash Mr. Briscoe for Bread. | | 4 | 6 | 8 |
|  | 16 | " 31 Galls. Canary | | 11 | 16 | 3 |
|  | 18 | " Cash pd. for 5 yds. Diaper for the Table | | 3 | 15 | 0 |
|  |  | " " " quarter Cask Canary | | 7 | 17 | 6 |
| Sept. |  | " " " cleaning Linen, &c. | |  | 12 | 6 |
| Oct. | 27 | " Sundry poor. | | 15 | 5 | 0 |
| Nov. |  | " quarter Cask Wine. | | 7 | 17 | 6 |
| Dec. | 5 | " Cash given to Mr. Goddard. | | 2 | 0 | 0 |
| 1726. Jan. | 3 | " Washing | |  | 8 | 6 |
|  |  | " Cash to Mr. Townsend 1 Bbl. Canary | | 12 | 0 | 0 |
|  |  | *Amount carried forward* . | | £232 | 5 | 9 |

|  |  |  | £ | s. | d. |
|---|---|---|---|---|---|
| 1720. | | | | | |
| Oct. | By Balance brought from Old Acct. | | 24 | 15 | 9 |
| Nov. to Feb. | " Contributions | | 22 | 0 | 3 |
| March & April. | " " | | 19 | 19 | 0 |
| May & June. | " " | | 15 | 7 | 11 |
| July & Aug. | " " | | 9 | 13 | 6 |
| Sept. Oct. & Nov. | " " | | 14 | 19 | 11 |
| 1721. | | | | | |
| Dec. to March. | " " | | 18 | 15 | 11 |
| April to June | " " | | 19 | 10 | 10 |
| July & Aug. | " " | | 10 | 14 | 10 |
| | | | £155 | 17 | 11 |
| 1722. | | | | | |
| Oct. 20 | By Balance brought from Old Acct. | | 58 | 15 | 8 |
| Sept. 17 | " Contribution | | 5 | 17 | 5 |
| Oct. 15 | " " | | 6 | 4 | 0 |
| Nov. 12 | " " | | 5 | 0 | 11 |
| Dec. 10 | " " | | 6 | 11 | 10 |
| 12 | " Fifty Pounds Recd. of Mr. Daniels, it being a legacy given by Mr. Simon Daniels for the poor of ye Old S. Church, to be disposed of accordg. to the direction of the Ministers and Deacons of s$^d$ Church (this is ye charge in ye Will) | | 50 | 0 | 0 |
| 1723. | | | | | |
| Jan. 7 | " Contribution | | 5 | 9 | 4 |
| Feb. 4 | " " | | 5 | 7 | 9 |
| March 4 | " " | | 6 | 14 | 6 |
| April 1 | " " | | 5 | 15 | 4 |
| 29 | " " | | 5 | 16 | 0 |
| May 29 | " " | | 6 | 7 | 9 |
| | " Cash for Wine for ye Ministers | | 1 | 7 | 10 |
| June 24 | " Contribution | | 5 | 17 | 6 |
| July 21 | " " | | 5 | 11 | 8 |
| Aug. 19 | " " | | 7 | 8 | 4 |
| Sept. 16 | " " | | 5 | 0 | 7 |
| Oct. 12 | " " | | 6 | 2 | 4 |
| Nov. 11 | " " | | 6 | 2 | 6 |
| Dec. 9 | " " | | 6 | 0 | 0 |
| 1724. | | | | | |
| Jan. 6 | " " | | 5 | 14 | 0 |
| Feb. 3 | " " | | 6 | 4 | 5 |
| | *Amount carried forward* . | | £223 | 9 | 8 |

|  |  |  |  |  |  |  | £ | s. | d. |
|---|---|---|---|---|---|---|---|---|---|
| 1726. |  |  |  |  |  |  |  |  |  |
|  |  | To amount brought forward | . | . | . | . | 232 | 5 | 9 |
| Jan. | 31 | " Sundry poor | . | . | . | . | 16 | 6 | 0 |
| March 28 |  | " Cleaning Linen and Plate | . | . | . |  | 8 | 0 |
|  |  | " Widow Webster . | . | . | . | . | 1 | 0 | 0 |
| April | 18 | " 21 Galls. Canary . | . | . | . | . | 7 | 17 | 6 |
| June | 8 | " Mr. Briscoe for Bread | . | . | . | . | 5 | 4 | 0 |
|  |  | " Poor | . | . | . | . |  | 10 | 0 |
| July | 18 | " 3 Galls. Wine | . | . | . | . |  | 19 | 6 |
| Aug. | 23 | " 35 Galls. Wine | . | . | . | . | 12 | 19 | 6 |
|  |  | " Cleaning Linen and Plate | . | . | . |  | 10 | 0 |
| Nov. | 3 | " Sundry poor | . | . | . | . | 28 | 13 | 0 |
| 1727. |  |  |  |  |  |  |  |  |  |
| Jan. | 3 | " Cleaning Linen and Plate | . | . | . |  | 9 | 0 |
| Feb. | 6 | " quarter Cask Canary | . | . | . | . | 7 | 17 | 6 |
| April |  | " Sundry poor | . | . | . | . | 2 | 0 | 0 |
| June | 6 | " Mr. Briscoe for Bread | . | . | . | . | 6 | 16 | 0 |
|  |  | " Cleaning Linen and Plate | . | . | . |  | 2 | 6 |
|  |  | " 32 Galls. Canary . | . | . | . | . | 12 | 0 | 0 |
|  |  | " Cleaning Linen and Plate | . | . | . |  | 4 | 6 |
| Aug. |  | " Sundry poor | . | . | . | . | 1 | 10 | 0 |
| Oct. | 8 | " Cleaning Linen and Plate | . | . | . |  | 10 | 0 |
|  |  | " 1 Cask Wine | . | . | . | . | 9 | 0 | 0 |
| 1728. |  |  |  |  |  |  |  |  |  |
| Jan. | 1 | " Sundry poor | . | . | . | . | 30 | 14 | 0 |
| April | 23 | " Townsend for Wine | . | . | . | . | 2 | 2 | 0 |
|  |  | " Cleaning Linen and Plate | . | . | . |  | 12 | 6 |
| June | 3 | " Briscoe for Bread | . | . | . | . | 6 | 18 | 6 |
|  |  | " Sundry poor | . | . | . | . | 7 | 15 | 0 |
| Aug. | 13 | " Cleaning Linen and Plate | . | . | . |  | 12 | 6 |
|  |  | " pd. Townsend for Wine . | . | . | . | 16 | 12 | 6 |
| Sept. | 2 | " Sundry poor | . | . | . | . | 5 | 0 | 0 |
|  |  | " Cleaning Linen and Plate | . | . | . |  | 12 | 0 |
| Nov. | 4 | " Townsend for Wine | . | . | . | . | 9 | 15 | 0 |
|  |  | " Sundry poor | . | . | . | . | 12 | 0 | 0 |
|  |  | " pd. Mr. Oliver for Wine . | . | . | . | 8 | 16 | 5 |
| 1729. |  |  |  |  |  |  |  |  |  |
| Feb. | 24 | " Cleaning Linen and Plate | . | . | . | 1 | 0 | 0 |
|  |  | " Townsend's Note for Wine | . | . | . | 13 | 1 | 6 |
| March 15 |  | " Sundry poor | . | . | . | . | 9 | 5 | 0 |
| June | 6 | " Townsend for Wine | . | . | . | . | 11 | 0 | 0 |
|  |  | " Mr. Briscoe for Bread | . | . | . | 6 | 18 | 6 |
|  |  | " Cleaning Linen and Plate | . | . | . | 1 | 10 | 0 |
|  |  | Amount carried forward | . | . | . | £491 | 8 | 2 |

|  |  |  |  |  |  |  |  | £ | s. | d. |
|---|---|---|---|---|---|---|---|---|---|---|
| 1724. |  |  |  |  |  |  |  |  |  |  |
|  |  | *By amount brought forward* | . | . | . | . | . | 223 | 9 | 8 |
| March | 2 | " Contribution | . | . | . | . | . | 6 | 10 | 0 |
|  | 30 | " " | . | . | . | . | . | 6 | 2 | 0 |
| April | 26 | " " | . | . | . | . | . | 5 | 11 | 8 |
| May |  | " " | . | . | . | . | . | 6 | 11 | 0 |
|  | 26 | " Money for Wine for ye Ministers |  |  | . | . | 1 | 8 | 0 |
| June | 26 | " Contribution | . | . | . | . | . | 6 | 6 | 2 |
| July | 21 | " " | . | . | . | . | . | 8 | 6 | 0 |
| Aug. | 17 | " " | . | . | . | . | . | 5 | 18 | 10 |
| Sept. | 14 | " " | . | . | . | . | . | 6 | 18 | 11 |
| Oct. | 12 | " " | . | . | . | . | . | 5 | 6 | 6 |
| Nov. | 9 | " " | . | . | . | . | . | 7 | 10 | 1 |
| Dec. | 7 | " " | . | . | . | . | . | 6 | 12 | 0 |
| 1725. |  |  |  |  |  |  |  |  |  |  |
| Jan. | 4 | " " | . | . | . | . | . | 5 | 15 | 1 |
|  |  | " Recd. of Mr. John Walley Twenty pounds m⁰, it being a legacy left by his father, to ye South Church for ye poor of s$^d$ church |  |  |  | . | . | 20 | 0 | 0 |
| Feb. | 1 | " Contribution | . | . | . | . | . | 6 | 1 | 1 |
| March | 1 | " " | . | . | . | . | . | 5 | 7 | 0 |
| May | 24 | " " at several times | . | . | . | 20 | 17 | 9 |
|  |  | " Wine taken out of stock for ye Ministers |  |  |  | . |  | 12 | 0 |
| 1726. |  |  |  |  |  |  |  |  |  |  |
| May | 23 | " Contributions at sundry times | . | . | . | 103 | 11 | 11 |
|  |  | " Canary for ye Ministers | . | . | . | . | 1 | 12 | 0 |
| 1727. |  |  |  |  |  |  |  |  |  |  |
| March | 27 | " Contributions at sundry times | . | . | . | 89 | 14 | 11 |
| Dec. | 3 | " " " | . | . | . | 71 | 8 | 11 |
| 1728. |  |  |  |  |  |  |  |  |  |  |
| Dec. | 30 | " " " | . | . | . | 126 | 17 | 5 |
| 1729. |  |  |  |  |  |  |  |  |  |  |
| Dec. | 29 | " " " | . | . | . | 87 | 6 | 2 |

*Amount carried forward* . . . £885 15 1

|  |  |  |  | £ | s. | d. |
|---|---|---|---|---|---|---|
| 1729. | | | | | | |
| | To Amount brought forward | . | . | 491 | 8 | 2 |
| Sept. 9 | " Townsend for Wine | . | . | 10 | 10 | 0 |
| | " Sundries | . | . | | 10 | 0 |
| 1730. | | | | | | |
| Jan. 26 | " Sundry poor | . | . | 13 | 10 | 0 |
| | " Cleaning Linen and Plate | . | . | 1 | 2 | 0 |
| March 2 | " Townsend for Wine | . | . | 15 | 0 | 0 |
| May 11 | " Sundry poor | . | . | 5 | 8 | 6 |
| | " Townsend for Wine | . | . | 7 | 13 | 0 |
| | " Mr. Briscoe for Bread | . | . | 6 | 0 | 0 |
| | " 2 Bbls. and 64 Galls. Wine | . | . | 29 | 0 | 6 |
| Oct. 5 | " Sundry poor | . | . | 15 | 15 | 8 |
| | " Balance to New Acct. | . | . | 346 | 8 | 5 |
| | | | | £942 | 6 | 3 |
| 1733. | | | | | | |
| Oct. 27 | To Cash pd. at sundry times for Wine to date | . | | 105 | 0 | 0 |
| | "    "    for Charitable purposes | . | | 293 | 6 | 0 |
| | " Balance to New Acct. | . | . | 422 | 3 | 6 |
| | | | | £820 | 9 | 6 |
| 1734. | | | | | | |
| Oct. 27 | To Cash pd. for Wine to date | . | . | 107 | 14 | 6 |
| | "    "    for Sundry Charitable purposes | . | | 198 | 1 | 7 |
| 1735. | | | | | | |
| Oct. 28 | " Balance to New Acct. | . | . | 441 | 11 | 0 |
| | | | | £747 | 7 | 1 |
| 1738. | | | | | | |
| Nov. 21 | To Cash pd. for Wine to date | . | . | 192 | 4 | 0 |
| | "    "    for Sundry Charitable purposes, &c. | . | | 261 | 14 | 10 |
| | " Balance to New Acct. | . | . | 549 | 6 | 10 |
| | | | | £1,003 | 5 | 8 |

|  |  |  | £ | s. | d. |
|---|---|---|---|---|---|
| 1730. | | | | | |
| | *By Balance brought forward* . . . . | | 835 | 15 | 1 |
| Feb. 23 | " Contributions at sundry times . . . | | 16 | 9 | 3 |
| March 19 | " Cash Recd. of Mr. Willard, a legacy left by Madam Saltonstall . . . . | | 20 | 0 | 0 |
| Nov. 2 | " Contributions . . . . . | | 70 | 1 | 11 |
| | | | £942 | 6 | 3 |

| | | | | | |
|---|---|---|---|---|---|
| 1730. | | | | | |
| | By Balance from Old Acct. . . . . | | 346 | 8 | 5 |
| 1733. | | | | | |
| March 5 | " Cash of Mrs. Manley, being a legacy left by Mr. Wm. Manley to the poor of So. Church . | | 20 | 0 | 0 |
| Oct. 1 | " Cash Recd. of John Maylem, it being so much given by his father Mr. Joseph Maylem, to be disposed of by the Deacons for the poor of the O. S. Church according to their best discretion. (Recd. Sept. 13) . . . | | 20 | 0 | 0 |
| 27 | " Contributions at sundry times . . . | | 434 | 1 | 1 |
| | | | £820 | 9 | 6 |

| | | | | | |
|---|---|---|---|---|---|
| 1733. | | | | | |
| Oct. 27 | By Balance from Old Acct. . . . . | | 422 | 3 | 6 |
| | " Contributions to date . . . . | | 325 | 3 | 7 |
| | | | £747 | 7 | 1 |

| | | | | | |
|---|---|---|---|---|---|
| 1735. | | | | | |
| Oct. 28 | By Balance from Old Acct. . . . . | | 441 | 11 | 0 |
| 1737. | | | | | |
| Nov. 3 | " Cash Recd. of Jonas Clark, it being so much left the poor of the church by Mrs. Abigail Duckaloone in her Will . . . . | | 5 | 0 | 0 |
| 1738. | | | | | |
| Oct. 20 | " Contributions to date . . . | | 556 | 14 | 8 |
| | | | £1,003 | 5 | 8 |

|  |  |  |  | £ | s. | d. |
|---|---|---|---|---:|---:|---:|
| 1743. | | | | | | |
| July | 9 | To Cash paid for Wine to date | . . . | 460 | 18 | 6 |
| Sept. | 4 | " Sundry poor, &c. . | . . . . | 120 | 8 | 7 |
| | | " Balance to New Acct. | . . . | 513 | 6 | 1 |
| | | | | £1,094 | 13 | 2 |
| 1746. | | | | | | |
| May | | To Cash paid for Wine to date | . . . | 289 | 1 | 0 |
| | | " Sundry poor, &c. . | . . . . | 165 | 15 | 8 |
| | | " Balance to New Acct. | . . . | 676 | 19 | 3 |
| | | | | £1,131 | 15 | 11 |
| 1746. | | | | | | |
| July | | To Cash paid for Wine to date | . . . | 641 | 4 | 1 |
| 1747. | | | | | | |
| May | 24 | " entertaining Ministers at Dr. Sewall's | . . | 7 | 13 | 0 |
| Nov. | | " Journey to Ipswich to Mr. Walley's ordination | . | 15 | 10 | 0 |
| 1748. | | | | | | |
| May | | " Cash for Convention at Ministers' houses | . | 8 | 15 | 0 |
| July | | "  "  " Horse hire for Com. to Ipswich . | . | 22 | 14 | 10 |
| Oct. | | "  "  "  "  "  " counsel to Medford | . | 10 | 0 | 0 |
| 1749. | | | | | | |
| June | | "  "  " Wine and for ministers at convention | . | 16 | 7 | 0 |
| July | 6 | "  " lent out of this stock July 6, 1747, to pay off the deficiency of our Ministers, as per Vote of the church | . . . . | 192 | 0 | 0 |
| | | " Sundry poor to date | . . . | 373 | 16 | 2 |
| | | " Balance to New Acct. | . . . | 330 | 1 | 0 |
| | | | | £1,618 | 1 | 1 |
| 1751. | | | | | | |
| Nov. | 4 | To Cash paid for Wine to date | . . | 447 | 14 | 0 |
| May | 19 | "  "  " 2 Horses and travelling expenses to attend the Council at Northampton | . | 56 | 3 | 2 |
| 1751. | | | | | | |
| Nov. | | " Sundry poor, &c. . | . . . | 256 | 4 | 0 |
| | | " Balance to New Acct. | . . . | 427 | 7 | 9 |
| | | | | £1,187 | 8 | 11 |

|   |   |   | £ | s. | d. |
|---|---|---|---:|---:|---:|
| 1738. | | | | | |
| Nov. 31 | By Balance brought from Old Acct. | . | 549 | 6 | 10 |
| 1743. | | | | | |
| Aug. 21 | " Contributions | . | 545 | 6 | 4 |
| | | | £1,094 | 13 | 2 |
| | | | | | |
| 1743. | | | | | |
| Sept. 4 | By Balance from Old Acct. | . | 513 | 6 | 1 |
| 1746. | | | | | |
| April 28 | " Contributions | . | 618 | 9 | 10 |
| | | | £1,131 | 15 | 11 |
| | | | | | |
| 1746. | | | | | |
| April 28 | By Balance from Old Acct. | . | 676 | 19 | 3 |
| 1749. | | | | | |
| May 29 | " Contribution | . | 941 | 1 | 10 |
| | | | £1,618 | 1 | 1 |
| | | | | | |
| 1749. | | | | | |
| June | By Balance from Old Acct. | . | 330 | 1 | 0 |
| 1751. | | | | | |
| Nov. 4 | " Contributions | . | 857 | 7 | 11 |
| | | | £1,187 | 8 | 11 |

|  |  |  |  | £ | s. | d. |
|---|---|---|---|---|---|---|
| 1753. |  |  |  |  |  |  |
| Oct. 13 | To Cash paid for Wine to date | . | . | 265 | 14 | 0 |
| 1752. |  |  |  |  |  |  |
| May 17 | " 360 £ Old Tenor, it was for Old Bills burnt, and Interest, Recd. from Treasurer Foye in dollars, and now vested in committee's notes to draw Interest from the Province, being $160 amº to 360 £ as above. | . | . | 360 | 0 | 0 |
| 1753. |  |  |  |  |  |  |
| Oct. | " Sundry poor | . | . | 241 | 19 | 0 |
|  | " Balance to New Acct. | . | . | 126 | 1 | 9 |
|  |  |  |  | £993 | 14 | 9 |

| 1755. |  |  |  |  |  |  |
|---|---|---|---|---|---|---|
| Jan. 12 | To Cash paid for Wine to date | . | . | 206 | 14 | 6 |
|  | " Sundry poor | . | . | 143 | 15 | 2 |
|  | " Balance to New Acct. | . | . | 716 | 9 | 5 |
|  | Memº, pd. Mr. Oliver £225 for a Province Note of £30 out of Stock. |  |  |  |  |  |
|  |  |  |  | £1,066 | 19 | 1 |

|  |  |  | £ | s. | d. |
|---|---|---|---|---|---|
| 1751. Dec. 1 | By Balance from Old Acct. | | 427 | 7 | 9 |
| 1752. May 17 | " Recd. from the Treasurer 20 £ Old Tenor, being for Int. of 340 £ Old Tenor burnt by committee, and Recd. Order on Mr. Foye for. | | 20 | 0 | 0 |
| 1753. Oct. 15 | " Contributions | | 546 | 7 | 0 |
| | | | £993 | 14 | 9 |

|  |  |  | £ | s. | d. |
|---|---|---|---|---|---|
| 1753. Oct. 15 | By Balance from Old Acct. | | 126 | 1 | 9 |
| 1755. Feb. 26 | " Contributions, including Province Notes in my hands which I made this Acct. Dr. for in 1752, £360 | | 940 | 17 | 4 |
| | | | £1,066 | 19 | 1 |

1755.
Feb. 28  By Balance of the foregoing Acct. adjusted with the committee this day, of which there is in my hands five hundred and eighty-five pounds Old Tenor in Province Notes to draw Interest. Old Tenor . . . . . £716 9 5

1755.
Feb. 28  We have examined the foregoing Acct. from the settlement in 1722, and find the same right cast.

       ANDREW OLIVER, ⎫
       ISAAC WALKER, ⎬ *Committee.*
       WILLIAM PHILLIPS, ⎭

|  |  |  |  |  | £ | s. | d. |
|---|---|---|---|---|---|---|---|
| 1755. |  |  |  |  |  |  |  |
| Feb. 28 | To Amount paid Mr. Oliver for a Note of £30 to draw Interest from Province . . . |  |  |  | 225 | 0 | 0 |
| 1757. |  |  |  |  |  |  |  |
| Nov. | " Cash pd. for Wine to date . . . |  |  |  | 526 | 15 | 3 |
| 1760–1. |  |  |  |  |  |  |  |
| April 4 | " " " " . . . |  |  |  | 882 | 5 | 6 |
| Dec. 7 | " 160 Dolls. included in a Province Note is . . . | £360. | 0s. | 0d. |  |  |  |
|  | " 80 Dolls. included in a Province Note is . . . | 180 | 0 | 0 |  |  |  |
|  | 2 Province Notes of £6. 2s. and 1 of £8. 5s. 1d. . . | 107 | 13 | 1 | 647 | 13 | 1 |
| Dec. | " Sundry poor, &c. . . . |  |  |  | 918 | 5 | 8 |
|  | " Cash paid Thos. Hubbard in full . |  |  |  | 239 | 1 | 8 |
|  |  |  |  |  | £3,439 | 1 | 2 |
| 1761. |  |  |  |  |  |  |  |
| Dec. 6 | To Cash paid for Wine . . . . |  |  |  | 272 | 16 | 3 |
|  | " Sundry poor . . . . . |  |  |  | 235 | 18 | 10½ |
|  | " Balance to New Acct. . . . |  |  |  | 219 | 11 | 5 |
|  |  |  |  |  | £728 | 6 | 6½ |
| 1763. |  |  |  |  |  |  |  |
| Nov. 1 | To Cash paid for Wine . . . |  |  |  | 458 | 15 | 0 |
|  | " Sundry poor . . . . |  |  |  | 240 | 14 | 0 |
|  | " Balance to New Acct. pd. to Dr. Jeffries |  |  |  | 315 | 10 | 0 |
|  |  |  | Old Tenor, | £1,014 | 19 | 0 |
| 1765. |  |  |  |  |  |  |  |
| Jan. 14 | To Cash paid for Wine, Old Tenor . |  |  |  | 94 | 10 | 0 |
|  | " Sundry appropriations, mostly to poor . |  |  |  | 418 | 18 | 9 |
|  |  |  |  |  | £513 | 8 | 9 |
|  | Which in Lawful Money is . . |  |  |  | 68 | 9 | 2 |
| Feb. 23 | " Cash paid for Wine . . | £157. | 10s. | 0d. |  |  |  |
|  | " Sundry appropriations . . | 66 | 10 | 0 |  |  |  |
|  |  | 224 | 0 | 0 | 29 | 17 | 4 |
| Sept. 1 | " Sundry appropriations . . | 106 | 17 | 0 |  |  |  |
|  | " Cash pd. Bro. Phillips and J. Sewall in addition to Church Stock | 195 | 10 | 1½ |  |  |  |
|  |  | 302 | 7 | 1½ | 40 | 6 | 3 |
|  | " Mending Flagon . . . |  |  |  |  |  | 8 |
| Nov. 25 | " Sundry appropriations . . . |  |  |  | 15 | 14 | 0¼ |
|  |  |  |  |  | £154 | 7 | 5¼ |
|  | To Balance due to Mr. Phillips . |  |  |  | £4 | 9 | 2¾ |

|  |  |  | £ | s. | d. |
|---|---|---|---|---|---|
| 1755.<br>Feb. 28 | By Balance brought forward as adjusted by the Committee . . . . . | | 716 | 9 | 5 |
|  | By Province Notes in my hands to draw Interest, part of the above Bal. £585., the remainder in Common Stock. | | | | |
| 1757.<br>Nov. 6 | " Contributions . . . . | | 1,091 | 17 | 9 |
| 1761.<br>Jan. 23 | " Int. of £360. and £225. to 1st June, 1758, ye date of ye Note . . £180. 0s. 0d. | | | | |
|  | " Int. one year of £116. 7s. 1d., or £872. 13s. 1d. . . . | 52  7  2½ | 232 | 7 | 2½ |
|  | " Contributions . . . . | | 1,398 | 6 | 9½ |
|  | | | £3,439 | 1 | 2 |
| 1761. | By Cash Recd. of former Treasurer . | | 239 | 1 | 8 |
| 1762.<br>Feb. 21 | " Contributions . . . . | | 489 | 4 | 10½ |
|  | | | £728 | 6 | 6½ |
| 1762.<br>Feb. 21 | By Balance from Old Acct. . . | | 219 | 11 | 5 |
| 1763.<br>Oct. 30 | " Contributions . . . . | | 795 | 7 | 7 |
|  | Old Tenor, | £1,014 | 19 | 0 |
| 1765.<br>Feb. 6 | By Contributions . . | £664. 11s. 10½d. | 88 | 12 | 2½ |
| Sept. 1 | "    " . . | 302  7  1½ | 40 | 6 | 3 |
| Dec. 22 | "    " . . | 157  8  0½ | 20 | 19 | 9 |
|  | " Balance carried to New Account . . | | 4 | 9 | 2¾ |
|  | | | £154 | 7 | 5¼ |
|  | By Balance Carried to Wm. Phillips, Cr. . | . | £4 | 9 | 2¾ |

Jan. 1, 1766. We have examined the above Acct., and find the same right cast and well vouched.   ANDREW OLIVER.
      THOS. HUBBARD.
      JOSHUA WINSLOW.

| | | | | | | £ | s. | d. |
|---|---|---|---|---|---|---|---|---|
| 1766. | | | | | | | | |
| Aug. | 31 | To sundry appropriations | . £261. 12s. 4½d. | | | 34 | 17 | 7¾ |
| Dec. | 30 | " Cash paid for Wine | | | | 50 | 0 | 0 |
| | | " Sundry appropriations | | | | 15 | 15 | 1 |
| | | | | | | £100 | 12 | 8¾ |

| | | | | | |
|---|---|---|---|---|---|
| 1767. | | | | | |
| Dec. | 29 | To Cash pd. for Wine | 19 | 5 | 0 |
| | | " Sundry appropriations | 41 | 2 | 4 |
| | | " Balance carried to New Acct. | 22 | 7 | 9¼ |
| | | Balance in the hands of D. J. is £0. 7s. 3½d. | | | |
| | | "      "      "    W. P. is 22 0 5¾ | | | |
| | | | £82 | 15 | 1¼ |

| | | | | | |
|---|---|---|---|---|---|
| 1769. | | | | | |
| Aug. | 28 | To Cash paid for Wine | 63 | 14 | 0 |
| | | " Sundry appropriations | 67 | 9 | 9½ |
| | | " Bal. carried to Debit of Wm. Phillips | 41 | 19 | 8½ |
| | | | £173 | 3 | 5 |

| | | | | | |
|---|---|---|---|---|---|
| 1771. | | | | | |
| Jan. | 8 | To Cash pd. for Wine | 37 | 16 | 0 |
| | | " Sundry appropriations | 88 | 7 | 3 |
| | | " Bal. carried to Debt. of Wm. Phillips | 18 | 1 | 6 |
| | | | £144 | 4 | 9 |

|  |  |  |  |  |  | £ | s. | d. |
|---|---|---|---|---|---|---|---|---|
| 1766. | | | | | | | | |
| Aug. 31 | By Contributions | . | . | . £368. 7s. 1½d. | | 49 | 2 | 3½ |
| | " " | . | . | . | . | 20 | 18 | 0½ |
| | " Bal. to Wm. Phillips, Cr. | . | . | . | | 30 | 12 | 4¾ |
| | | | | | | £100 | 12 | 8¾ |

Jan. 1, 1767. We have examined the above Acct., and find the same right cast and well vouched.      ANDREW OLIVER.
                 THOMAS HUBBARD.
                 JOSHUA WINSLOW.

1767.
Aug. 30   By Recd. of Bro. Sewall £2. 9s. 9⅖d., being the
      Bal. of his Acct., for which I am accountable.
Dec. 20   " Contributions   .   .   .   .   .    82   15   1¼

                  £82   15   1¼

1768.
Jan.    By Balance from Old Acct.   .   .   .    22   7   9¼
Aug.    " Contributions   .   .   .   .    150   15   7¾

                  £173   3   5

1771.
Dec. 16   By Contributions   .   .   .   .   .    144   4   9

                  £144   4   9

* Boston, Jan. 8, 1771. We have examined the above Acct., and find the same right cast and well vouched.     ANDREW OLIVER.
                 THOMAS HUBBARD.
                 JOHN WINSLOW.

|  |  |  | £ | s. | d. |
|---|---|---|---|---|---|
| 1771. Jan. | } To sundry appropriations | . . . | 38 | 2 | 3 |
| 1773. June | } " Cash for Wine . . . . | | 79 | 9 | 0 |
| | | | £117 | 11 | 3 |

| 1771. May 11 | } To sundry appropriations . . | . £31 | 18 | 7 |
|---|---|---|---|---|
| 1772. June 30 | | | | |

| 1771. May | } To sundry appropriations, including a Catalogue of Dr. Sewall's Library, £3. 12s. 0d. . | . £20 | 3 | 7 |
|---|---|---|---|---|
| 1773. Aug. 31 | | | | |

| 1772. Sept. | } To this sum brought from above . . . | 31 | 18 | 7 |
|---|---|---|---|---|
| 1773. Sept. | } " Sundry appropriations, including expenses of Pastors and Delegates to Bolton in June and Aug. £5. 15s. 6d. . . . | 26 | 3 | 4½ |
| | | £58 | 1 | 11½ |

| To Cash paid, &c., per David Jeffries, as per Acct. | 58 | 1 | 11½ |
|---|---|---|---|
| " " per Jona. Mason . . . . | 20 | 3 | 7 |
| " " " Wm. Phillips . . . . | 117 | 11 | 3 |
| " Bal. carried to the Debt. of Wm. Phillips's Acct. | 21 | 13 | 3¾ |
| | £217 | 10 | 1¼ |

|  |  | £ | s. | d. |
|---|---|---|---|---|
| 1771.<br>Jan. 13<br>1773.<br>April 3 } By Contributions. | | 71 | 1 | 4 |
| | | £71 | 1 | 4 |

| 1771.<br>Sept.<br>Nov. } By Contributions. | £26 | 10 | 9¼ |
|---|---|---|---|

| 1771.<br>May 5<br>1773.<br>Aug. 23 } By Contributions in Old Tenor money. | £445. 1s. 11½<br>247 12 0 | £92 | 7 | 2 |
|---|---|---|---|---|

| 1772.<br>Sept. 20<br>Dec. } By this Sum from above. | | 26 | 10 | 9¼ |
|---|---|---|---|---|
| " Collections. | | 27 | 10 | 10 |
| | | 54 | 1 | 7¼ |
| 1773.<br>Sept. 29 " Cash of Dea. Phillips. | | 4 | 0 | 4¼ |
| | | £58 | 1 | 11½ |

| By Contributions Recd. by David Jeffries as per the above Accounts | 54 | 1 | 7¼ |
|---|---|---|---|
| " ditto per Jona. Mason | 92 | 7 | 2 |
| " " " Wm. Phillips | 71 | 1 | 4 |
| | £217 | 10 | 1¼ |

Boston, September 30, 1773. We have examined the above Account, and find the same right cast and well vouched.     JOHN SCOLLAY.
HENDERSON INCHES.
THOMAS DAWES.

|  |  |  | £ | s. | d. |
|---|---|---|---:|---:|---:|
| 1773. Sept. 1774. Aug. | } To sundry appropriations | | 32 | 17 | 6 |
| 1775. March | "   "   "   not added up in Old Book | | 13 | 0 | 0¾ |
| | | | £45 | 17 | 6¾ |

| | | | | | |
|---|---|---|---:|---:|---:|
| 1774 to 1778. | To sundry appropriations | | 35 | 7 | 11 |
| | " Cash pd. for Wine | | 37 | 16 | 0 |
| 1779. Feb. | 13 | " pd. David Jeffries in part Sac. Coll., as per receipt | 25 | 0 | 0 |
| Nov. | 8 | " do. as per receipt for Bal. of his Acct. | 85 | 10 | 9 |
| Dec. | 15 | "   "   " | 31 | 0 | 0 |
| 1780. Aug. | 14 | " Saml. Conant, Bread Bill | 50 | 8 | 0 |
| Sept. | 15 | " Jona. Williams 2½ Galls. [casks?] Wine, £28. | 70 | 0 | 0 |
| | | Amo. of the above four last entries paid in Paper Money .   £236. 8s. 9d. | £335 | 2 | 8 |
| | | To Balance Lawful Money, £1. 11s. 11d., 75 for 1 | 119 | 13 | 6 |
| | | | £454 | 16 | 2 |

| | | | | | |
|---|---|---|---:|---:|---:|
| 1783 to 1784. | To sundry appropriations | | 3 | 11 | 8 |
| | " David Jeffries as per Acct. | | 15 | 0 | 0 |
| July | 31 | " Wine, Rum, Sugar, Lemons, Pipes, and Tobacco, sent by D. J. to Rev. Mr. Eckley on the convention, as per Bill. | 2 | 13 | 0 |
| 1783. April | 1 | " D. Jeffries, as per Acct. | 20 | 4 | 8 |
| | | " Balance carried to Debt. of W. Phillips | 31 | 12 | 6 |
| | | | £73 | 1 | 10 |

| | | | | | |
|---|---|---|---:|---:|---:|
| 1785. May | | To Wine, Spirit, Pipes, &c., supplied Rev. Mr. Eckley by Bro. Jeffries — convention | 2 | 5 | 8 |
| | | " pd. for 1 cask Lisbon Wine | 9 | 12 | 0 |
| | | " Sundry Contributions. | 38 | 15 | 2 |
| | | | £50 | 12 | 10 |

|   |   |   |   |   |
|---|---|---|---|---|
| 1773. } By Collections, Old Tenor | £194. 16s. 2½d. | | £ s. d. | |
| 1774. Dec. 11 | | 167 11 6 | | |
| | | £362 7 8½ | 48 6 4½ | |
| | | | £48 6 4½ | |
| 1774 to 1780. By Collections | £454. 16s. 2d. | | | |
| 1778. Aug. " Recd. in Paper Money | 409 13 1 | | | |
| Amo. as above | | | 454 16 2 | |
| | | | £454 16 2 | |
| 1781. By Balance of Acct. in lawful money | | | 1 11 11 | |
| 1783. Dec. " Collections | | | 71 9 11 | |
| | | | £73 1 10 | |
| 1785. By 13 Collections at the Sacrament the year past, as appears by the Contribution Book | | | 45 2 3 | |
| 1789. Feb. 23 " Bal. carried to Cr. of Wm. Phillips | | | 5 10 7 | |
| | | | £50 12 10 | |

## Old South Church to Thos. Hubbard.

| 1763. | | Old Tenor. | £ | s. | d. |
|---|---|---|---|---|---|
| To Bal. of Friday evg. Lecture Acct. of Light, | | £29. 6s. 0d. | | | |
| " Bal. of Thanksgiving Collection | | 6 14 5 | 4 | 16 | 0¾ |
| " Cash paid Minister's Salary, Wood, &c., since last Ex. | | 13,825 0 2½ | | | |
| " Cash pd. Coms. for Repairing Dr. Sewall's house, Bal. | | 334 7 4 | 1,887 | 18 | 4 |
| " Cash in hand, being Stock in Bonds, Notes, &c. | | | 513 | 14 | 3 |
| " Bal. due to church, which waits their order | | | 72 | 14 | 4 |
| | | | £2,479 | 2 | 11¾ |

### David Jeffries.

| | £ | s. | d. |
|---|---|---|---|
| To Sundries belonging to So. Church Stock, Recd. of Dea. Hubbard; viz.,— | | | |
|     James Mirrick's Bond | 17 | 7 | 9 |
|     Joseph Garfield's " | 22 | 16 | 8 |
|     Daniel Whitney's " | 29 | 4 | 0 |
|     Wm. Smith's " | 22 | 5 | 10 |
|     Roger McKnight's Note | 4 | 0 | 0 |
|     Treasurer's Notes | 418 | 0 | 0 |
|     Cash Bal. of Sacramental Stock, Folio 6, £315. 10s. is | 42 | 1 | 4 |
|     Bal. of Acct. of Int. Folio | 35 | 9 | 0¾ |
| | £591 | 4 | 7¾ |
| From which deduct £4. 16s. 0¾ chgd. in Mr. Hubbard's Acct. settled, which is copied in this book, Folio | 4 | 16 | 0¾ |
| | 586 | 8 | 7 |
| To Receipts at sundry times:— | | | |
|     Mrs. Mary Ireland's Legacy | 133 | 6 | 8 |
|     John Simpson's " | 30 | 0 | 0 |
|     Pious and Charitable fund | 2 | 13 | 2¼ |
|     Rev. Dr. Sewall's donation | 20 | 0 | 0 |
|     Int. Recd. of Whitney | 8 | 13 | 1¾ |
|     " " Mirrick | 1 | 0 | 11 |
|     " " McKnight | | 4 | 9½ |
|     Int. on Treasurer's Note to June 30, 1764 | 21 | 1 | 10 |
| | £803 | 9 | 1½ |

## Contra.

| 1763. | | £ | s. | d. |
|---|---|---|---|---|
| Dec. 1 | By Stock belonging to the South Church, in Bonds, Notes, &c. | 513 | 14 | 3 |
| | " Cash Recd. per contra since the last Acct. was settled | 1,887 | 18 | 4 |
| | " Bal. of Sacramental Stock | 42 | 1 | 4 |
| | " Bal. of Acct. of Int. Recd. | 35 | 9 | 0¾ |
| | | £2,479 | 2 | 11¾ |

Boston, 1 Dec., 1763.
    Errors excepted.             THOMAS HUBBARD.

## Contra.

| 1764. | | £ | s. | d. |
|---|---|---|---|---|
| Nov. | By Cash, Bonds, and Notes, as per Dea. Phillips's receipt. | | | |
| | " Mrs. Mary Ireland's Legacy | 133 | 6 | 8 |
| | " A Treasurer's Note | 460 | 0 | 0 |
| | " James Mirrick's Bond | 17 | 7 | 9 |
| | " Joseph Garfield's " | 22 | 16 | 8 |
| | " Daniel Whitney's " | 29 | 4 | 0 |
| | " Wm. Smith's " | 22 | 5 | 10 |
| | " Roger McKnight's Note | 4 | 0 | 0 |
| | " Rev. Dr. Sewall's donation | 20 | 0 | 0 |
| | " John Simpson's Legacy | 30 | 0 | 0 |
| | " Int. paid by Mr. Mirrick | 1 | 0 | 11 |
| | " Int. " " Mr. Whitney | 8 | 13 | 1¾ |
| | " Int. " " McKnight | | 4 | 9½ |
| | " Charitable Fund, £19. 19s. 0d. Old Tenor | 2 | 13 | 2¼ |
| | " 170 Dolls. | 51 | 0 | 0 |
| | " Bal. of the cost of a Flagon given by the late John Simpson | | 6 | 0 |
| | " Cash paid his Bro. Phillips Bal. hereof | | 10 | 2 |
| | | £803 | 9 | 1½ |

## William Phillips.

| | | | £ | s. | d. | £ | s. | d. |
|---|---|---|---|---|---|---|---|---|
| 1764. | | | | | | | | |
| Nov. 6 | To Cash Recd. of Bro. Jeffries, per recpt.; viz.,— | | | | | | | |
| | Rev. Dr. Sewall's Gift | £20. 0s. 0d. | | | | | | |
| | John Simpson's Legacy | 30 0 0 | | | | | | |
| | Int. Recd. of D. Whitney | 8 13 1¾ | | | | | | |
| | " " " Mirrick | 1 0 11 | | | | | | |
| | " " " McKnight | 4 9½ | | | | | | |
| | Charitable Fund | 2 13 2¼ | | | | | | |
| | 170 Dollars | 51 0 0 | | | | | | |
| | | 113 12 0½ | | | | | | |
| | To Mary Ireland's Legacy | 133 6 8 | | | | | | |
| 29 | " Pious and Charitable Fund | 2 6 0 | | | | | | |
| 1765. | | | | | | | | |
| March 7 | " One quarter's Int. on Treasurer's Note No. 15 | 6 0 0 | | | | 255 | 4 | 8½ |
| 11 | " A Treas. Note payable to him | 460 0 0 | | | | | | |
| | " 8 m. 11 days' Int. on do. from 4 June | 19 4 10 | | | | | | |
| | " 1 payable to John Gould | 16 0 0 | | | | | | |
| | " 9 m. 7 days' Int. on do. | 14 9 | | | | | | |
| | " 1 Treas. Note payable to A. Oliver | 100 0 0 | | | | | | |
| | " 20 days' Int. on do. from 19 Feb. | 6 8 | | | | 596 | 6 | 3 |
| Oct. 2 | " Cash Recd. of Bro. Sewall | 26 1 4 | | | | | | |
| 23 | " " 1 yr.'s Int. on 2 Treas. Notes, Nos. 126 and 376, amt. £779. | 46 14 9 | | | | | | |
| | " 1 yr.'s Int. on J. Mirrick's, due 19 Sept., 1764 | 1 0 11 | | | | | | |
| | " 1 yr.'s Int. on Jona. Simpson's, due 11 March, 1764 | 1 6 10 | | | | 75 | 3 | 10 |
| | | | | | | £926 | 14 | 9½ |
| | To Bal. of above Acct. | | | | | 9 | 11 | 0 |
| Dec. 5 | " Pious and Charitable Fund | | | | | 2 | 0 | 0 |
| 22 | " Cash Recd. of Bro. Jeffries, Bal. of his Acct., folio 35 | | | | | | 10 | 2 |
| 1766. | | | | | | | | |
| Aug. 31 | " Cash of Bro. Sewall | | | | | 21 | 4 | 0¾ |
| | " " for a Treasurer's, No. 126 | | | | | 49 | 0 | 0 |
| | " Int. on do. from June 10, 1765, to July, 1766 | | | | | 3 | 4 | 10 |
| | " Treasurer's Note, No. 376 | | | | | 730 | 0 | 0 |
| | " Int. on do. from Oct. 23, 1765, to July 17, 1766 | | | | | 32 | 2 | 5 |
| | " 1 yr.'s Int. of James Merrick | | | | | 1 | 0 | 11 |
| Dec. 15 | " A Treasurer's Note, No. 108 | | | | | 820 | 0 | 0 |
| | " Int. on do. from July 17, 4 mos. 28 d. | | | | | 16 | 17 | 0 |
| | " Bal due to Wm. Phillips to New Acct. | | | | | 60 | 0 | 11¾ |
| | | | | | | £1,745 | 11 | 4½ |

## Contra.

| 1764. | | | | £ | s. | d. |
|---|---|---|---|---|---|---|
| Aug. 21 | By a Treasurer's Note, No. 126, dated June 10, 1763, payable to Eleazer Porter, Esq. £49. 0s. 0d. | | | | | |
| | " Int. 2 m. 11 days on do. | | 11 6½ | 49 | 11 | 6½ |
| Nov. 26 | " 1 Note payable to Jno. Gould | | 16 0 0 | | | |
| | " Int. 5 m. 22 days | | 9 0 | | | |
| | " 1 Note payable to Andrew Oliver. | | 100 0 0 | | | |
| | " Int. 9 m. 7 days | | 4 12 4 | 121 | 1 | 4 |
| 1765. | | | | | | |
| March 11 | " 1 Note, No. 376, dated 23 Oct., 1764, payable to Richd. Lechemere, Esq. | | 730 0 0 | | | |
| | " Int. 4 mos. 6 days | | 16 10 11 | 746 | 10 | 11 |
| | " Bal. carried to New Acct. | | | 9 | 11 | 0 |
| | | | | £926 | 14 | 9½ |

| | By Int. arising on Mary Ireland's Legacy, Cr. in that Acct. as per page | | 8 | 0 | 0 |
|---|---|---|---|---|---|
| | " Bal. of Contribution, folio 27 | | 4 | 9 | 2¾ |
| 1766. | | | | | |
| July 17 | " A Treasurer's Note of this date, No. 108, payable to Wm. Phillips, with 5 % Int. per an. | | 820 | 0 | 0 |
| Dec. 15 | " A Treasurer's Note, No. 113, dated 17 July, 1766, payable to Wm. Phillips | | 301 | 0 | 0 |
| | " Int. on do. | | 6 | 3 | 9 |
| | " Cash pd. Stephen Minot, for which have his Bond and Mortgage of this date | | 575 | 0 | 0 |
| | " Cash Ezekiel Goldthwaite, drawing Bond | | | 6 | 0 |
| | " Bal. of Contribution Acct., folio 29 | | 30 | 12 | 4¾ |
| | | | £1,745 | 11 | 4½ |

## *Wm. Phillips.*

| 1767. | | £ | s. | d. |
|---|---|---|---|---|
| Jan. | To Cash Recd. of his Bro. Jeffries, contributed to the Charitable Fund last Thanksgiving | 6 | 0 | |
| 24 | " Cash Recd. 3 yrs'. Int. on R. McKnight's Note | | 14 | $4\frac{1}{2}$ |
| Feb. 11 | " Cash " 1 " " of S. Mirrick | 1 | 1 | $7\frac{1}{4}$ |
| May 17 | " Cash Recd. on Treasurer's Note, No. 113 | 301 | 0 | 0 |
| | " Int. on do. from 17 July to 11 May, when let S. Minot £125. as per Contra, is 9 m. 24 days @ 5 % is . . . . £12. 5s. 9d. | | | |
| | £176. from 11 May to 17 July is 2 m. 6 days . . . . 1 12 3 | | | |
| | 13 18 0 | | | |
| | Deduct 1 yr.'s Int. on £60. 0s. $11\frac{3}{4}d$. for the Bal. due to him out of the above Note as per Contra . 3 0 0 | 10 | 18 | 0 |
| Sept. 21 | " Cash Recd. of Joseph Gearfield and Bro. Sewall in part of his Bond | 22 | 12 | $11\frac{3}{4}$ |
| Oct. 20 | " Cash of J. Mirrick in full for Int. to 19 ult. | 1 | 0 | 3 |
| | " Bal. due W. Phillips to Cr. of New Acct. | 54 | 14 | $5\frac{1}{4}$ |
| | | £392 | 7 | $7\frac{3}{4}$ |
| 1769. | | | | |
| June 16 | To Cash of S. Miller, Esq., in part of Int. . | 13 | 0 | 0 |
| | " " " S. Minot, for 2 yrs.' Int. of his Bond £575 | 69 | 0 | 0 |
| | " " " " " " " " 125 | 15 | 0 | 0 |
| | " " " S. Mirrick, due Sept. 19, 1768 . | 1 | 0 | 11 |
| | " " " Thos. Hubbard, Esq., for John Osborn, Esq., Legacy . | 13 | 0 | 0 |
| | " " " Jas. Mirrick, 1 yr.'s Int. due Sept. 19, 1769 | 1 | 0 | 11 |
| | " " " S. Miller in part of Int. . . | 4 | 16 | 8 |
| | " Bal. of Contribution Acct. from folio 28 . | 41 | 10 | $8\frac{1}{2}$ |
| | | £158 | 9 | $2\frac{1}{2}$ |
| 1770. | | | | |
| | To Bal. Brought from Old Acct. . | 88 | 8 | $1\frac{1}{4}$ |
| Feb. 19 | " Cash quarter's Int. on S. Minot's Bond, £575 | 34 | 10 | 0 |
| April 17 | " " 6 yrs.' Int. on D. Whitney's Bond to Oct. 20, 1769 . | 10 | 10 | 3 |
| Oct. 2 | " " 1 yr.'s Int. on S. Minot's Bond | 7 | 10 | 0 |
| Nov. 2 | " " of Roger McKnight in part of his Note | 1 | 13 | 7 |
| Dec. 1 | " " 1 yr.'s Int. of J. Mirrick, due Sept. 19, 1770 | 1 | 0 | 11 |
| 1771. | | | | |
| Jan. 1 | " Bal. of Contribution Acct., folio 28 . | 18 | 1 | 6 |
| | | £161 | 14 | $4\frac{1}{4}$ |

## Contra.

| 1767. | | £ | s. | d. |
|---|---|---|---|---|
| Jan. 1 | By Balance of Acct. and per S. Church stock | 60 | 0 | 11¾ |
| | " Int. on Mary Ireland's legacy Cr. in that Acct. as per folio | 7 | 6 | 8 |
| May 11 | " Cash paid Stephen Minot, for which have his Bond and a second Mortgage of this date | 125 | 0 | 0 |
| July 24 | " Cash paid Stephen Miller, Esq., of Milton, for which have his Bond and Mortgage of this date | 200 | 0 | 0 |
| | | £392 | 7 | 7¾ |

| 1768. | | | | |
|---|---|---|---|---|
| Jan. | By Balance of above Acct. | 54 | 14 | 5¼ |
| | " Int. Cr. in Mr. Ireland's legacy folio | 7 | 6 | 8 |
| 1769. | | | | |
| Jan. | "    "        "      "      " | 8 | 0 | 0 |
| | " Balance to New Acct. | 88 | 8 | 1¼ |
| | | £158 | 9 | 2½ |

| 1770. | | | | |
|---|---|---|---|---|
| Nov. 23 | By Balance of Contribution Acct. | 36 | 4 | 1 |
| Dec. 8 | " Cash pd. Josiah Quincy, Jr., | 1 | 13 | 8 |
| 1771 | | | | |
| Jan. 9 | " Balance due Church | 123 | 16 | 7¼ |
| | | £161 | 14 | 4¼ |

## *William Phillips.*

| 1771. | | | £ | s. | d. |
|---|---|---|---:|---:|---|
| Jan. | 9 | To Balance of Old Acct. . . . . | 123 | 16 | 7¼ |
| Feb. | 1 | " Cash, 1 yrs. Int. on S. Minot's Bond . | 34 | 10 | 0 |
| April | 7 | " " " " of S. Miller, Esq., to July 24, 1770 | 18 | 3 | 4 |
| July | 13 | " " " Stephen Minot . . | 7 | 10 | 0 |
| 1772. | | | | | |
| Jan. | 29 | " " 1 yrs. Int. of Joseph Allen and others on their Bond of £100., due 21st inst. . . . | 6 | 0 | 0 |
| April | 21 | " Cash ½ yrs. Int. on J. Merrick's Bond . . | 1 | 11 | 5 |
| June | 24 | " " of S. Miller, in part Int. . . | 13 | 16 | 0 |
| Sept. | 26 | " " 1 yrs. Int. of S. Minot on £575., due 15 Dec. 1771, £34. 10s. 0d., and 1 yr.'s Int. on £125., due 11 May, 1772, £7. 10s. 0d. . | 42 | 0 | 0 |
| Dec. | 24 | " Cash of D. Whitney in discharge of his Bond, £29. 4s. 0d., 3 yrs. 2m. 14d. Int. on do. £5. 11s. 4d. . . . . . | 34 | 15 | 4 |
| | 31 | " Cash of Bro. Jeffries, Pious and Char. Fund . | 1 | 6 | 8 |
| 1773. | | | | | |
| Feb. | 16 | " " " S. Minot in discharge of his Bond of £125. 0s. 0d., and 9m. 5d. Int. on do., £5. 14s. 7d. . . . . . | 130 | 14 | 7 |
| | | " Cash of S. Minot, 1 yr. 2m. 1d. Int. on his Bond £575., to 15th inst., £40. 6s. 11d. | | | |
| | | " Rec'd. part of Principal of above, £150. 0s. 0d. | 190 | 6 | 11 |
| April | 7 | " Cash of Joseph Allen and others, 1 yr.'s Int. on their Bond of £100. due 21 Jan. 1773, per T. Ruggles . . . . . | 6 | 0 | 0 |
| May | 8 | " Cash in discharge of Jas. Mirrick's Bond, £17. 7s. 9d., Int. from May 19, 1773 [?], 13⅔m. £1. 3s. 9d. . . . . . . | 18 | 11 | 6 |
| July | 6 | " Cash of S. Miller, in part of Int. . . | 17 | 5 | 0 |
| Aug. | 17 | " " " Ex. of the late Thos. Hubbard, Esq., for his legacy to the Pious and Char. Fund . | 50 | 0 | 0 |
| Sept. | 15 | " Cash of S. Miller in part of Int. . . | 3 | 10 | 0 |
| | 30 | " Balance of Contribution Acct., folio 30 . . | 21 | 13 | 3¾ |
| | | " Balance to New Acct., folio 58 . . . | 30 | 9 | 4 |
| | | | £752 | 0 | 0 |

*Contra.*

|  |  |  | £ | s. | d. |
|---|---|---|---|---|---|
| 1771. | | | | | |
| Jan. | 1 | By Cash pd. Joseph Allen, Danl. Fay, and Joseph Safford, all of Hardwick, for which they have given their Bond payable with Interest, Jan. 21, 1772 . . . . . | 100 | 0 | 0 |
| | 26 | " 2 yrs.' Int. Cr. Mary Ireland's legacy, folio | 16 | 0 | 0 |
| 1772. | | | | | |
| Feb. | 6 | " 1 " " " " " . | 8 | 0 | 0 |
| 1773. | | | | | |
| Feb. | 24 | " Cash pd. Amasa Davis and Robert Pierpont, for which have their Bond of this date and said Davis Mortgage . . . . | 300 | 0 | 0 |
| May | 15 | " 1 yr.'s Int. Cr. Mary Ireland's legacy . . | 8 | 0 | 0 |
| Aug. | 16 | " Cash pd. Nathan Parker of Reading, for which have his Bond of this date on Interest, and a Mortgage of two old dwelling houses with the land in Hanover Street . . . | 120 | 0 | 0 |
| | 17 | " Cash pd. Benj. White and Ebenr. Davis of Brookline, for which have their Bond of this date on interest, being taken for the late Thos. Hubbard, Esq.'s legacy to the Charitable and Pious Fund of the Old South Church in Boston . . . . . | 50 | 0 | 0 |
| | | " Cash pd. Ebenr. Farrar, for which have his Bond with five other persons, and John Flint's obligation to discharge said Bond in case of the default or neglect of the said Farrar and others, dated July 26, 1772, on interest . . . . . | 150 | 0 | 0 |

£752 0 0

## *William Phillips.*

| Date | | Description | | | £ | s. | d. |
|---|---|---|---|---|---:|---:|---:|
| 1774. | | | | | | | |
| Feb. 7 | To | Cash of Amasa Davis and R. Pierpont, 1 yr.'s Int. | | | 18 | 0 | 0 |
| | " | Cash of Jos. Allen and others, 1 yr.'s Int. on their Bond, $100., due Jan. 1, 1774, pd. Timothy Ruggles, Esq. | | | 6 | 0 | 0 |
| Sept. 5 | " | Cash of Stephen Minot, 1 yr.'s Int. due 15th Feb. | | | 25 | 10 | 0 |
| 12 | " | Cash of White & Davis, 1 yr.'s Int. due 17th Aug. | | | 3 | 0 | 0 |
| 1775. | | | | | | | |
| May 9 | " | Cash of A. Davis and R. Pierpont, 1 yr.'s Int. due 24th Feb. | | | 18 | 0 | 0 |
| 1777. | | | | | | | |
| Feb. 17 | " | Cash of White & Davis, principal £50., Int. | 7 | 8  4 | 57 | 8 | 4 |
| 1782. | | | | | | | |
| Feb. 1 | " | Cash of Henry Gardner's Note, as per contra | 50 | 0  0 | | | |
| | | Deduct 7½ per cent for depreciation | 3 | 10  0 | | | |
| | | | 46 | 10  0 | | | |
| | | Int. and premium to this date | 18 | 2  9 | 64 | 12 | 9 |
| 1783. | | | | | | | |
| Jan. 1 | " | Cash of Amasa Davis and R. Pierpont on acct. of Int. | | | 73 | 10 | 0 |
| May. 5 | " | " Saml. Whitwell and Jona. Mason, Executors of the Will of Benj. Pemberton, Esq., deceased, for his legacy to the Old South Church | | | 20 | 0 | 0 |
| Sept. 23 | " | Cash recd. of Treas. Ives 9 mos. Int. on Note 5,906 for £64. 12s. 9d. | | | 2 | 18 | 1 |
| Nov. 17 | " | Cash of John Fenno on acct. of Int. on S. Parker's Bond | | | 15 | 0 | 0 |
| | " | Cash on Stock Note, 5,906, £64. 12s. 9d. | | | 3 | 17 | 7 |
| 1784. | | | | | | | |
| July 2 | " | Amasa Davis and R. Pierpont on acct. of Int. | | | 27 | 0 | 0 |
| | " | Bal. of Contribution acct. brot. from folio 32 | | | 31 | 12 | 6 |
| Aug. 20 | " | Cash of John Fenno in discharge of Nathl. Parker's Bond | 120 | 0  0 | | | |
| | | Interest | 92 | 3  4 | 212 | 3 | 4 |
| Mch. 21 | " | Cash of Jona. Mason, Jr., Esq., Principal and Int. of Ebenr. Farrar and others' Bond | | | 251 | 5 | 0 |
| | " | Cash for dividend Nos. 1 and 2 on two shares in the Bank as per Contra recd. Jan. 13, 1785 | | | 4 | 10 | 0 |
| July 30 | " | Cash for div. No. 2 on four shares in the Bank | | | 11 | 15 | 0 |
| Aug. 15 | " | " 1 yr.'s Int. on State Note 5,096, £64. 12s. 9d. | | | 3 | 17 | 7 |
| 1787. | | | | | | | |
| Jan. 4 | " | " dividend No. 3 on four shares in the Bank, 2 % | | | 12 | 0 | 0 |
| 28 | " | " " " " 4 " " " 3 % | | | 18 | 0 | 0 |
| May 8 | " | " Stephen Minot's heirs on acct. Int. | | | 30 | 0 | 0 |
| 23 | " | " of Davis and Pierpont " | | | 45 | 0 | 0 |
| Aug. 8 | " | " " Stephen Minot's heirs | | | 30 | 0 | 0 |
| July 26 | " | " " Davis and Pierpont | | | 55 | 0 | 0 |
| Oct. 10 | " | " " Div. No. 5 on four shares in Bank 3½ % | | | 21 | 0 | 0 |
| Nov. 9 | " | " " Stephen Minot's heirs on acct. Int. | | | 30 | 0 | 0 |
| | | *Amount carried forward* | | | £1,091 | 0 | 2 |

*Contra.*

|  |  | £ | s. | d. |
|---|---|---:|---:|---:|
| 1773. |  |  |  |  |
| Sept. 30 | By Bal. due to Wm. Phillips as per last Acct. | 30 | 9 | 4 |
| 1774. |  |  |  |  |
| Feb. 7 | " 1 yr.'s Int. Cr. Mary Ireland's Legacy | 8 | 0 | 0 |
| 1775. |  |  |  |  |
| Feb. | "   "   "   "   "   "   " | 8 | 0 | 0 |
| 1777. |  |  |  |  |
| Feb. 7 | " Cash pd. H. Gardner, State Treas. for his Note of this date, No. 827, Principal Recd. of White & Davis as per Contra | 50 | 0 | 0 |
| 1782. |  |  |  |  |
| Feb. 1 | " Cash H. Gardner, State Note for the above Note renewed, No. 5,096, see Contra | 64 | 12 | 9 |
| 1783. |  |  |  |  |
| Sept. 23 | " Cash Distributed to sundry persons, June, Cash on Acct. of Mrs. Ireland's Legacy as appears by Quarterly Charity Book, folio 5 | 18 | 18 | 0 |
| Nov. | "   "   "   "   "   " | 19 | 10 | 0 |
| 1784. |  |  |  |  |
| March | "   "   "   "   "   " | 16 | 4 | 0 |
| Aug. 7 | " Cash supplied Thomas Moulin |  | 12 | 0 |
| 20 | "   " for 2 Shares in Mass. Bank, Nos. 191, 192 | 300 | 0 | 0 |
| Mar. 23 | "   " for 2   "   "   "   " 412, 413 | 300 | 0 | 0 |
|  | "   " Distributed to sundry persons this month on Acct. of Mrs. Ireland's Legacy as appears by Quarterly Charity Book, folio 5 | 20 | 0 | 0 |
| 1786. |  |  |  |  |
| May 10 | "   "   "   "   "   "   " 8 | 13 | 8 | 0 |
| 1787. |  |  |  |  |
| April 10 | "   "   "   "   "   "   "  " and added thereto as below . £8. 0s. 0d. Then follow sundry names to which were given . . . 10 6 0 | 18 | 6 | 0 |
| 1788. |  |  |  |  |
| Jan. 1 | " Do. folio 8 and added thereto as below 8 0 0 Then follows the Amt. given sundry persons . . . . 15 8 0 | 23 | 8 | 0 |
| Feb. 5 | " Cash Sundry Donations | 6 | 18 | 0 |
| Sept. 2 | "   " for Treas. Hodgdon's Note, No. 43, Sept. 1, 1788, on Int. | 109 | 13 | 9 |
| Dec. 29 | "   " Sundry Donations | 54 | 12 | 0 |
| 1789. |  |  |  |  |
| Jan. 1 | "   " Treas. Hodgdon's Note, No. 105 on Int. | 300 | 0 | 0 |
|  | "   "   "   "   "   " 117   " | 100 | 0 | 0 |
| Feb. 23 | "   " Distributed to sundry persons on Acct. of Mrs. Ireland's Legacy as per Quar. Charity Book, 8 | 8 | 0 | 0 |
|  | " Bal. of his Contribution Acct. brought from fol. 33 | 5 | 10 | 7 |
| May 8 | " Cash pd. Jona. Mason, Jr., Esq., costs on sundry obligations as per Acct. | 11 | 10 | 4 |
| 9 | " Balance due the Church carried to the debit of his new Acct. | 114 | 14 | 10 |
|  | *Amount carried forward* | £1,602 | 7 | 7 |

## *William Phillips.*

| 1789. | | | | £ | s. | d. |
|---|---|---|---|---|---|---|
| | | *Amount brought forward* . . . | . 1,091 | 0 | 2 |
| Feb. 24 * | To Cash | of A. Davis and R. Pierpont on Acct. of Int. | 34 | 10 | 0 |
| May 1 | " " | Thos. Bromfield's Legacy, see extract of his Will, folio . . . . . . | 33 | 6 | 8 |
| | " " | 4 mos. Dis. on £400. according to the rules of the Bank, which sum is now included in our note dated April 26, 1789 . . | 8 | 16 | 0 |
| 1788. | | | | | |
| Feb. 25 | " " | for Div. No. 6, on 4 Shares in the Bank, 3 per cent . . . . . | 18 | 0 | 0 |
| May 8 | " " | Stephen Minot's Heirs on Acct. of Int. . | 30 | 0 | 0 |
| Sept. 2 | " " | " " by Treas. Hodgdon's Note, Int. | 109 | 13 | 9 |
| Dec. 2 | " " | for Div. No. 7, on 4 Shares in the Bank, 4 per cent . . . . . | 24 | 0 | 0 |
| 1789 | | | | | |
| Jan. 1 | " " | of Treas. Hodgdon, in discharge of this Note . . . £109. 13s. 0d. 4 mos. Int. on the above . 2 3 9 | 111 | 17 | 6 |
| | " " | Div. on 4 Shares in the Bank, No. 8, 3½ per cent . . . . . | 21 | 0 | 0 |
| Feb. 15 | " " | of Jona. Danforth and others in part per Jona. Mason, Jr., Esq., by him the 9th inst. | 100 | 12 | 8 |
| 23 * " | " | of Dea. Dawes, being part of the Contributions on the Communion Sabbaths for 1788 | 19 | 10 | 10 |
| | | | £1,602 | 7 | 7 |

## Contra.

|  | £ | s. | d. |
|---|---|---|---|
| *Amount carried forward* . . . . | 1,602 | 7 | 7 |

£1,602 7 7

Boston, May 9, 1789. We have examined the above Account and find the same right cast and properly vouched; and that there is a balance due the South Society, in the hands of Dea. Phillips, of one hundred and fourteen pounds, 14s. 10d. L. Money.

JONA. MASON, JR.
WILLIAM PHILLIPS, JR.

## William Phillips.

| 1789. | | | £ | s. | d. |
|---|---|---|---:|---:|---:|
| May 9 | To Balance of above Acct. carried back to folio | | 114 | 14 | 10 |
| July 18 | " div. No. 9 on 4 shares in the Bank 3½% | | 21 | 0 | 0 |
| Oct. 7 | " Stephen Minot's heirs on Acct. of Int. | | 87 | 6 | 10 |
| Nov. 9 | " Jona. Danforth and others pd. Jona. Mason, Jr. in part of Int. and Principal. | | 7 | 10 | 0 |
| 1790. | | | | | |
| Feb. 7 | " div. No. 10 on 4 shares in the Bank 5%. | | 30 | 0 | 0 |
| March 1 | " 10 mos. dis. on £400., see Treas. Hodgdon's note, folio | | 22 | 0 | 0 |
| April 24 | " Stephen Minot's heirs on Acct. of Int. | | 30 | 0 | 0 |
| 26 | " A. Davis and R. Pierpont on Acct. of Int. | | 36 | 0 | 0 |
| Sept. 23 | " div. No. 11 on 4 shares in the Bank 4½% | | 27 | 0 | 0 |
| Oct. 18 | " Stephen Minot's heirs on Acct. Int. | | 30 | 0 | 0 |
| Nov. 22 | " Jno. Danforth and others pd. Jona. Mason, Jr. for Int. 1 yr. | | 7 | 10 | 0 |
| 1791. | | | | | |
| Jan. 6 | " div. No. 12, profits arising on withdrawn shares | 66 0 0 | | | |
| | " " No. 13, profits on discts. the last 6 mos. | 37 10 0 | | | |
| 8 | " 10½ mos. disct. on £600., see Treas. Hodgdon's note as per contra, March, 1790 | 45 13 0 | | | |
| | " Treas. Hodgdon in discharge of his note as above | 600 0 0 | 738 | 3 | 0 |
| March 21 | " A. Davis and R. Pierpont on Acct. Int. | | 28 | 13 | 0 |
| April 5 | " Stephen Minot's heirs on Acct. of Int. | | 30 | 0 | 0 |
| July 2 | " div. No. 14, on 8 shares in the Bank, 387 Dolls. is | | 116 | 2 | 0 |
| Aug. 12 | " Stephen Minot's heirs in full of Prin. and Int. to 15th. | | 446 | 5 | 0 |
| Nov. 22 | " Danforth and others on Acct. of Int. of Nath. Page | | 7 | 6 | 11 |
| 1792. | | | | | |
| Jan. 7 | " div. No. 15 on 8 shares in the Bank @ 10% | | 120 | 0 | 0 |
| May 16 | " Amasa Davis and R. Pierpont in full of their Bonds | | 339 | 4 | 4 |
| July 9 | " Div. No. 16 on 8 shares in Bank 16% | 192 0 0 | | | |
| | " " No. 17 on 7 shares in Bank 16% | 115 14 9 | 307 | 14 | 9 |
| 23 | " Edward H. Robbins for land mortgaged by Stephen Miller, Milton, July 22, 1767, as per folio. Principal and Int. recd. this day | | 283 | 1 | 0 |
| Dec. 24 | " Bro. Jona. Mason, Esq. | | 46 | 12 | 7 |
| 29 | " Jona. Danforth and others on Acct. Int. of Martin Kinsley. | | 6 | 1 | 3 |
| 1793. | | | | | |
| Jan. 5 | " Div. on 16 shares in the Bank 4% | | 96 | 0 | 0 |
| | | | £2,978 | 5 | 6 |

## *Contra.*

| 1789. | | | £ | s. | d. |
|---|---|---|---|---|---|
| May 29 | By Cash suplied Dr. Eckley at Convention | | 3 | 0 | 0 |
| July 30 | " " John Sweetser's expenses to New Concord for instalment of Mr. Evans | | 10 | 16 | 4 |
| Nov. 2 | " Donations to sundry persons | | 58 | 16 | 0 |
| Dec. 6 | " Added to Quarterly Collections the year past | | 18 | 8 | 6 |
| 1790. | | | | | |
| May | " Treas. Hodgdon, for which have his Note with the £400. included, total £600. | | 200 | 0 | 0 |
| Dec. 5 | " Donations to sundry persons | | 146 | 17 | 7 |
| 1791. | | | | | |
| Jan. 7 | " 4 additional Shares in the Bank | | 660 | 0 | 0 |
| Dec. 4 | " Distributed to sundry persons | | 157 | 17 | 10 |
| 1792. | | | | | |
| June 19 | " 6 additional Shares in the Bank | | 900 | 0 | 0 |
| July 9 | " 2 " " " | | 300 | 0 | 0 |
| Sept. 4 | " Distributed the same as Nov. '91, and additions | | 57 | 0 | 0 |
| Dec. 4 | " Added to Quarterly Collections | | 8 | 10 | 2 |
| 29 | " Tax on land at Milton, sold E. H. Robbins | | | 13 | 5 |
| 1793. | | | | | |
| Feb. 25 | " Distributed same as Sept. 4, '92, with additions | | 62 | 8 | 0 |
| March 3 | " Distributed to sundry persons on Acct. Mrs. Ireland's Legacy | | 8 | 0 | 0 |
| Sept. 2 | " Added to Quar. Collection, as entered Dec. 4 to this day | | 5 | 11 | 10 |
| Nov. 19 | " Paid Bro. Jona. Mason, Esq., Treasurer | | 380 | 5 | 10 |

£2,978 5 6

*South Church to*

|  |  |  |  |  | £ | s. | d. |
|---|---|---|---|---|---|---|---|
| 1793. | | | | | | | |
| Nov. | 20 | To Cash for Trunk . . . . . | | | | 9 | 3 |
| | 21 | " " pd. Jos. Fosdick for Certificate $2,300 U.S. 3 % Stk. . . . . | | | 379 | 10 | 0 |
| Dec. | 4 | " " Distributed . . . . | | | 60 | 18 | 0 |
| 1794. | | | | | | | |
| Jan. | 8 | " " pd. for Bread . . . . | | | 2 | 12 | 0 |
| May | 1 | " " Distributed . . . . | | | 55 | 10 | 0 |
| | 13 | " " Mass. Note as per Contra for $33 $\frac{90}{100}$, loaned at Treas. Davis's office for $38.97, Cr. in Church Stock . . . | | | 10 | 3 | 4 |
| June | 2 | " Amo. Distributed . . . . | | | 5 | 4 | 9 |
| Sept. | 10 | " Cash Distributed with Quar. Collection . | | | 7 | 3 | 8 |
| | | " the Society Stock in Notes as per folio . . | | | 2,678 | 18 | 5 |
| | | " so much Cr. before on the Note loaned at Treas. Davis's office . . . . . | | | 1 | 10 | 2 |
| | 12 | " Cash on hand Cr. to New Acct.. . . | | | 203 | 0 | 1 |

£3,404 19 8

## Jonathan Mason, Treasurer.

| 1793. | | £ | s. | d. |
|---|---|---:|---:|---:|
| Nov. 19 | By Cash of Bro. Phillips | 380 | 5 | 10 |
| " | " Shares in Mass. Bank, 16 shares | 2,460 | 0 | 0 |
| " | " John Danforth and others, Notes and Bond | 125 | 0 | 0 |
| " | " one certificate 6 % Funds for $121.88 | 36 | 10 | 8 |
| " | " " " 3 % " " 91.40 | 27 | 8 | 4 |
| " | " " " in deferred Stock, 60.93 | 18 | 5 | 7 |
| " | " " " Mass. Stock, 33.90 | 10 | 3 | 4 |
| " | " loaned and Cr. in Church Stock, £21. 13s, 10d. as below. | | | |
| | N.B. — The above certificate for Dea. Hubbard's legacy to the poor of ye Church. | | | |
| " | " Cash of Bro. Phillips for Int. on above | 3 | 15 | 0 |
| 20 | " Int. I recd. at the office this day on the above certificates | 1 | 9 | 10 |
| Dec. 4 | " Cash recd. at Mass. Bank for Div. No. 19, $28.00 | 8 | 8 | 0 |
| " | " " " " " " " 20 | 96 | 0 | 0 |
| 14 | " Int. and part principal on Jona. Danforth's Bond. | 16 | 3 | 6 |
| 1794. | | | | |
| Jan. 11 | " Cash quarter's Int. on 3 % $2,300, $17.50 | 5 | 3 | 6 |
| " | " " " " " Mr. Hubbard's legacy, Church | | 15 | 1 |
| M'ch 15 | " " Div. No. 21 Mass. Bank | 96 | 0 | 0 |
| April 4 | " " quarter's Int. on Mr. Hubbard's legacy | | 15 | 1 |
| " | " " Int. on 3 %, $2,300 | 5 | 3 | 6 |
| May 3 | " Note unassumable at Appleton's office, principal $33.90, reloaned to this Commonwealth at Treas. Davis's office | 11 | 13 | 10 |
| July 10 | " one yr.'s Int. on Thos. Hubbard's legacy | | 15 | 1 |
| " | " Int. on $2,300, 3 % Stock | 5 | 3 | 6 |
| " | " Div. No. 22, Mass. Stock | 96 | 0 | 0 |
| | | £3,404 | 19 | 8 |

## South Church with

| 1794. | | | £ | s. | d. |
|---|---|---|---|---|---|
| May 9 | To Cash distributed. | | 57 | 1 | 3 |
| April 14 | " " pd. Thos. Dawes, Esq., for Thos. Davis, Esq., Treas., Note No. 2,582 for $670.40 @ 15s. 9d. per £.. | | 158 | 7 | 9 |
| Dec. 29 | " Cash distributed. | | 126 | 13 | 0 |
| | | | £342 | 2 | 0 |
| | Reduced to dollars is. | | $1,140 | 33 | |
| 1796. | | | | | |
| Jan. 19 | To Cash to Poor | | 5 | 00 | |
| | " " pd. John Marston for certificate in the 5 % U. S. Stock, signed by Nathan Appleton for  $1,000.00 | | | | |
| | Certif. No. 9, Disct. 20 % (page 61)  200.00 | | 800 | 00 | |
| March 8 | " Cash to Poor | | 6 | 90 | |
| Oct. 18 | " " " | | 208 | 20 | |
| 28 | " " pd. John Jackson for 42 shares in the Union Bank at 59 % | | 417 | 92 | |
| Dec. 27 | " Cash to Poor | | 271 | 00 | |
| 1797. | | | | | |
| | " Balance to new acct. | | 26 | 07 | |

$2,875 42

## Jonathan Mason.

| 1794. | | | £ | s. | d. |
|---|---|---|---:|---:|---:|
| | | By Balance from Old Acct. . . . | 203 | 0 | 1 |
| Oct. | 9 | " 1 yr.'s Int. of Mr. Hubbard's legacy . . | 0 | 15 | 1 |
| | | " Int. on $2,300, 3 % . . . . | 5 | 3 | 6 |
| 1795. | | | | | |
| Jan. | 2 | " Bal. of Sacramental, from J. Mason . . | 42 | 13 | 4½ |
| | 6 | " Cash of Dea. Dawes . . . . | 18 | 13 | 0 |
| | 9 | " quarter Int. on $2,300, 3 % . . | 5 | 3 | 6 |
| | | "    "    "    " Hubbard's donation . . | | 15 | 1 |
| | | " Mass. Bank, 23d Dividend .  $320.00 | | | |
| | | "    "    "   24    "   .  200.00 | | | |
| | | 520.00 | 156 | 0 | 0 |
| | 10 | " Int. on Treas. Davis's note . . . | | 5 | 9 |
| March | 12 | "   " 1 year on Thos. Danforth and others' Bond, | | | |
| | | Recd. of Jonathan Winthrop . . | 7 | 2 | 4 |
| April | 4 | " quarter's Int. of U. S. A. .  $19.75 | 5 | 18 | 6 |
| July | 10 | " 25th Div. Mass. Bank . . . . | 96 | 0 | 0 |
| | 13 | " quarter's Int. U. S. . . . . | 5 | 18 | 6 |
| | | " Int. of Treas. Davis . .  $17.74 | 5 | 6 | 4 |
| Oct. | 19 | " quarter's Int. U. S. . . . . | 5 | 18 | 6 |
| | | | £558 | 13 | 6½ |

| | Reduced to Dollars is. . . . | $1,862 | 25 |
|---|---|---:|---:|
| 1706. | | | |
| Jan. 7 | " Int. of Thomas Dawes . . . . | 17 | 73 |
| | " quarter's Int. on Funded Debt . . . | 19 | 47 |
| | " 2 % on one quarter of principal of 6 % stock . | 2 | 42 |
| 13 | " 6 mos. Div. Mass. Bank . . . . | 360 | 00 |
| 19 | " Sacramental Money from Bro. Salisbury . | 77 | 40 |
| April 15 | " quarter's Int. U. S. Debt . . . | 33 | 47 |
| May 5 | " 1 yr.'s Int. on J. Danforth's Bond . . | 21 | 72 |
| July 8 | " 6 mos.' Int. of Treas. Davis . . . | 17 | 73 |
| 21 | " quarter's Int. of U. S., and what was short last | | |
| | quarter . . . . . | 33 | 52 |
| 25 | " 6 mos. Div. Mass. Bank Stock . . . | 360 | 00 |
| Oct. 10 | " quarter's Int. of U. S. . . . . | 33 | 51 |
| 1797. | | | |
| Jan. 23 | " quarter's Int. of U. S., and 2 % principal . | 35 | 93 |
| | | $2,875 | 42 |

*South Church with*

| | | |
|---|---|---:|
| 1797. | | |
| March 30 to Jan. 4, '98. | To Cash distributed to Poor . . | $592 00 |
| May 22 | "   " in full paid Wm. Phillips, Jr., Treasurer . . . . | 603 91 |
| | | $1,195 91 |

## *Jonathan Mason.*

| 1797. | | | |
|---|---|---|---|
| Jan. 4 | By Bal. from Old Acct. | $26 | 07 |
| 7 | " 6 mos. dividend Mass. Bank Stock, deposited then as per Bank Book | 360 | 00 |
| 11 | " Interest of Treas. Davis | 17 | 73 |
| 16 | " Cash of Dea. Phillips, Jr., Bal. of Sac. Coll. | 109 | 00 |
| April 15 | " 6 mos. div. Union Bank | 17 | 00 |
| | " " " U.S. 3 % | 33 | 51 |
| July 12 | " " " Mass. Bank, deposited | 360 | 00 |
| | " Quarter's Int. of U.S. | 33 | 51 |
| 27 | " Int. of Treas. Coffin | 17 | 73 |
| Oct. 7 | " " " U.S. | 33 | 51 |
| | " " " Union Bank | 17 | 00 |
| 1798. | | | |
| Jan. | " 2 % as Principal | 2 | 45 |
| | " Quarter's Int. | 33 | 51 |
| April | " " " | 33 | 51 |
| 16 | " Cash Bal. of Sacramental Collection | 101 | 38 |
| | | $1,195 | 91 |

## South Church

| | | £ | s. | d. | | | |
|---|---|---|---|---|---|---|---|
| 1734. | To Cash given to sundry persons at ye discretion of ye Minister, &c. | 112 | 3 | 9 | | | |
| 1752. | Memorandum:— To shut up this Acct. of Int. of the Bonds, and to balance it, being £43. 8s. 3d., have laid by a $20 Note, dated March 18, to draw Int. from the Province | 43 | 8 | 3 | | | |
| | | £155 | 12 | 0 | | | |
| 1766. Jan. | To Balance as per Contra | £874 | 14 | 3 | | | |
| | | £874 | 14 | 3 | | | |

Rise of and increase of the Church Stock is as follows:—

| | | | | | | | |
|---|---|---|---|---|---|---|---|
| Rev. Mr. Pemberton's Legacy | £17 | 7s. | 9d. | | | | |
| Mr. Cunningham's " | 66 | 13 | 4 | | | | |
| Mrs. Mills's " | 100 | 19 | 10 | | | | |
| Mrs. Elizabeth Loring's " | 13 | 6 | 8 | | | | |
| Capt. John Armitage's " | 13 | 6 | 8 | | | | |
| Mr. Farr Tolman's " | 40 | 0 | 0 | | | | |
| Daniel Henchman's " | 66 | 0 | 0 | | | | |
| Mr. John Simpson's " | 30 | 0 | 0 | | | | |
| Mrs. Mary Ireland's " | 133 | 6 | 8 | | | | |
| Rev. Dr. Sewall's " | 20 | 0 | 0 | 501 | 0 | 11 |
| Pious and Charitable Fund | 63 | 12 | $6\frac{1}{4}$ | | | | |
| Ministers and Widows | 3 | 6 | 8 | 66 | 19 | $2\frac{1}{4}$ |
| Sacramental Stock | 186 | 19 | $5\frac{1}{4}$ | | | | |
| Int. Recd. on the above | 119 | 14 | $8\frac{1}{2}$ | 306 | 14 | $1\frac{3}{4}$ |
| | | | | £874 | 14 | 3 |

## South Church.

| | | | £ | s. | d. |
|---|---|---|---|---|---|
| 1728. | | | | | |
| | By six Bonds from sundry persons for | | 280 | 0 | 0 |
| | " a Note underhand and Cash, | | 2 | 3 | 1¼ |
| | | | 282 | 3 | 1¼ |

The sum of £282. 3s. 1¼d., as above, is the one-quarter part of the residue of the estate of Mrs. Ann Mills, late of Watertown, deceased, which she gave by her last Will and Testament to be improved for the relief of the poor of the Old South Church and Congregation at the discretion of the Ministers and Deacons of said Church.

| | | | £ | s. | d. |
|---|---|---|---|---|---|
| 1743. | | | | | |
| Feb. 19 | By Int. Recd. of sundry persons as per Mem. | | 155 | 12 | 0 |
| | | | £155 | 12 | 0 |
| | | | | | |
| 1756. | | | | | |
| Oct. 20 | By Daniel Whitney's Bond, Int. pd. to Oct. 20, 1763 | | 29 | 4 | 0 |
| 1752. | | | | | |
| March 17 | " Joseph Garfield's Bond, Int. pd. to March 17, 1763 | | 22 | 16 | 8 |
| 1755. | | | | | |
| Sept. 19 | " James Mirrick and others' Bond, Int. pd. to Sept. 19, 1764 | | 17 | 7 | 9 |
| 1765. | | | | | |
| March 11 | " Jona. Simpson and others' Bond, Int. pd. to March 11, 1764 | | 22 | 5 | 10 |
| Jan. 24 | " R. McKnight's Note, Int. pd. to Jan. 20, 1764 | | 4 | 0 | 0 |
| | " a Treas. Note, No. 126, dated 10th June, 1763, payable to Eleazer Porter, Int. pd. to June 10, 1765 | | 49 | 0 | 0 |
| | " a Treas. Note 376, dated Oct. 26, 1764, payable to Richard Lechemere, Int. pd. to Oct. 23, 1765 | | 730 | 0 | 0 |
| | | | £874 | 14 | 3 |

January 1, 1766. We have examined the above and find it to be the true state of the Church Stock in the Deacons' hands at this time, being eight hundred and seventy-four pounds, fourteen shillings, and three pence, lawful money.

ANDREW OLIVER.<br>THOS. HUBBARD.<br>JOSHUA WINSLOW.

## South Church Stock.

|  |  |  | £ | s. | d. |
|---|---|---|---|---|---|
| To Wm. Phillips, as per his acct., viz.:— |  |  |  |  |  |
| Balance due to him Dec. 22, 1765, | £0. | 8s. 0¾d. |  |  |  |
| "  " Contribution acct. | 30 | 12  4¾ |  |  |  |
|  | 31 | 0  5½ |  |  |  |
| Deduct pd. him by his brother Sewall | 21 | 4  0¾ |  |  |  |
|  | 9 | 16  4¾ |  |  |  |
| Paid Ezekiel Goldthwait, Esq., drawing Stephens's Mortgage | 0 | 6  0 |  |  |  |
|  |  |  | 10 | 2 | 4¾ |
| 1767. Jan. 1 Balance due as per Contra |  |  | 911 | 13 | 3¼ |
|  |  |  | £921 | 15 | 8 |

| | £ | s. | d. |
|---|---|---|---|
| To Wm. Phillips for Bal. of his acct. as per folio 36 | 60 | 0 | 11¾ |
| Balance as above | 911 | 13 | 3¼ |
|  | £971 | 14 | 3 |

*Contra.*

| 1766. | | | £ | s. | d. |
|---|---|---|---:|---:|---:|
| Jan. | 1 | By Balance from folio 54 . | 874 | 14 | 3 |
| July | 17 | " Int. on Treas. Note, No. 126 . | 3 | 4 | 10 |
| | | "    "      "    "    376 . | 32 | 2 | 5 |
| | | "    "      "    "    108 . | 16 | 17 | 0 |
| | | "    "  Jas. Mirrick's Bond . | 1 | 0 | 11 |
| | | | £927 | 19 | 5 |
| | | Deduct for Int. due on Treas. Note, No. 113 . | 6 | 3 | 9 |
| | | | £921 | 15 | 8 |

| | £ | s. | d. |
|---|---:|---:|---:|
| By Balance of the above accounts in obligations, as follows; viz., 4 Bonds and 1 Note, as per folio 34 . . . . . . | 95 | 14 | 3 |
| " a Treasurer's Note, No. 113, dated 17 July, 1766, payable to Wm. Phillips . . | 301 | 0 | 0 |
| " Stephen Minot's Bond, with a Mortgage, Dec. 15, 1766 . . . . . | 575 | 0 | 0 |
| | £971 | 14 | 3 |

Jan. 1, 1767. We have examined the above account, and find it to be the true state of the Church Stock in the Deacons' hands at this time, being nine hundred and eleven pounds, fourteen shillings, three pence, one farthing.

ANDREW OLIVER.<br>THOS. HUBBARD.<br>JOSHUA WINSLOW.

## South Church Stock.

|  |  |  | | £ | s. | d. |
|---|---|---|---|---:|---:|---:|
| | | To 3 yrs.' Int. on the Ireland legacy, per folio . | | 22 | 13 | 4 |
| | | " Loss by James Garfield, Recd. short of principal | | | 3 | 8¼ |
| | | " Loss John Simpson and others, from whom payment is not likely to be obtained . | | 22 | 5 | 10 |
| | | " Cast of Court *vs.* Simpson, as per folio . | | 1 | 13 | 8 |
| | | | | £46 | 16 | 6¼ |
| | | " Bal. now in the following obligations and Cash:— | | | | |
| 1755. Sept. | 19 | " Jas. Mirrick and others' Bond, Int. pd. to Sept. 19, 1770 . . . . | | 17 | 7 | 9 |
| 1756. Oct. | 20 | " Danl. Whitney's Bond, Int. pd. to Oct. 20, 1769 | | 29 | 4 | 0 |
| 1766. Dec. | 15 | " Stephen Minot's Bond, Int. pd. to Dec. 15, 1769 | | 575 | 0 | 0 |
| 1767. May | 11 | " Stephen Minot's Bond, Int. pd. to May 11, 1770 | | 125 | 0 | 0 |
| July | 24 | " Stephen Miller's Bond, Int. 3s. 4d. since Jan. 24, 1769 . . . . | | 200 | 0 | 0 |
| Sept. | 15 | " Roger McKnight's Note . . . | | 1 | 0 | 0 |
| 1771. Jan. | 9 | " Wm. Phillips, Cash in his hand, as per folio | | 123 | 16 | 7 |
| | | | | £1,118 | 4 | 10¼ |

|  |  |  | | | | | £ | s. | d. |
|---|---|---|---:|---:|---:|---:|---:|---:|---:|
| | | To 4 yrs.' Int. on Mrs. Ireland's legacy, folio . . | £32. | 0s. | 0d. | | | | |
| | | Loss on Roger McKnight's Note . . . | 1 | 0 | 0 | | 33 | 0 | 0 |
| | | Balance now in the following obligations:— | | | | | | | |
| 1766. Dec. | 15 | Stephen Minot's Bond, Int. pd. to Feb. 15, 1773 | £575. | 0s. | 0d. | | | | |
| | | Deduct principal paid . | 150 | 0 | 0 | | | | |
| | | | 425 | 0 | 0 | | | | |
| 1767. July | 24 | Stephen Miller, Esq., short, July 9, 1773 . . | 200 | 0 | 0 | | | | |
| 1771. Jan. | 21 | Joseph Allen and others' Bond, Int. pd. to Jan. 1, 1773 . . . | 100 | 0 | 0 | | | | |
| 1773. Jan. | 24 | Davis & Pierpont Bond . | 300 | 0 | 0 | | | | |
| July | 26 | Ebenr. Farrar and others' Bond . . . | 150 | 0 | 0 | | | | |
| Aug. | 26 | Nathan Parker's Bond . | 120 | 0 | 0 | | | | |
| | 17 | White & Davis's Bond . | 50 | 0 | 0 | | | | |
| | | | £1,345 | 0 | 0 | | | | |
| | | Deduct Bal. due to Wm. Phillips, folio 40 . . | 30 | 9 | 4 | | £1,314 | 10 | 8 |
| | | | | | | | £1,347 | 10 | 8 |

## Contra.

| | | | | | £ | s. | d. |
|---|---|---|---|---|---|---|---|
| 1767. | | | | | | | |
| Jan. 1 | By Balance then settled, as per folio 56, which lay in the following obligations: — | | | | | | |
| | Daniel Whitney's single Bond | | | | 29 | 4 | 0 |
| | Joseph Garfield's " " | | | | 22 | 16 | 8 |
| | James Mirrick and others " | | | | 17 | 7 | 9 |
| | John Simpson and others " | | | | 22 | 5 | 10 |
| | Stephen Minot and others " and Mortgage | | | | 575 | 0 | 0 |
| | Roger McKnight's Note | | | | 4 | 0 | 0 |
| | A Treasurer's Note | . | £301. 0s. 0d. | | | | |
| | Deduct, being more than the church had in stock, folio 56 | . | .. | 60 0 $11\frac{3}{4}$ | 240 | 19 | $0\frac{1}{4}$ |
| | | | | | 911 | 13 | $3\frac{1}{4}$ |
| | By Contribution to the Charitable Fund, folio 56 | | | . | | 6 | 0 |
| | " Hon. John Osborn's Legacy, folio | | | . | 13 | 0 | 0 |
| | " Interest, per folio | | | . | 181 | 18 | $7\frac{3}{4}$ |
| | " Bal. of Sacramental Stock, folio 62 | | | . | 21 | 6 | $11\frac{1}{4}$ |
| | | | | | £1,118 | 4 | $10\frac{1}{4}$ |

Jan. 9, 1771. We have examined the Acct. above, and find it to be the true state of the Church Stock in Deacon's hands at this time, being £1,071.-8s. 4d. lawful money.

ANDREW OLIVER.<br>THOS. HUBBARD.<br>JOHN WINSLOW.

| | | | £ | s. | d. |
|---|---|---|---|---|---|
| 1771. | | | | | |
| Jan. 9 | By Bal. settled as above | . | 1,071 | 8 | $4\frac{1}{4}$ |
| | " Contribution to Pious and Charitable Fund | . | 1 | 6 | 8 |
| | " Thos. Hubbard's Legacy | . | 50 | 0 | 0 |
| | " Interest, per folio | . | 203 | 2 | 4 |
| | " Bal. of Sacramental Stock, folio 62 | . | 21 | 13 | $3\frac{3}{4}$ |

Boston, Sept. 30, 1773. We have examined the above Acct., and find it to be the true state of the Church Stock in the Deacon's hands at this time, being one thousand three hundred and forty-seven pounds ten shillings and eight pence, lawful money.

JOHN SCOLLAY.<br>HENDERSON INCHES.<br>THOS. DAWES.

£1,347 10 8

*The Stock belonging to the Old South Church*

| 1793. | | | £ | s. | d. |
|---|---|---|---|---|---|
| Dec. | 14 | To Recd. and Cr. in Acct. of Cash received and paid on Acct. Saml. Hinkley and Danforth's Bond . . . . . . | 16 | 3 | 6 |

## In hands of Jonathan Mason, Treasurer.

|  |  | £ | s. | d. |
|---|---|---:|---:|---:|
|  | By 16 Shares in Mass. Bank | 2,460 | 0 | 0 |
|  | " Saml. Hinkley and Co. Bond for Bal. | 125 | 0 | 0 |
|  | " $121.88 in 6 % Stock | 36 | 10 | 8 |
|  | "      91.40 in 3 % Funds | 27 | 8 | 4 |
|  | "      60.93 in deferred Stock | 18 | 5 | 7 |
| 1793. Nov. | " $2,300 in 3 % Stock purchased with Money Recd. of Bro. Phillips | 379 | 10 | 0 |
|  | " $33.90 of unassumed debt reloaned at Treasurer Davis's office, Principal and Int. amo. $38.97, @ 5 % | 11 | 13 | 10 |
| 1795. April 14 | " Treasurer Davis's Note for $670.40 | 201 | 2 | 5 |
| 1796. Jan. 18 | " *Certificate in 5 % Stock of Debt of U. S., for $1,000 | 300 | 0 | 0 |
|  | " 42½ Shares in the Union Bank, purchased by J. M., Treasurer, @ 59s. | 125 | 6 | 6 |
|  |  | £3,684 | 17 | 4 |

* N. B. This certificate was by a mistake carried to my credit in Mr. Appleton's books, and is now transferred by me to the Ministers and Deacons of the Old South Church.

## Sacramental Stock

| | | | £ | s. | d. |
|---|---|---|---|---|---|
| 1761. | | | | | |
| Oct. 31 | To South Church Stock invested in a Note of this date | | 134 | 0 | 0 |
| | | | £134 | 0 | 0 |

| | | | £ | s. | d. |
|---|---|---|---|---|---|
| From 1767 to 1771. | To Cash for the following from Jan. 1, 1767, to Jan. 1, 1771:— | | | | |
| | Wine for the Sacrament | | 120 | 15 | 0 |
| | Bread " " | | 10 | 0 | 0 |
| | Roulstone & Moulton | | 4 | 13 | 4 |
| | A Basket | | | 3 | 0 |
| | Distributed to the poor, &c. | | 179 | 2 | 7½ |
| | Sundries to Ministers at the Convention | | 3 | 2 | 8 |
| | A Book to record Church votes | | | 6 | 8 |
| | Balance to Church Stock, folio 59 | | 21 | 6 | 11¼ |
| | | | £339 | 10 | 2¾ |

| | | £ | s. | d. |
|---|---|---|---|---|
| To Cash for the following, from Jan. 1771 to Sept. 1773:— | | | | |
| Wine for the Sacrament | | 79 | 9 | 0 |
| Bread | | 5 | 16 | 0 |
| Roulstone & Moulton, ye service | | 2 | 13 | 4 |
| Distributed to poor | | 100 | 2 | 3½ |
| Expenses 2 Journeys to Boston | | 4 | 4 | 2 |
| Rev. Mr. Walley, taking Catalogue | | 3 | 12 | 0 |
| Bal. Carried to Cr. of Church Stock | | 21 | 13 | 3¾ |
| | | £217 | 10 | 1¼ |

## Contra.

|  |  | Old Tenor. |  |  | £ | s. | d. |
|---|---|---|---|---|---|---|---|
| 1758. June 1 | By out of the stock let out in 1752 | £360. | 0s. | 0d. |  |  |  |
|  | " Int. to this day | 150 | 6 | 0 |  |  |  |
|  | " more money let out, 1775 | 225 | 0 | 0 |  |  |  |
|  | " Int. on same | 29 | 14 | 0 |  |  |  |
|  |  | £765 | 0 | 0 |  |  |  |
|  | £765. old tenor invested in Prov. Note to draw Int. |  |  |  | Lawful 102 | 0 | 0 |
|  | " a note for 1 year |  |  |  | 6 | 2 | 4 |
|  | " " " |  |  |  | 8 | 5 | 1 |
|  | " Int. recd. on £116. 7s. 5d., to 31 Oct. 1761 |  |  |  | 16 | 13 | 11 |
| 1761. Oct. 31 | " the Sacramental Stock to make an even sum |  |  |  |  | 18 | 8 |
|  |  |  |  |  | £134 | 0 | 0 |
| 1767. | By Contributions, as per folio |  |  |  | 82 | 15 | 1¼ |
| 1768. | "    "    " |  |  |  | 85 | 14 | 1½ |
| 1769. | "    "    " |  |  |  | 89 | 18 | 8 |
| 1770. | "    "    " |  |  |  | 81 | 2 | 4 |
|  |  |  |  |  | £339 | 10 | 2¾ |
| 1771. | By Contribution |  |  |  | 77 | 18 | 6¼ |
| 1772. | "    " |  |  |  | 81 | 9 | 1 |
| 1773. | "    " |  |  |  | 58 | 2 | 6 |
|  |  |  |  |  | £217 | 10 | 1¼ |

*The Pious and Charitable Fund belonging to the*

| 1761. | | | | | £ | s. | d. |
|---|---|---|---|---|---|---|---|
| | To South Stock invested in 1 Note of £58. of this date | | | | | | |
| | | Ministers' and Widows' fund | £3. 6s. 8d. | | | | |
| | | Charitable and Pious | 54 13 4 | | 58 | 0 | 0 |
| | | | | | £58 | 0 | 0 |

| Oct. | 31 | " Cash pd. Mrs. Deborah Prince the Int. of Ministers' fund to this day | £0. 12s. 0d. | | | |
|---|---|---|---|---|---|---|
| 1763. | | | | | | |
| Oct. | 31 | "       "       " | 0 8 0 | | | |
| | | " Acct. of Int. Balance carried thither | 9 11 11 | 10 | 11 | 11 |
| | | | | £10 | 11 | 11 |

| 1764. | | | | | |
|---|---|---|---|---|---|
| Nov. | 26 | To the per contra £19. 19s. 0d. carried to the Dr. of Dea. Phillips's Acct. of Church Stock . | 2 | 13 | 2½ |
| | 29 | " the per Contra, £17. 5s. 0d. | 2 | 6 | 0 |
| 1765. | | | | | |
| Dec. | 5 | "    "         "   £15. 0s. 0d. | 2 | 0 | 0 |
| | | | £6 | 19 | 2½ |

**South Church** (Is Small Stock for Ministers' Widows and Children).

| | | | | £ s. d. |
|---|---|---|---|---|
| 1758. | | | | |
| Jan. 1 | The money having been put out to Old Tenor. Int. am. to in the whole . . £333. 15s. 7d. | | | |
| | A Bal. in the Books not put out to Int. | 32 0 0 | | |
| | Money collected for Ministers' Widows and Children . . . | 25 0 0 | | |
| | | 390 15 0 | | |
| | The sum of £390. 15s. 0d., old tenor, in a Province Note dated Jan. 1, 1758, to draw Int., is, lawful money . . . . . | | 52 0 0 | |
| | Mem. Nov. 23, 1758, put into the Box on the Thanksgiving, 40s. lawful money, for the Pious and Charitable Fund. Nov. 29, 1759, 40s. Nov. 27, '60, 40s. . . . . . | | 6 0 0 | |
| | | | £58 0 0 | |
| | Recd. Int. for 1 yr. £3. 2s. 5d. and lyes in Stock . . . £3. 2s. 5d. | | | |
| 1761. Oct. 31 | By Int. recd. to time . . . | 7 9 6 | | 10 11 11 |
| | | | | £10 11 11 |
| 1763. Dec. 8 | By Cash contributed this Thanksgiving day . . . . | Old Tenor. 19 19 0 | | |
| 1764. Nov. 29 | " Cash chd. Wm. Phillips . . | 17 5 0 | | |
| 1765. Dec. 5 | " " " " " . . | 15 0 0 | | 6 19 2½ |
| | | | | £6 19 2½ |

## South Church to Thomas Hubbard.

| | | £. | s. | d. |
|---|---|---|---|---|
| 1761. May. | To Cash pd. for sundry charitable purposes from Nov. 1, 1757, to date . . . . | 36 | 13 | 9 |
| | | £36 | 13 | 9 |

### Account of Interest of Bonds and Notes.

| | | £ | s. | d. |
|---|---|---|---|---|
| 1763. Nov. 21 | To Cash to sundry poor . . . . | 30 | 10 | 0 |
| | " Bal. lawful money as per Dea. Hubbard's acct., and pd. to Dr. Jeffries . . . | 35 | 9 | 0¾ |
| | | £65 | 19 | 0¾ |
| 1764. July | To the per Contra Int., £21. 1s. 10d., is included in a Treas. Note of £460., lawful money, which Treas. Note, also the several Treas. Notes on the foregoing side am. to £418. . ☞ Said £460. Note also includes £20. 18s. 2d. I paid Bro. Phillips to complete said Note. | 21 | 1 | 10 |
| | " the per Contra £8. 13s. 1¾d., 20s. 11d., and 4s. 9½d. carried to the Debit of Dea. Phillips's acct. in this Book, folio . . . | 9 | 18 | 10¼ |
| | | £30 | 0 | 8¼ |

*(Interest Acct.)* **Contra.**

| 1757. | | £ | s. | d. |
|---|---|---|---|---|
| April 15 | By Cash Recd. for Int. of Mr. Nathl. Cunningham to 10th . . . . . | 4 | 4 | 9 |
| | Mrs. Eliza Loring's legacy to 11th . . | 2 | 8 | 0 |
| Dec. 27 | Rev. Mr. Pemberton's legacy to 19 Sept. . | 2 | 1 | 9 |
| 1758. | | | | |
| April 27 | Mr. Nathl. Cunningham, to this day . . | 6 | 3 | 8 |
| Nov. 14 | Rev. Mr. Pemberton, to Sept. 19 . . | 1 | 0 | 11 |
| 1759. | | | | |
| Jan. 1 | Mr. Nathl. Cunningham, and Exchange of Notes | 1 | 13 | 4 |
| March 1 | Mrs. Eliza Loring's . . . . | 1 | 12 | 0 |
| 1760. | | | | |
| July 30 | Mr. Cunningham's and Mrs. Loring's . . | 4 | 16 | 0 |
| Oct. 7 | Rev. Mr. Pemberton's . . . . | 2 | 1 | 9 |
| 1761. | | | | |
| Nov. 10 | Mr. Cunningham's and Mrs. Loring's . . | 4 | 16 | 0 |
| Oct. 31 | "        "        "   to this day | 3 | 15 | 4 |
| | Bal. charged in Church Acct. £15. 1s. 10½d. | 2 | 0 | 3 |
| | | £36 | 13 | 9 |

**Contra.**

| 1762. | | | | |
|---|---|---|---|---|
| Feb. 2 | By Cash of Jas. Mirrick, Recd. Int. to 19 Sept. 1761 | 1 | 0 | 11 |
| Nov. 2 | "    "    "    "    " 1762 | 1 | 0 | 11 |
| 1763. | | | | |
| April 2 | " Cash £418. Treas. Note belonging to the stock | 25 | 1 | 6 |
| May 7 | "    " Wm. Smith, Jr., 1 yr.'s Int. . . | 1 | 7 | 6 |
| June 18 | "    " Joseph Garfield, 2 yrs.' " . . | 2 | 14 | 10 |
| July 5 | "    " £106. Treas. Note, Int. of Messrs. Henchman & Tolman. . . . | 6 | 7 | 2 |
| Oct. 31 | "    " Pious and Char. fund, folio 22, for Bal. . | 9 | 11 | 11 |
| | "    " Int. £312. Treas. Notes . . . | 18 | 14 | 3¾ |
| | | £65 | 19 | 0¾ |

| 1764. | | | | |
|---|---|---|---|---|
| Feb. 23 | By Cash Recd. Int. D. Whitney's Bond to Oct. 20, 1763 . . . . . | 8 | 13 | 1¾ |
| March 6 | "    " Recd. Int. J. Mirrick's Bond to Sept. 19, 1763 . . . . . | 1 | 0 | 11 |
| April 2 | "    " Roger McKnight's note of hand . . | | 4 | 9½ |
| July 2 | "    " of Bro. Phillips on Sundry Prov. Notes . | 21 | 1 | 10 |

£30 0 8¼

## Stock belonging to South Church in Boston, at Interest.

| 1761. | | | | | | | £ | s. | d. |
|---|---|---|---|---|---|---|---|---|---|
| Oct. | 31 | Jas. Mirrick's Bond, dated Sept. 17, 1755, Rev. E. Pemberton's legacy | | | | | 17 | 7 | 9 |
| | | Jas. Garfield's Bond, March 17, 1752, £22. 6s. 8d. | | | | | | | |
| | | Danl. Whitney's Bond, Oct. 20, 1756, 29 4 0 | | | | | | | |
| | | Wm. Smith, Jr.'s Bond, March 11, 1758 | | 22 | 5 | 10 | 74 | 6 | 6 |
| | | Treasurer's Notes; viz., — | | | | | | | |
| | | 1 of £80., of which is Nathl. Cunningham's legacy | | 66 | 13 | 4 | | | |
| | | Eliza Loring's legacy | | 13 | 6 | 8 | 80 | 0 | 0 |
| | | 1 of £40., of which is Capt. Armitage's legacy | | 13 | 6 | 8 | | | |
| | | Mrs. Mills's legacy | | 26 | 13 | 4 | 40 | 0 | 0 |
| | | 1 of £58., of which is Pious and Char. Fund | | 54 | 13 | 4 | | | |
| | | Ministers' and Widows' | | 3 | 6 | 8 | 58 | 0 | 0 |
| | | 1 of £40., Mr. Francis Tolman's legacy | | | | | 40 | 0 | 0 |
| | | 1 of £66., Danl. Henchman's " | | | | | 66 | 0 | 0 |
| | | 1 of £134., Sacramental Stock | | | | | 134 | 0 | 0 |
| 1763. | | | | | | | | | |
| Jan. | 24 | Roger McKnight's note of hand, Pious and Char. Fund | | | | | 4 | 0 | 0 |
| | | | | | | | £513 | 14 | 3 |

## Memo. of Money given to our poor out of ye Interest.

| 1758 to 1762. | To Sundry persons whose names are recorded | 23 | 2 | 4 |
|---|---|---|---|---|

£23 2 4

*Extract of the late Thomas Bromfield's Will, dated Dec. 14, 1764.*

*Item.* I give to the Old South Church in Boston, New England, whereof the Rev. Doct. Joseph Sewall is now Pastor, the sum of twenty-five pounds lawful money of Great Britain, to be paid into the hands of the Deacons of said Church, and to be by them let out at interest, and the interest applied to the poor of said church.

Received and entered folio —, May 1, 1783.

*Memo. of Interest Recd. on Acct. of Bonds.*

|  |  |  |  |  |  |  |  |
|---|---|---|---|---|---|---|---|
|  | Recd. from | Joseph Garfield. | June 13, 1755 | 1 | 4 | 0 |
|  | " | " | " | " | March 17, 1758 | 3 | 0 | 0 |
|  | " | " | Danl. Whitney. | April 8, 1758 | 1 | 16 | 0 |
|  | " | " | Joseph Garfield. | June 13, 1759 | 1 | 6 | 9 |
|  | " | " | " | " | March 17, 1759 | 1 | 4 | 0 |
|  | " | " | " | " | " 12, 1760 | 3 | 6 | 0 |
|  | " | " | Danl. Whitney. | April 19, 1760 | 1 | 16 | 0 |
|  | " | " | Stimpson. | " 3, 1760 | 1 | 6 | 9 |
| 1761. |  |  |  |  |  |  |
| Dec. 16 | " | " | Stimpson. | March 11, 1761 | 1 | 6 | 9 |
| 17 | " | " | Joseph Garfield. | " 17, 1761 | 5 | 11 | 4 |
| 1762. |  |  |  |  |  |  |
| April 15 | " | " | Stimpson. | " 11, 1762 | 1 | 6 | 9 |
|  |  |  |  | £23 | 2 | 4 |

## Memo. of Bonds, part of Mrs. Mills's Legacy

|  | £ | s. | d. |
|---|---|---|---|
| To South Church Stock | 74 | 6 | 6 |

|  | £74 | 6 | 6 |
|---|---|---|---|

## Part of Mrs. Mills's of Watertown Legacy, and Capt. Armitage's

1759.

Nov. 2, 1761. To Cash pd. sundry persons whose names are mentioned . . . . . 10 1 0
" South Church Stock invested in 1 Note of £40., dated 21 Oct. 1761; viz., —
Capt. Armitage's Legacy,
Mrs. Mills's " in part . . 40 0 0

£50 1 0

## to the South Church.

| | £. | s. | d. |
|---|---|---|---|
| Joseph Garfield's Bond, of Waltham, for lawful money, March 17, 1753 . . . . | 22 | 16 | 8 |
| Daniel Whitney of Watertown, Bond Oct. 20, 1756, | 29 | 4 | 0 |
| Wm. Smith, Jr., James and John Stimpson . | 22 | 5 | 10 |
| | £74 | 6 | 6 |

### Legacy. Contra.

1758.
June 1. By part of Mills, being money recd. of Mr. Spring's Bond, and given up, with Int. on it, am. to in old tenor . . . £138. 14s. 0d.
" Money remaining on hand with Int. . . . . 61 6 0
" Capt. Armitage's donation and four yrs. Int. . . . 124 0 0   Lawful Money.
    taken in a Province Note . 324 0 0   43 4 0

1759.
" Bal. Recd. 1 yr.'s Int. of the Treasurer . . 2 8 4
1761.
Oct. 21 " Cash Recd. for Int. . . . . 4 8 8
                                                        £50 1 0

*On a loose scrap of paper in Old Book, folio 42, is the following Item:* —

."I give and bequeath unto the Old South Church, that I now belong to, one hundred pounds old tenor, or thirteen pounds six and eight pence lawful money of the Province aforesaid, forever to put out at interest by the minister and deacons of the aforesaid church, and the interest of it to be given to the poor members of the aforesaid church as the ministers and deacons shall think fit.

May, 1754.                                                       CAPT. ARMITAGE."

## Mary Ireland's Legacy.

|  |  | £ | s. | d. |
|---|---|---|---|---|
| 1766. Feb. | To Cash given to sund. persons whose names are ment'd | 8 | 0 | 0 |
| 1767. Jan. | "         "         " | 7 | 6 | 8 |
| 1768. Jan. | "         "         " | 7 | 6 | 8 |
| 1769. Jan. | "         "         " | 8 | 0 | 0 |
| 1770–71. Jan. | "         "         " | 16 | 0 | 0 |
| 1772. Jan. | "         "         " | 8 | 0 | 0 |
| 1773. Jan. | "         "         " | 8 | 0 | 0 |
| 1774. Feb. | "         "         " | 8 | 0 | 0 |
| 1775. Feb. | "         "         " | 8 | 0 | 0 |
| " Sundry persons as appears by Quarterly Charity Book, p. 15, 17th June, 1783, £18. 18s. 0d.; Nov. £19. 10s. 0d.; May, 1784, £16. 4s. 0d.; March, 1785, £20. 0s. 0d.; and p. 8, May, 1786, £13. 8s. 0d. | | 88 | 0 | 0 |
| " April 10, 1787, £8. 0s. 0d.; Jan. 10, 1788, £8. 0s. 0d.; Feb. 23, 1789, £8. 0s. 0d. | | 24 | 0 | 0 |
| " March 14, 1790, £8. 0s. 0d.; May 7, 1791, £8. 0s. 0d. | | 16 | 0 | 0 |
|  |  | £206 | 13 | 4 |

## Mrs. Mary Ireland's Legacy.

|  | £ | s. | d. |
|---|---|---|---|
| Recd. of Nathl. Glover and Thomas Gray, Executors to her Will, as per David Jeffries and Saml. Sewall's acct., £1,000, is | 133 | 6 | 8 |
| Treas. Note 260, dated June 30, 1764, payable to Wm. Phillips, Esq., for £460., in which are included the above-mentioned Treasurer's Notes amounting to £418.; also the Int., £21. 1s. 10d. thereon to June 30, 1764; also £20. 18s. 2d. pd. Bro. Phillips to complete said sum of £460. | 460 | 0 | 0 |
| Bonds as mentioned above am. to | 91 | 14 | 3 |
| Roger McKnight's Note of hand | 4 | 0 | 0 |
| Oct. 29 Gift of the Rev. Dr. Joseph Sewall, £20., the income of said sum to be distributed to the poor of the Old South Church in Boston, yearly, by the deacons of said Church. | 20 | 0 | 0 |
|  | £575 | 14 | 3 |

## 231

*Contra.*

| | | £ | s. | d. |
|---|---|---|---|---|
| 1766. Jan. | By Int. arising on her legacy, £133. 6s. 8d., included in a Treas. Note as per Stock Acct. p. 1 yr. @ 6 % . . . . . | 8 | 0 | 0 |
| 1767. Jan. | " 6 mos. Int. @ 6 % and 6 mos. @ 5 % . . | 7 | 6 | 8 |
| 1768. Jan. | " " " " " " . . | 7 | 6 | 8 |
| 1769. Feb. | " 12 mos., 6 % . . . . . | 8 | 0 | 0 |
| 1770, 1771. Jan. | " 2 yrs., 6 % . . . . . | 16 | 0 | 0 |
| 1772. Jan. | " 12 mos., 6 % . . . . . | 8 | 0 | 0 |
| 1773. Jan. | " " " " . . . . | 8 | 0 | 0 |
| 1774. Jan. | " " " " . . . . | 8 | 0 | 0 |
| 1775. Jan. | " " " " . . . . | 8 | 0 | 0 |
| 1786. Feb. | " 11 yrs., 6 % . . . . | 88 | 0 | 0 |
| 1789. Feb. | " 3 " " . . . . | 24 | 0 | 0 |
| 1791. Feb. | " 2 " " . . . . | 16 | 0 | 0 |
| | | £206 | 13 | 4 |

**Mr. John Simpson** (*Son of Deacon Simpson of Boston*), **his Legacy.**

|  |  |  | £ | s. | d. |
|---|---|---|---|---|---|
| 1764. | | | | | |
| Oct. 20 | To Cash pd. Saml. Minot for Silver Flagon, weight 52oz. 16, making per acct. and receipt | . | 24 | 6 | 0 |
| | " Thos. Johnson for engraving the coat-of-arms and the inscription, which is, "The gift of Mr. John Simpson of Boston, Merchant, to the South Church in said town; who died at sea, July 12, 1764, on his return to his native land." . . . | . | 1 | 0 | 0 |
| Nov. 26 | " the per Contra £30., lawful, carried to the Dr. of Deacon Phillips's acct., folio . | . | 30 | 0 | 0 |

£55 6 0

## Contra.

| | | | £ | s. | d. |
|---|---|---|---|---|---|
| 1764. | | | | | |
| Oct. | 9 | By £30. lawful money to the poor of the Church whereof Dr. Sewall is Minister, to be paid to the Deacon or Deacons of said Church to be by them distributed among said poor | 30 | 0 | 0 |
| | | " £25. lawful money to the said Church in Boston whereof the Rev. Dr. Sewall is Minister, to purchase a piece of Plate for the use of said Church | 25 | 0 | 0 |
| | | Received the above-mentioned two legacies of £30. and £25. of Mr. John Simpson, the Father, and surviving partner of the late Company, of John and Jonathan Simpson, pr. David Jeffries. | | | |
| Nov. | 26 | Bal. hereof to Cr. of Dr. Jeffries's acct. | 0 | 6 | 0 |
| | | | £55 | 6 | 0 |

# OFFICERS OF THE OLD SOUTH CHURCH AND SOCIETY, 1868.

### PASTORS.
GEORGE W. BLAGDEN.         JACOB M. MANNING.

### DEACONS.
CHARLES STODDARD.         LORING LOTHROP.
AVERY PLUMMER.

The above five persons are *ex-officio* trustees of the Poor-Fund, now established as a public charity.

### CLERK OF OLD SOUTH CHURCH.
GEORGE F. BIGELOW.

### STANDING COMMITTEE.
GEORGE HOMER, *Chairman*.         SAMUEL JOHNSON, JR.
JABEZ HOWE.         JACOB A. DRESSER.
SAMUEL R. PAYSON.         WILLIAM HILTON.
J. B. KIMBALL.         GEORGE P. DAVIS.
GEORGE H. LANE.

### TREASURER.
CHARLES STODDARD.

### CLERK OF SOCIETY.
LORING LOTHROP.

### SUPERINTENDENT OF CHAMBERS-STREET CHAPEL.
LORING LOTHROP.

### COMMITTEE ON PEWS.
LINUS M. CHILD.         CHARLES STODDARD.
LORING LOTHROP.

Printed in Dunstable, United Kingdom